A GRAYWOLF REDISCOVERY

The Graywolf Rediscovery Series aims to give new life
in paperback to previously out-of-print literary favorites.
We are pleased to bring these books back to a
wider readership and are grateful to all those who
have brought the titles to our attention.

KABLOONA

GONTRAN DE PONCINS

In Collaboration with Lewis Galantière

Illustrated by the Author

GRAYWOLF PRESS

Originally published by Reynal & Hitchcock, Inc.

Publication of this volume is made possible in part by a grant provided by the
Minnesota State Arts Board through an appropriation by the Minnesota State
Legislature, and by a grant from the National Endowment for the Arts.
Significant additional support has been provided by the Andrew W. Mellon
Foundation, the Lila Wallace–Reader's Digest Fund, the McKnight
Foundation, and other generous contributions from foundations, corporations,
and individuals. Graywolf Press is a member agency of United Arts, Saint Paul.
To these organizations and individuals who make our work possible,
we offer heartfelt thanks.

Published by Graywolf Press
2402 University Avenue, Suite 203
Saint Paul, Minnesota 55114
All rights reserved.

Printed in the United States of America

ISBN 1-55597-249-7

2 4 6 8 9 7 5 3 1
First Graywolf Printing, 1996

Library of Congress Catalog Card Number: 96-75792

Special thanks to David Fettig for bringing this book to Graywolf's attention.

Series design by Foos Rowntree.
Cover design by Don Leeper.
Cover black-and-white photo and interior line drawings by Gontran de Poncins.

Cut off from the surrounding world by ice-filled seas and trackless wastes, a little handful of men calling themselves the Netsilikmiut (the Seal Eskimos) have been suffered to live their own life entirely untrammelled by outside influence, up to the present time.   —RASMUSSEN.

To all those who made it possible
this book is dedicated
in gratitude

Foreword

THE story of my journey into the North and out again is a long one, and I have no wish to write a long book. Between the time I left Ottawa on my way in, and the day I reached Vancouver at the end of the voyage out, fifteen months elapsed. Whole blocks of that journey of 20,000 miles will not appear in this record—for example, the fifty-seven days of ice, fog, and storm in the 106-foot *Audrey B.* in which I sailed home from Coppermine into the Glacial Ocean, round Alaska and through the Strait into the Bering Sea, to the whaling station in the bay at Akutan, to Dutch Harbor, and then due east eighteen hundred miles until we rode through Seymour Narrows and into the friendly port of Vancouver. As at the front in a great war, there were weeks, sometimes many of them, of enforced idleness and hebetude about which no one would wish to hear. For as I travelled with nothing of my own, I was constantly dependent upon the journeyings of others to furnish my chance means of transport. A Royal Canadian Police boat, a Hudson's Bay Company supply vessel, might or might not be present at a given moment to give me a lift in a given direction; and if it was not, I was forced to wait until it turned up. If, myself staying at a Hudson's Bay post, an Eskimo arrived who was about to join others at a seal-camp thirty or sixty miles away, I seized the occasion, and, for the value in trade of a few fox-skins, was able to share the life of the camp. And once there, it was again a matter of chance whether or not I should find another native to take me either back to my base or to another point I wished to reach. All this, I hope, will be clear enough in the pages that follow.

Even in the most sophisticated of us there is a deposit of human naïveté that is ineradicable. "To think," a man will say to himself as he lies on a sub-tropical beach in February, "to think that three days ago I was fighting my way against a snowstorm at home!" My own reflections were often of this simpleminded order, but with a higher degree of intensity. I, a child of civilization, had wandered in the course of a few weeks into the stone age. This was I who squatted beside a stone vessel in which seal-oil burned and gave off its warmth and light. I who had so lately been surrounded by Paris, by all that Paris means, sat here clad in the skins and furs of animals in a shelter built of snow, in a land and a season where a temperature of forty degrees below zero was the normal thing—and I was relaxed, content, happy. I was at peace with myself; and surely of all things in the world the rarest is a civilized man at peace with himself. Grant that it was simple. Say it was as simple as getting from Boston to Nassau, or from London to Cannes, in February (which it was not). Still, it was no less strange for that. If this was I, where was that other I that belonged to France, loved ease and warmth, read and argued and was the prey of intellectual restlessness? And if that other was I, who was this that sat chatting and laughing with the Eskimos in the igloo?

Let me excuse this intrusion of the first person singular by a word of explanation. My concern, in this book, is not primarily with my own wanderings or state of mind. My concern is with the Eskimo, with his life and traits, his broodings and ruminations, his invincible serenity in the face of the hardest physical existence lived by man anywhere upon earth. It was because of the simplicity and directness of his existence that I went into the Arctic to live with him; and living with him was not easy. Hardest of all was not the severity of the climate, not the intensity of the cold, not the physical anguish which, often, I endured as every man from Outside must endure it. The cold was a problem; but a very much more difficult problem was the Eskimo mentality. There was no getting on with the Eskimo except on his own terms; and as I was not a tourist concerned with externals, but a man concerned to find himself with the aid of the Eskimo, I had to get on with him. The Eskimo was not in my eyes an "interesting species" nor was I, in my own mind, a diligent "scientist." The stake was bigger than that. I sought to *live* the Eskimo life, not to measure it with instruments of precision.

A good part of this book, therefore, becomes of itself the story of the encounter of two mentalities, and of the gradual substitution of the Eskimo mentality for the European mentality within myself. Of course this substitution never became entire for long at a time. Again and again the European in me would protest, would rage; and particularly when the physical strain seemed too great to be borne, would refuse abruptly to accept the need for the adoption of the Eskimo view of life—and would suffer certain consequences. But within the limits of what was possible for me, I believe I succeeded.

From all that I have said, it will I hope be clear that there is no fiction in this book. Here and there I have made assumptions concerning what was going on in the mind of one or other of the Eskimos with whom I lived. It is possible that an assumption here or there is inaccurate: if so, the inaccuracy is the product of ignorance and not of intent. As for the physical and material life of the Eskimo, I have set that down as I saw it with my own eyes. I do not insist that other travellers may not have seen other Eskimos proceed differently.

A few pages of this book contain scenes or references that will offend the sensibility of the delicate reader. I regret them as much as anybody does; but what, of this sort, I have allowed to stand seems to me essential to the presentment of the Eskimo.

G. de P.

Part One
King William Land

Chapter I

In the spring of 1938 I stood one afternoon before the house of the Oblate Fathers in the Rue de l'Assomption in Paris. The day was fine, the street deserted and still, the house-front blank with that anonymity characteristic the world over of the city dwellings of priestly communities. I was about to embark upon a long trek into what was for me the unknown. If those within were willing to help me, my first step would be taken without stumbling. If not . . . well, I should go forward somehow.

Whether it was a photograph in a shop-window that had first prompted me, or a chance remark negligently dropped in my hearing, I do not now remember nor does it much signify. I know only that some time before that spring day the word Eskimo had rung inside me and that the sound had begun to swell like the vibrations of a great bell and had eventually filled the whole of my subconscious being. I had not been possessed instantly by a conscious and urgent need to go into the Arctic and live with a primitive people. These things operate slowly, like the germ of a cancer. They brood within, they send out tentacles and grow. Their first effect is not decision but restlessness. You find yourself feeling that something is obscurely yet radically wrong with your life.

You fidget. Your world becomes progressively more stuffy, less tolerable. Probably you show it, and show it unpleasantly; for your friends seem to you more and more to be talking nonsense, leading a meaningless existence, content with a frivolity and a mediocrity to which you find yourself superior. In their eyes, very likely, unbearably superior. But no matter. The thing is at work in you. Finally, there comes a moment when you waken in the middle of the night and lie still, eyes wide open in the dark. Life, you sense, is about to change. Something is about to happen. And it happens: you have made your decision.

There I stood, then, with my finger on the bell at the door of the Oblate Fathers. It is the particular mission of the Oblate Fathers to evangelize the most distant and disinherited peoples of the earth. For generations, Christian priests have gone out of this house to the confines of the world—to central Africa, to the Brazilian jungles, to the Arctic. Here in this house you would never have guessed it. Not a footfall sounded, not a map hung on a wall. Someone, a shadow, had opened a door and vanished, shutting the door behind me. I stood alone in an old-fashioned reception room, waiting in the company of three green chairs and, on the wall, the enlarged photograph of a dead bishop.

A man came in: obviously a religious, and one look at his face and bearing told me that he was a chief. He signed to me to sit down, and we sat in two of the three straight-backed chairs. Without a preliminary word, I blurted out the purpose of my visit, which was to go live with the Eskimos. Not those of Greenland, who, I gathered, were domesticated under governmental tutelage; nor those of Alaska, who carved souvenirs for tourists; but the Canadian Eskimos, those of the Central Arctic who, because they inhabited regions so remote and difficult to reach, still lived their primitive life of thousands of years ago, knowing of the white men only an occasional solitary missionary. I knew that their islands in the Glacial Ocean formed part of the immense diocese of that Oblate father who was celebrated in Canada as "the Bishop of the Wind"; that the bishop toured his diocese in his own airplane; and what I wanted was to be flown in by the bishop. Could the Oblate Fathers help me to realize my wish?

The man had not stirred. A proposal that had seemed to me, as I made it, monstrous, childish in its effrontery, seemed to him entirely normal. "You have only to write to the bishop," he said in a curiously depersonalized voice; "he will reply." As if the Arctic lay round the corner! This was my first lesson in humility, and I had been taught it even before leaving Paris. In a single word this religious, for whom neither time nor space existed, had reduced my vainglorious project to the dimensions of a Sunday picnic. But the bishop did not know me, I had ventured to say; the recommendation of the House would perhaps be necessary. . . . With a wave of the hand my objection was dismissed. "Not at all. It will be much better if you write direct. Here is the address. Good afternoon." And silently this imperturbable servant of Christ had left me, shutting himself back into that eternity out of which he had for an instant emerged.

It was in April that I wrote, addressing my letter to the bishop's episcopal seat at Fort Smith, on the sixtieth parallel. At the end of May came the bishop's reply. His Grace would be pleased to fly me in, provided there was space; "for," he wrote, "the plane is small and there will be another passenger. Meet me at McMurray, in northern Alberta, at the beginning of July." And he added a charming postscript: "You may wish to bring along a camera: there are things here worth photographing."

This precious letter, and equally essential documents from the Paris Geographic Society and the Director of the Trocadéro Museum attesting to the Canadian authorities my status of ethnographer, were virtually all my baggage. I had not much more money than baggage, for it was no great American foundation that had subsidized me. I had no equipment, for I was not an expedition. No agents were buying dogs for me; none were preparing in advance caches of food and feed, hiring interpreters, engaging native women to sew the skins and furs I would be wearing, fitting out a boat to meet me in season at this point or that in the Glacial Ocean. I had not even made plans, for I had long ago discovered— in India, in China, in the South Seas—that Life abhors our plans and knows better ones than we can imagine.

I had left Paris on June 11, 1938. It was on the 9th of July that I took off from Fort McMurray with Bishop Breynat, his chaplain, and Bisson, his pilot. At nearby Waterways I had left my last train—a wonderful train with a stove in each car on which the passengers heated their tins of food; a train that carried trappers, Indians, and colonizers of every speech and nation into the North, cautiously covering the three hundred miles from Edmonton in twenty-two weary hours, for it drew an endless row of cars filled with explosives for the mines. At Waterways, also, I saw my last hotel and the last Canadian banknote of a higher denomination than five dollars, for we were moving into a moneyless land, a land where furs were bartered for food and equipment without the intervention of the banks.

My seat in the bishop's plane was a sort of platform jutting inward from the instrument board, and here I crouched as we galloped over the surface of Lake La Biche, all four of us tense and leaning forward, like jockeys urging on a horse.

As the plane rose finally above the tree-tops Bisson made a sign with his hand; we fell back, and I, looking behind, saw the chaplain purple with tenseness and the bishop quietly absorbed in his breviary.

Below us spread a wide land of forest sown with thousands and thousands of shining pools, an unfinished world from which the waters had still to recede, and where you would have said that no man lived. But the airplane is radioactive and itself a creator of life. We did not drop down from time to time because life suddenly appeared below us, for wherever we looked no life was to be seen. Yet wherever we stopped, life sprang up as if spontaneously generated by our coming; and it died again when we rose as if we were carrying off the seed of life.

In this wise I saw Goldfields born and die again, where the bishop left, by way of gift, a haunch of beef. I saw Fond-du-Lac spring into existence and then vanish, where, on a little knoll, Brother Cadoret knelt, and the Indians with him, to kiss the bishop's ring. It was there that an Indian had ventured to speak to the bishop.

"You go to see the Great Seated One,"—the Pope—he said. "Take him this, and when you have seen him, pray for Higine." He had put three dollars into the bishop's hand; and as we sat again in the plane and the earth darkened and the lakes below us shone like metal in the darkening earth, the bishop still held in his hand the three dollars, forgetting in his emotion to put them into his purse.

After Goldfields, Fort Smith and the Mackenzie River, the Mississippi of the Northwest Territories, its muddy waters a mile wide, the great highway up and down which pass the barges of the Hudson's Bay Company, carrying in supplies and bringing out furs. And then Fort Rae where as we came down a lurid sun sent a weird light over the land, and clouds of smoke trailing on the surface of the earth seemed to say that the geologic fires beneath the crust of our globe were only now dying out.

We had flown fifteen hundred miles when I saw one night, shining in the Arctic sun, a pool bigger than any I had seen before. This was the sea, the Glacial Ocean. Again the pilot dived, again a little cluster of huts sprang up; and exactly at midnight on the 14th of July I was set down in Coppermine. Father Delalande took us to his mission house, and without a word the old bishop climbed the wooden ladder into the attic and went to bed. Next day he was off. He had done what he could for me in dropping me here at the last outpost of civilization.

At Coppermine, the white man's world ended. Here money, though only a little, could still be spent. Here the most northerly radio station stood, a Government station that broadcast on Sunday afternoons in happy-go-lucky fashion, hoping but not certain that its messages would reach those scattered missionaries, policemen, and Hudson's Bay post managers for whom they were intended. Here a dentist turned up once a year, with an Eskimo boy carrying his pedal drill. Here there was not even an inn, and I was housed by the grace of the Roman Catholic missionary.

Yet Coppermine, which I had reached after seven thousand miles of travel, was not to be my base. It was still too remote from the regions inhabited by the Eskimos I had come to live among. My ultimate base, the Hudson's Bay post at Gjoa Haven, on the island called King William Land, lay seven hundred miles north and east from here; and to reach it I had still to travel—such were the fortunes of wandering in the Arctic—twenty-one hundred miles.

A world lay ahead of me, but when and how I was to

enter that world, I did not know. As far as Coppermine, man is master in the North. Whether on skis or on floats, he can come this far by plane. Beyond, it is Nature that is the stronger. You may go north from here only in certain seasons, and of them all summer is the worst. It is the season between seasons, and there is no telling what the Glacial Ocean, through which you must sail or over which you must fly, will be like. If the summer is late, the sea may not have opened up yet; and your boat will not get through the ice, the pontoons on your plane will not allow you to land. The sea may be open, but then you have still to reckon with the wind. If it is blowing up from the south, your boat will have free passage, for it will be driving the broken ice north. But the Arctic wind veers unpredictably, and it may bring the ice back down and crush your boat in mid-passage as it crushed the *Bay Chimo,* the *MacPherson,* the *Fort James.*

It was one o'clock in the morning of July 15th, and I lay sleepless in the mission house thinking these thoughts. Through the open door the light of the sun was streaming over my blanket. I could hear the native children playing on the seashore, and southward I could see through a window the brilliantly lighted hills that rose inland. This warmth, these mosquitoes born overnight on the still-present ice, mosquitoes that descend in clouds so thick that the men of the North wear veils against them—all this would be gone in a couple of weeks; and I should have to be off too.

It was almost exactly two weeks before I was able to get away. Meanwhile I lived at the mission with Father Delalande, a priest whose religious spirit was as profound as his Parisian gaiety was infectious; and I helped with the housekeeping. One day I came in and found him on all fours,

scrubbing the floor and chanting the Ave Maris Stella. He
began to soliloquize.

"What a trade ours is!" he said as he scrubbed vigorously.
"We go from our breviary to dog-disease and back again,
from prayers to the Primus stove, from Christian charity to
a sound thwacking of the huskies because they are fighting
out-of-doors and their howling annoys us. Thou shalt not
kill, we repeat; and we take our 30-30 and bring down as
many caribou as we can, because even a priest must eat, and
so must his dogs. I tell you, it's enough to make a man die
laughing." And into my boots he flung half the contents of
his water-bucket.

I was cook, among other things, and every day, when
time came to eat, my Parisian missionary would say to me
solemnly:

"Monsieur de Poncins, what are you preparing for us to-
day? Did you say roast turkey? Or was that lobster Ther-
midor I heard you rolling over your tongue?" With that we
would finish off the remains of a tin of chipped beef. We
were able to make some toast one day: it brought France
to mind, and I asked Father Delalande if he ever thought
of going home. He was in high spirits, playing old French
airs on his harmonium, but at the question he stopped,
shook his head soberly, and said:

"No, I think probably it wouldn't suit me. I might as well
end here. The snow, the dogs, everything . . . there's nothing like it."

He went on. "The only thing that is painful for me," he
said, "is that I haven't a parish. We priests like to say a fine
Mass from time to time, you know. It makes us happy.
When I think that in the mission at Burnside I didn't even
have a proper censer! I had to make one out of an old
kerosene lamp and a dog-chain. The incense vessel was a

biscuit box, complete with lead spoon. Here at Coppermine, one Easter Sunday, we had a high Mass: Bishop Fallaize officiated and another missionary and I served him, chanting like the damned. We were all alone, too, except for an old Eskimo woman, and she was deaf. I'd like the Cardinal to come up here some time: he'd never get over it."

A frequent visitor to the mission was a police sergeant called Frenchy Chartrand. He and Father Delalande were the best-liked men on Coronation Gulf; and there was nobody like Frenchy to look after a sick dog or set nets under the ice at forty below. When the post had to be carried through blizzards to Cambridge Bay, three hundred miles off, it was Frenchy who took it out. When a family of natives was reported to be starving, he was off with his sled, his great voice lifting the team over the trail. He loved the priest and he loved the priest's sacramental wine, so we saw a lot of him.

"Monsieur Chartrand," we would say when this colossus came in, "will you have something?"

"Just a touch," he would answer; and four spoonfuls of sugar would go into his cup of tea.

When we passed him an apple pie that I had baked that morning, he would say:

"Hand me that spoon so that I can tackle this properly," and half the pie would go in three mouthfuls.

Then he would seize the tobacco box; and by the time he had left it didn't take you long to draw up your inventory.

Sometimes we had six or seven visitors at the mission, all of them trappers. They came into Coppermine every year at this season, returning to their shacks when the snow fell. Art Watson was one, Slim Purcell was another. Bill Store turned up here from Stypleton Bay; Big Slim Semmler from

Krusenstern; Old Charlie Levin from the upper reaches of the Rae River; Ole Andreasen on his schooner out of the east.

They would sit on the floor or on one of the few chairs, Charlie looking like an old Englishwoman with a green mosquito-veil over his battered hat; Ole rosy and round, his bright eyes winking as he told story upon story; all of them on holiday and in holiday mood, and all giants with hands so big that when, for emphasis, one put his hand on my leg, the leg disappeared from view.

But Frenchy was the dominant figure, and he would sit running with sweat while his great head came forward across the table and his great laugh shook the spoons in the drawer and the dust in the attic.

"One afternoon," Frenchy would roar, "I found seven hundred fish in my net, each one as big as that,"—and his hands would be up, two feet apart.

"Take it easy, Frenchy! We've heard that one before."

"No! I mean it! That year I caught three thousand fish in three weeks. And if you think that's anything, one year off Hershel Island we bagged thirteen thousand fish, four hundred and fifty seal, and three white whales, one of them living, for she had caught her fin in the net and couldn't get out.

"That was in the days of old Bill Seymour, when Cap Pederson was only a cabin boy. That was something! Hershel Island was full of whale carcasses, anchors, harpoons; and all day long you could hear the cat-o'-nine-tails whistling on deck. As soon as a man said anything, they strung him up to the mast by his thumbs, and you'd better not ask how he happened to be dead when they untied him."

He would pour himself another cup of sacramental wine:

"Those days are over. You don't find men like that any more. Compared to them we're a lot of cream-puffs!"

Poor Father Delalande would sit blinking sleepily and thinking of the Mass he had to say in another couple of hours, for they sat and talked until five in the morning, long after the briefly set sun had climbed the sky again, and while the dogs on their line whimpered like babies as the mosquitoes all but hid their hair from view.

They would talk now and then of the Eskimos, and the Eskimos they talked of were invariably "no good." "No good" meant that the natives were failures as white men; and I said to myself how curious it was that these same white men, so far from winning over the Eskimo to their way of life, had been won over to his—in the nature of things. Only the Arctic existed for them; and everything that lay below the Mackenzie River was to them the remote, the virtually non-existent "Outside." Their concerns, even their words, were quasi-Eskimo. The subject of their discourse was Eskimo—the freeze, the break-up, the sled, dog-disease, the price of furs. A sick leader of a dog-team was infinitely more significant than the peace of Europe; for in the North a leader is everything. Father Delalande himself had been here six years, he told me, before getting a good leader, and now he talked about the dog constantly and never made a plan to visit the outlying natives without bringing the prowess of his leader into the conversation.

He was, in this respect, no different from the others. Often, as we chatted together, his eyes would stray to the window, and in the middle of a sentence he would go out of doors to see if that was really a seal he had caught sight of on the water. Seal meant food, and food was more important than conversation. When Father Delalande soliloquized to himself in the next room, the subject of his

soliloquy was always dog or fish; and when he spoke of
fish it was always about the quantity he would have to send
up in advance and cache at different points on his winter
route. Eat and keep warm were the two rules by which men
lived in the North.

The more I listened to Father Delalande and his visitors,
the clearer it became that for me, on this journey, the earth
was not round but flat. There was first, in the foreground,
the civilized world, the world I had come from. Beyond it
lay the white man's world of the North. And hidden behind that world, stretching into infinity as far as thought
could reach, was the Eskimo world. I distinguish between
"life" and "world." The trappers and hunters of the white
man's North live the Eskimo life, up to a point. They travel
on sleds, fish through ice, wear furs, and even, on rare occasions, build igloos. But into the Eskimo *world,* which is a
mental fact, they never penetrate. Apart from every other
difference between them and me—priest and trapper on the
one side, I on the other—there was the difference that I had
come here to penetrate into a world to which they were
indifferent.

At Ottawa the Canadian authorities had examined my
credentials and given me the various licenses without which
a white man may not go into the North. At Edmonton I
had been able to fit myself out almost completely. But I still
lacked the proper clothing for Arctic life, and Father Delalande advised me to buy my skins here in Coppermine, for
caribou had been rare on King William Land and I might
find that I had no wardrobe when I reached Gjoa Haven.
He sent for Krilamik, the best seamstress in the village, and
told her what was wanted.

Limping, grinning, smoking cigarette upon cigarette, the

old Eskimo woman walked with me to the Store. There are few sights more engaging than a craftsman practising his craft, displaying his professional resource upon wood, or marble—or hides. Krilamik bowed over the piles of hides inspired confidence. Half the skins were rejected at a glance, not even touched. Here was one her eye judged possible, but when she had rubbed it between her fingers, hefted it in one hand, turned it over to peer at the nether side, it was discarded. One by one, she went over the whole stock, and after two hours a good-sized pile had been set aside. Out of this pile a second selection was made; and finally she straightened up, waved a careless hand to indicate that she had made her choice, and we counted the lot. There were seventeen full hides, three white bellies, and thirty legs, all of caribou. In addition, one big sealskin for boots, a moose-skin, and, for trimming, a wolverene skin. My sleeping-bag and other odd pieces would be made for me at Gjoa Haven.

We bought also a packet of caribou sinew that looked to me like a dead flounder and was a common article of stock in the Hudson's Bay posts. From my flounder, Krilamik would draw out the nerves, one by one, and, twisting them with her teeth, would make the strongest possible kind of thread.

All this was carried off to her tent; and without a word to me about measurement she proceeded with her sewing. Not to have been measured for my clothes worried me, and I spoke of it to Father Delalande. He laughed and said I need not fret. "She's had a good look at you. Eskimo seam-stresses never go wrong. As tailors, they beat even the Chinese."

I had been twelve days at Coppermine when it became clear that I could reach King William Land only by shipping with Art Watson in the *Audrey B.* Not that the *Audrey B.* would take me straight to Gjoa Haven. She was not bound for King at all, and would drop me at her terminus, Perry River, two hundred and fifty miles from King. But better than that: before she went east to Perry River she would sail west to Tuktuyaktuk, at the mouth of the Mackenzie; only thereafter would she return practically within sight of Coppermine and proceed to Perry. Thus, in order to go five hundred miles (Coppermine to Perry), I should sail seven hundred miles west to Tuk, the same distance back to within sight of Coppermine, and then proceed, doing a total of nineteen hundred miles to reach a point five hundred miles distant!

The explanation was as simple as the journey was complicated. I have already said that the Mackenzie River is the single highway down which supplies in bulk can be brought into the Arctic. Those supplies are landed at Tuk. There, a part is transshipped on board the *Audrey B.,* and by the *Audrey B.* distributed to certain posts on the Glacial Ocean.

Had we been in mid-winter, and had I possessed my own sled and team, the journey would have been hard but relatively swift. We were in July; there was no other way out; and in the circumstances I was in great luck to be able to sail with Watson, Bill Store, and Big Slim Semmler on this 28-day cruise.

It was at Tuktuyaktuk on the 12th August that I saw something which no man has the right to expect to see—a bishop in shirt-sleeves loading coal. I said as much to Bishop Fallaize, and he laughed.

"Had you come up two years ago," he said, "you would have found me in a mine, swinging a pick-axe."

Back and forth went Bishop Fallaize and Father Griffin,

carrying sacks of coal between them to a hand-cart pulled by Father Binamé and Father Buliard, both dressed in French workmen's blouses.

Sixteen days later, on the 28th, we dropped anchor before the Hudson's Bay post at Perry River, and on the 29th the *Audrey B.* was off again. One month had brought change in the Arctic summer. Sleet and snow were falling; there was not a moment to lose if the vessel was to be back at Coppermine before the freeze came. The chill of a wind that whipped us, the swell at sea, spoke of an early winter; and all of us working in a sort of frenzy, we tumbled the cases overboard and heaped them up on shore, our hands freezing while the August storm blew. Next morning the whistle of the *Audrey B.* cut the air, and I ran to the point of the island and watched her glide heavily and noiselessly along the horizon. As she moved out of sight, I thought of Big Slim's casually dropped farewell ("So long: I feel sorry for you already"), and I thought also of the bishop's warning at Tuk: "Your lungs will freeze. You will be locked up in an icy prison, unable to get out." The *Audrey B.* was mere smoke on the horizon when I walked back to the Hudson's Bay post, aware that my last tie with the Outside had been snapped.

Yet even Perry was not the end of the trail. I spent a week there as the guest of Angus Gavin, the able and philosophic Post Manager, before a half-civilized Eskimo named Angulalik took me in his motor boat over the two hundred and fifty miles that still separated me from King William Land. On the 9th of September, finally, at five in the afternoon, we rode into the tranquil and majestic bay of Gjoa Haven, the first true harbor I had seen in the Arctic.

The bay was the shape of a long bean, surrounded on three sides by low ridges cut with deep gullies. Spread wide in every direction lay a colorless plain, static, stony, void of life, empty of every promise except the promise of solitude. On shore as we moved slowly in, two white men stood. They did not wave, they did not call out: they stood waiting. One of these men, I knew, would be going out next day with Angulalik. But the other! What sort of man was he? In that brown shack that rose among its out-buildings on the ridge, that man and I were to spend days and weeks together, cut off from all the world.

I stepped out of the boat and shook hands for the first time with Paddy (born William) Gibson. One look at his face told me there was nothing to fear. We should get on.

Chapter II

THE morning after my arrival I stood at a window and stared at a bird as it tacked and wheeled in the storm over the wide and empty tundra. It was a hawk, flying with the swiftly beating wings of a whale-bird at sea, skirting the ridge, dipping into the hollows, vanishing from sight. The hawk was hunting; its game was the snowbird; and because the snowbirds were still here, the hawk was here. Soon they would move southward, and in their wake would go the hawk picking them off one by one, for they were its source of life.

Everything in this place was a link in the chain of death. Man was here because the white fox was here. The white fox was here because it hunted the lemming. And the lemming, that diminutive Arctic rat, was here because of a still smaller prey. Inland it was the same: the wolves followed in the track of the caribou; behind came the fox to eat what the wolf left, and then the wolverene who cleaned up what the fox disdained. Along the ice floes the polar bear hunted the seal, and the knowing fox followed the bear because the bear—that ice-inhabiting gourmet—ate only the blubber and left the rest. And once again behind the fox came man, setting his traps.

Life in the Arctic is governed by the sign of the implac-
able, and wherever I turned my eyes I met its symbols.
Across the creek, three hundred yards south of the Post,
rose two cairns, two heaps of stones carefully piled up by
Amundsen in 1905 to mark his passage here. His camp-site
was still discoverable on two little mounds out of which
straggled a few thin clumps of yellow weed. Southwest
across the bay was Fram Point, named for Amundsen's ship,
and on that point rose another landmark—two beams nailed
together in the shape of a cross, topped by an empty overturned gasoline drum and held in place by wires. If you
came close enough, you could hear it screech in the wind
and rattle like dry bones. Northward, solitary on the wide
plain, a Hudson's Bay man lay buried. He had become lost
as I was soon to lose myself in the autumn blizzard, and
had been found dead. The little white fence built round the
grave was visible through the window. "Funny thing,"
Paddy Gibson said as I stared at it, "that grave draws the
white fox. Makes trapping easier. Rather handy, what?" I
saw myself suddenly a potential object of "handiness." Not
that any one wished my death; but after all, why should I
not be good for four or five foxes a season, if it came to it?

Once again my world had shrunk. From the wide Arctic
it had narrowed to the dimensions of this little bay, Gjoa
Haven, where in this season three-quarters of a mile was as
far as the eye could see. (It was to shrink, later, down to the
circumference of the Post itself, and even to the tiny circle
round the stove.) A little like a detention camp, I thought;
and wherever I set my eyes the limits were visible, as if the
whole thing were a décor planted there to serve for a film
and then be taken apart. It was grim, barren, inexorable,
and virtually lifeless. There was an owl, a single white owl
that hunted the lemming and spoke of death and desolation.

It flitted from beacon to beacon—a beacon here is not a
light, but a landmark, a pole held in place by heavy stones
at its base—and this winged menace, companion to the Post
as long as the autumn lasted, was so ominous a sight that
somehow no one dared to shoot it.

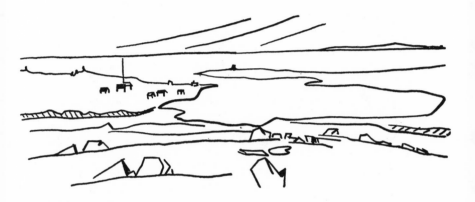

My thoughts went back to yesterday, to Sturrock and his
clippers, cutting the wires of his radio set. Sturrock was a
Hudson's Bay apprentice who had left King William Land
in the boat that had brought me in. I had watched him as
he got his effects together, and they seemed to consist mainly
of his radio—an old B battery to which was hooked a tele-
phone set. He had made it himself; and though it could
not have cost him more than a couple of dollars, it was his
all, and he wrapped it carefully away in an old egg-crate
as if it were the most resplendent jewel in the world.

Sturrock had accomplished marvels with his toy, feats
proper to rouse the jealousy of a power station. For the ether
is like a woman: it is not enough to have instruments of
price and power: you must amuse it, cajole it, invoke it in
your dreams. Anyone who has seen an amateur radio-

operator retire to a corner of a room and dream for hours
with that shy preoccupied air they all have, knows how
true this is. Living in the solitude of the Post, Sturrock had
prayed to the goddess of the radio tenderly and with respect,
and she had come to him and stayed with him. Elsewhere
she had come and fled, or had not come at all; but she had
never deserted Sturrock. Thus the young man had grown
famous in the Arctic, and it was to him that the whole of
the North had sent forth its appeals. With his sensitive
hands—there are hands in the world that confer grace, and
he had them—Sturrock would rescue messages that were
dying in the air; he would revive them and relay them to
their destination.

Small wonder, then, that on his last day Sturrock had not
drunk with us, had stuck his mail into his pocket without
looking at it, and that I remember him best squatting beneath the table that had been the altar raised to his goddess,
cutting the ground wire and leaving in the wall a little hole
like a wound.

The boat left, and with it Sturrock and his toy. We had
a receiving set at the Post, but no sending apparatus; and it
was not until the next day that I was struck by the destitution in which Sturrock had abandoned us. What were we
to do now? If I went mad, to whom could Paddy appeal?
If Paddy's appendix went bad, over what wire or by what
wireless could I cry out to the nearest surgeon, at Aklavik
fourteen hundred miles away, "Tell me: how do you open
an abdomen with a kitchen knife?" There were certain
inalienable privileges of man which had nevertheless been
alienated from us. We had surrendered the right of man
to have recourse to his kind. We had not the right to fall
ill, to become restless, to ask to be diverted. All that by
which the life of civilized man is made bearable and is borne

up, had gone with Sturrock's two-dollar toy and the sailing of
the boat that had brought me to this far-off corner of the
world, this last trail, this more than Scythian wilderness.

Paddy and I stood side by side at the water's edge as the
boat moved down the bay, and I marvelled that he said no
word, made no gesture of farewell. Not one. Gestures are
good enough for people on railway platforms who wave to
travellers certain to come home again. Here they were super-
erogatory. Paddy turned on his heel without waiting for the
boat to disappear, and walked with long strides up the rise
that led to the Post. Distraught, I walked behind him.

Then there was the matter of incoming mail. As soon as
we had got back, Paddy had buried himself in it. He was
to do hardly anything else for two days. Letters and papers
were strewn on the floor. Sitting in an armchair, dressed in
sealskin boots and an old sweater, Paddy bent down and
rummaged in the pile. He would open an envelope, begin
a letter, read a page or two, toss it aside, open the next
envelope. There is an eagerness for contact which has nothing to do with eagerness for information. Whom is this
from? What is he saying that I care to hear? . . . The
magazines are piled to one side. They will be read in the
course of the winter.

I had no letters, but sat looking at Gibson. Suddenly he
picked up an envelope and gasped; and this letter he read
carefully through to the end. It was from his father. But his
father—he had had the news by radio—had died in Ireland
six months before. He sat motionless, and I looked away.
Here, I thought, is a corner of the world where the dead
still write letters; a place where no man knows what has
happened to his country, his village, his father. If war comes
to-morrow, I shall not know it. If a sidereal cataclysm de-
stroys half the surface of the globe, I shall not hear of it.

Man's pride lies in feeling himself one with his kind, in the knowledge that he is a member of human society; we, at Gjoa Haven, have not this honor. We are the tail of the lizard, cut off from the body and continuing to wriggle.

Gibson said nothing, but put the letter into his pocket. The thought pursued me, and in the evening, when each of us had retired to sleep in his own cubicle, I could imagine him the other side of the partition, lying in his bed, opening the letter again, and reading those words: "My dear son . . ."

All such thoughts—the roving hawk, the grisly owl, the sense of isolation—were, I know now, the frettings of a man from Outside; no man of the Arctic let them upset him. Even in me, they were to vanish and be replaced by other and more immediate concerns, by reflections better adapted to life near the Pole; and this transformation was to take place with a rapidity so great that I cannot now say when the change came. What was grim and strange was soon to be familiar. What was dreary, as those lightless beacons had at first seemed to me dreary, was shortly to bear a friendly cast in my sight. The snow would be my shelter, the blizzard an enemy I should learn to deal with, and the notion of death itself would grow as familiar as a cat before a fireplace.

But I had not yet reached this point. Winter had not yet come with its feeling of permanence and of something settled. We were in the fall of the year, the dread season of squall and high wind, of cold without snow and of shivering discomfort (the only season in which men shiver in the North), when the motionless Eskimo crouches in his flapping tent and prays for the coming of winter as we outside long for the signs of spring.

Somewhere inland the Eskimo has cached his riches, that is, buried in the earth under heaps of stones his sled, his harpoons, his harness, and all the paraphernalia of the rich and severely magnificent winter months. As a great lady of the world, once the season is over, sends her jewels to her banker for safe custody, so the Eskimo confides his treasures to the earth until the revolution of the seasons calls for disinterment in October. Until that time the Eskimo is a miserable creature, a wretched gipsy clad in rags and waiting for purification by snow. And when the snow comes, the shabby tent is abandoned, the white igloo is built, the skins and furs are sewn into handsome clothes, and a metamorphosis takes place: the seedy gipsy becomes a hunter, the beggar round the Post is now an *Inuk*—"a Man, preeminently," as these Eskimos call themselves.

For the time being, however, the Eskimo is unimpressive and King William Land is flat, desolate, and storm-swept. Sown with millions of skull-shaped stones, this barren ground is as sinister as an antique battlefield, a dead earth almost colorless in its brown monotony. The heart sinks as the eye moves round this cheerless expanse, this sapless and skeletal space. This is not even the Sahara. Nothing here exalts the spirit, comforts the eye, or challenges man's strength. Was it for this that I had come ten thousand miles by ship, by rail, by plane, by river-boat?

And who were these Eskimos I had come so far to see? From the inner room of the Post, the "white man's room" into which the native does not penetrate, I had been called by Gibson into the outer room where, on benches round the wall, the Eskimos were permitted to loiter, there to see my first member of the Netsilik people. Tutiak was his name, a man already old—forty years old, probably, and looking sixty. He sat in his rags on a bench, empty sleeves dangling and arms folded across his chest inside his coat. (It makes scratching oneself easier.) As I came in, he raised his bowed head and widened his mouth in a grin that was no more than a movement of human flesh, for the whole face—eyes, cheeks, nose, lips—remained completely expressionless. For the first time in my life, I found myself face to face with a human being who disconcerted me beyond explanation. He spoke no word. No current flowed between him and me. I could not say what this was that sat there before me. I searched in my memory: Fiji Islanders, Tahitians, African Negroes, Arabs, up-river Chinese—never had a gleam of recognition failed to come into their eyes when first they saw me, a spark that told me that they were men as I was a man. The grin itself of this Eskimo was nonhuman, might have been the facial contortion of a fox staring at the sun, an animal reflex. I was nonplussed.

Later, when I knew a little more of the Eskimo mind, the thing became clear to me. Tutiak was about to go off fishing. In this season when no sleds run for want of snow, the Eskimo dogs carry packs. Tutiak had come up to the Post to wheedle a length of rope out of Gibson. The mind of this truly elementary being could contain no more than this thought; and obsessed by it, there was no room in his mind for the fact—which ought to have been prodigious and was not—that he was in the presence of the fourth or fifth white man he had seen in his whole life. And I, in my ignorance, stood there seeking vainly a way into this man's consciousness which could not open to receive me. I was seeking him: he was seeking a length of rope.

He had come a long way from inland for that bit of rope, and no sooner had he got it than he was off again. I watched him through the window as he crossed the horizon, long hair flying in the wind, his rags blowing about him, inconceivably the picture of a mediaeval mendicant. He was trotting after his two dogs as if fearful of losing them; and the dogs, badly packed, ran with long tufts of hair like his own, though theirs hung from their bellies. Tutiak trudged behind, the pack on his back tied under his arms and held in place by a strap that went round his forehead. There was something pitiful in his silhouette against the sky as he trotted with feet flat and head and chest straining forward. The dogs stopped at the creek to lap the icy water, and the old man moved on ahead of them. With a bound, they caught up, then passed him, one dog moving easily under a load of caribou skins, the other dragging a couple of tent-poles behind as if unhappy over the shiftlessly adjusted burden. They disappeared behind a knoll and there was left nothing but the wind over the deserted scene.

Utak was the name of my second Eskimo. Gibson, who was all kindness, had let me know that there was a fish-camp thirty miles away where I might make my first acquaintance with the Eskimo world. Utak had been engaged to guide me there and bring me back, and at the first sight of the man, at his first grin, I had been released from the vague despondency into which the meeting with Tutiak had plunged me. Here was a younger man, and, I thought, a friendly man. Though there was something sly and almost subtle in his glance, I felt I should get on with him and regretted that I knew so little of his language. To Gibson I said, "Thank heaven they are not all like Tutiak. I like this fellow. He'll do very well, I think."

"Mm, yes," Gibson said dubiously. "He knows a fair lot about white men. Been round quite a bit. Killed his step-father, you know. Spent three years in prison at Aklavik,

over near Alaska. Learnt how to smoke tailor-mades, and
two or three words of English. Not a dangerous chap, probably, but he's rather well known for his fits of temper. I
dare say you'll get on with him all right. Anyway, there's
nobody else round to take you to the fish camp."

Not very consoling. I took a sharper look at my man.
Each time that I looked at him, he grinned. I did not need
to be told that the Eskimo grin was a mental attitude, a
convention, a sign of good breeding. There was nothing
awkward about Utak. He felt perfectly at home with the
white man. Rolling himself a cigarette, he sat squinting and
smoking while Gibson and I talked. There was hardly a
word of our conversation that he understood, but he guessed
what we were talking about, and with the intuitiveness of
primitives everywhere he pointed to the clock:

"Sikisi!" he said, pronouncing "six" as well as an Eskimo
could.

If we were to be off at six, I should have to be out of bed
at five.

Next morning I was up at seven, rather ashamed of myself. Utak must be waiting impatiently for me. I looked out
of the window and saw no sign of life. Paddy Gibson said
nothing. He was enjoying the adventures of his tenderfoot.
"Ublako!" the Eskimos say: "To-morrow early." It is always
ublako with them; they are always full of good resolutions,
particularly just after the white man had fed them—given
them what is called in the North a "mug up."

It was nine o'clock before anything began to stir round
the shack provided for the natives in the summer months.
Stir, did I say? A man flew out like a projectile in one direction: a woman ran through the doorway, followed by two
more, and all three began to shout and call. There was an

air of bustle and agitation as of late risers fearful of missing a boat.

The philosophic Gibson said calmly, "It will be a good two hours before you get away. No hurry."

I shall have more to say later about how the Eskimos make a start on the trail. What I was witnessing here was the packing of the dogs in preparation for an autumn journey. The process is almost comically laborious. First, you must catch your dogs. Eskimo dogs love to pull a sled, and with equal intensity they hate to carry a pack. When they smell the coming of a pack they are off in all directions. There was one now running over the plain, followed by two women who were employing all the ruse and cunning of the Red Indian to catch him. Another had slipped on his belly under the shack and was being dragged out by one paw while he howled like a man being murdered in a cellar. A third saw a native coming towards him with a carefully balanced pack ready for his back, and he rolled over barking and squealing while the man kicked him again and again until the dog surrendered, stood up, and let the pack be strapped on his back. And Utak, as if there were now not a minute to lose, flew among the dogs, kicking, strapping, shouting, while his wife went into and out of the shack again and again, bringing out each time a single object, as if she could think of only one thing at a time and no one in the world had ever thought of carrying more than one object at a time in his hands.

The poverty of the natives of King William Land is so wretched that the least bit of string, the least stick of wood is a treasure in their existence. There was a time when they were rich, when they hunted the whale and killed hundreds of caribou every summer. All this is in the past. The land here has risen, the waters have become shallow, the whale comes no more and the caribou trail is far away. These Netsilik are now the most abjectly poor people in the world. Yet they stay, they do not think of migrating to better hunting grounds. King William is their land, the land of their ancestors. As tramps and gypsies rummage through the dust-bins on the outskirts of towns, so these sharp-eyed Eskimos find scraps of treasure in this barren landscape; and especially here round the Post this sort of hunting is good. Whenever they come here to trade their white foxes, they wander round and round, scrutinizing the ground, and their wives and children follow the shores of the bay ready to pick up any stray bit of timber, of wire, of rope. All this goes back to their camp, where of an old crate they will make a treasure chest, of a broken file the point of a harpoon.

It is the fruit of this patient rummaging that the dogs carry, along with hides and tent-poles and harpoons—a broken kettle, three sticks of wood, torn bits of tar-paper; and the dogs disappear under their loads, moving on unseen legs like ambulatory junk-shops.

Finally this comical bustle was ended and we were ready to be off. I shouldered my pack. Utak, for the honor of the Eskimo, carried more than any of us: piled up on his small tent was mine, big enough to shelter four people. And perched atop of my tent sat his little son. We started . . . and at that moment one of the dogs burst his strap (these straps are all, almost without exception, made of bits of cord tied together, and of sealskin always on the point of breaking). The whole load had to come down. The dog had to be beaten while all the animals howled in sympathy with their howling brother, and Utak had to be re-packed. We did get off, then, Utak trotting in the lead, his wife at his

heels—but literally with her toes at the heels of his boots—
the child perched high, and I bringing up the rear.

Once over the low ridge that skirts the bay we marched
through an endless plain that stretched as far as the eye
could see. This was the Arctic tundra, a land indescribable
because there is literally nothing to describe, nothing that
holds the eye, that exalts, that gives promise of anything
whatever at the end. If there is a landscape in the world in
which no thrill of romance can be evoked, it is this. Sombre
brown, not colorless but dead in color, except for an occasional low ridge this world is flat and void. One ridge
crossed, the same world is here again and the same low
ridge lies ahead. There is no vegetation, none at all; and
the pools of water cannot even be called pools, for a pool
implies something fresh and alive, whereas these are dead
waters, waters which have not yet receded from the earth.
I thought as we walked on, Is this a land out of which life
has died, or a land to which life has not yet come? It induced a strange impression of lassitude, so that one was
weary even before one had begun to march. And walking
here was painful, for either there were limestone rocks that
tore one's soft sealskin boots, or one slipped and sank into
greasy humid marshland. Meanwhile, we trotted on, nose
to the ground under the burden of the pack.

Yet where I saw space devoid of life, my Eskimos saw life.
Again and again Utak and his wife—who seemed to be his
double, so extraordinarily did she reproduce all his gestures
—would stop, bend forward, stare at the ground, or leave
the trail and go to the right and the left, then come back
smiling. What had they seen? A lemming's hole, and the
lemming may be in it. We wait ten minutes. No, he is not
there: we go on. Or they see traces, droppings of a fox or a
bird. Nothing escapes them and their observation is inces-

sant. For a stone that is not in its normal position they will
stop, murmur, discuss; and then on they go with me behind.

When we stop for a breather, instead of resting and rolling a cigarette, as I do, they are off exploring. The instinct
of destruction drives them on. They find a couple of bird's
eggs: there must be a bird. The wife runs off to a near-by
pool with a .22 rifle and brings back a dead plover which
they tear apart with their hands and eat raw on the spot.
They paddle in the shallow waters, carefully lifting up
stones under which tiny fish are hidden, and in a moment
they have caught a dozen of these fish, the biggest as long
as my hand. They eat them raw, and the child cries out that
he too wants a fish. The fish is too big for him and it sticks
out of his mouth, the tail flapping while he tries to bite off
the head. Quickly his mother runs to his rescue, chews up
the fish for him, and feeds it back to him, mouth to mouth.
She slakes his thirst in the same way while Utak sucks an
icicle as if it were a sherbet.

Trudging along, watching the play of these people, absorbed by the charming picture of the mother's bird-like
feeding of the child, seeing the lad enthroned upon his
father's pack, all thought of the monotony of the landscape
went out of my mind. It came to me suddenly—and this
discovery preoccupied me entirely—that here was unity, here
was the eternal and primitive family, the family of the
Bible: father, mother, child, beasts of burden, all composing
one body with multiple heads. As the Touaregs in the Sahara form with their dogs and camels and children a wandering island of life in the desert, so these Eskimos, in these
barren immensities, kept themselves alive only by virtue of
their compact solidarity. They clung to one another as if in
constant fear that otherwise this single body might fall apart.
The wife trotted in the footsteps of the husband, though

from time to time she would move up abreast of him in order to talk to the child. The husband turned round now and again to throw a look at the dogs; and if one of the dogs lingered, they waited for him to come up, as if the degree of elasticity in this body was limited. Then once again they would collect into a block. Thus they advanced over the plain, as brown and colorless as the tundra itself, so that if they had not stirred, it would have been hard for me to distinguish them in this landscape.

It was clear that the child was master in the Eskimo family. Perched high with widespread legs, as if riding a camel, he spoke forth his edicts and he was obeyed. When he sent down a question to his father, he was answered without impatience. When he signified that he pre- ferred to walk, they stopped, the world stopped. Each took the child by a hand, and half holding, half carrying him, the three moved with slow steps down the trail. There was no irritability in these parents, no complaint over time lost. The child's desires were as orders, and the parents obeyed. Back on the pack again, the little boy spoke two or three words, and the father, to amuse the child, re- peated them over and over again, like a nurse in a family where the heir is prince and tyrant.

All this, I say, I watched, but I was not of it. They ignored me completely, and to my great pleasure, for I did not wish to be drawn into their body. I was too happy watching them and, by this time, too happy in my thoughts. They had in the end isolated me with such success that I walked in a world of fancy, of dreams, and one after another there

passed through my mind a hundred comforting pictures out
of the Bible.

The sun sank, and of a sudden the earth grew dark. Light,
which was all the life of this land, had gone out of it, and
the land was dead. Now my Eskimos were hardly discernible, and the night came down and blotted out the
world. We had done perhaps fifteen or eighteen of thirty-
five miles, and time had come to make camp. We pitched
our tent on the flank of a ridge while the chilly air grew
colder. On the frozen ground we spread our caribou skins,
stuck a lighted candle on an empty box, and lit the Primus
stove. Utak stripped to the waist; the child, naked, was
already playing on the skins, and his mother had taken off
her outer garments. By signs, Utak let me know that I must
do as he had done, and dry my clothes lest I freeze in the
chilled sweat.

The Primus was going, and soon we would eat. I slipped
out. Seen from fifty yards away the tent was tiny and the
glow of the candle was a faint gleam. Without, the world
seemed endless and our habitation less than a dot upon its
face. I drew a long breath, the extent of my weariness came
suddenly over me, and I went back into the tent.

We brewed tea and drank it with boiled rice and raw
fish. I lay on the ground dazed with fatigue, but they were
as fresh as when we started. Supper was no sooner over than
they began to play with the child, hiding little things round
the tent which he never failed to find and hold up in triumph. This went on for two hours in the midst of noisy
laughter while I looked on at them and at the swift and
silent flow of their huge shadows on the tent walls. They
were still at their game when I fell asleep, thinking as I

dozed off how strange was this gaiety in the midst of infinity.

It was the afternoon of the next day that we reached our destination. This time my disappointment was really great. I had been told that I would be taken to a fish camp: what I saw, on the edge of a creek, was three miserable tents and not a soul in sight. Dogs barked to signal our approach, however, and two or three men came out of the tents. A canvas boat was solemnly unfolded and the big man of the camp crossed the creek to row me back while the others forded the stream on foot.

Once on the other side, my astonishment was great to see my hosts suddenly vanish. They had returned to their tents, and now each sat in his own, awaiting my visit. Eskimo etiquette is not elaborate, but it is strict. It demanded that I pay the first visits and leave in each tent a gift, however small. And until I, the newcomer, had done this, life in the camp was suspended. What was more, Utak and his wife would not accompany me on my round of calls: I must go alone.

No man being chief among the Eskimos, there was no speech from the throne, no seat of honor for the guest, no ceremonial cup of welcome, not even a word of thanks for the canister of tea I presented to the wife of Ohudlerk, the packet of needles that constituted my credentials in the second tent, the plug of tobacco I left with the mistress of the third. Each object was taken from my hand and swiftly concealed beneath a heap of rags on the ground. The visits lasted but a moment, and I was back with Utak and his family.

They were on my heels, all of them, returning my visits before I had time to sit down. And what a difference there

was now in their faces, their attitude! In their own tents
they had been solemn, stony; in mine they were buzzing
with activity and good cheer. They had the right, it appeared, to handle everything I owned, open whatever was
shut, test the strength of whatever might be breakable. Paper
fascinated them, particularly, and they spent minutes over
it, feeling it, rubbing it, turning it over and over, trying to
get to the bottom of its mystery. Where could this thing
come from? they seemed to ask. Why was it so light?
What was it used for? You could almost see through it,—
though this was a discovery of the children, who put it over
their faces and insisted it would be wonderful for masks.

Invaded, inundated by my visitors, I saw suddenly that
Utak, radiant with joy, was serving as butler, giving away
my tea, my tobacco, my biscuits. The visit lasted exactly the
length of time required to clean me out of provisions; for
it is again a matter of Eskimo etiquette that nothing be left
unconsumed. And when they had manifested full obedience
to their code, my visitors withdrew.

It was by now very late. Lacking all experience of Eskimo
society, I had not taken Utak's hospitality in good part. For
one thing, I was far from suspecting that he had not been
pillaging me, but had rather been helping me, acting in my
behalf. For another, my mind was troubled by a question:
Had I been right to allow the sacking of my grub? Would
not this compliance be seen by them as a sign of weakness?
Had I not started my Eskimo life under a severe handicap?
I was tired, I was annoyed, I was dissatisfied with myself,
and in this sour mood I was trying to get to sleep when of
a sudden the child, lying between its parents under their
only blanket, began to cry. He wept, and then he howled.
The toothache, I thought; he must have the toothache. Not
at all. It was tea he wanted. At one in the morning. And

would his parents silence him? Punish him? By no means. His mother got up, got the Primus going again—in the dark, in order not to disturb me—and brewed tea for him. All this to content a whim. Had the child cried for the moon his father would have shot at it with the native bow and arrows that lay near by on the ground.

I woke next morning with the impression that living among these people was not going to be easy. It was not so much that I had trouble sleeping, that the inside of my bag was chill and humid and the outside covered with frost, that the sky was grey, cheerless, and the landscape actively repellent. What worried me most of all was the Eskimos themselves. I had not expected them to be actually sordid, physically repugnant, and possessed by a nature in which I could see none of the generous hospitality of primitive peoples elsewhere, none of the frankness I had known in other parts of the world, but only suspicion, cunning, slyness. And not an atom of even the most "practical" intelligence! Fifty yards off, on a gentle slope above the stream, the ground was perfectly dry; yet they chose to pitch their tents in the mud of the river bank. And I could not forget how my grub had been pillaged. Not that it mattered materially; but I could not make up my mind whether it had been deliberately or innocently done.

Most of that day, two children came and went in my tent. They would arrive, would plant themselves in front of me, and would stare. One was really astonishingly dressed. A great part of both his inner and outer clothing seemed to have been gnawed away, and I could see a bit of hide over his pudgy belly and a pair of pants that hung as if hooked to his navel. The pants were once his father's, and so much too big for him that an enormous pocket covered his knee.

For the rest, he was not unattractive, and in this lugubrious place it was pleasant to see his grin and hear the clatter of Eskimo consonants in his childish voice.

The other was a little girl with an absolutely expressionless glance. She was the youngest daughter of Tutiak, and her greasy hair hung like his over her face and down to her shoulders. As is common with the Eskimos, particularly the women, her arms were not in her sleeves but were clasped across her chest, where they served to keep her warm. When she left to go back to her father's tent, I watched her as she skirted the ridge. It was like watching a scarecrow on its way to bed. The girl was eleven years old. She had long been promised in marriage, and her young man had come last year from Pelly Bay, two hundred and fifty miles away, to claim his bride. Tutiak had put him off till next year, saying the girl was still too young. The man had travelled five hundred miles to no purpose.

In the evening, as we squatted round the tent of the man of great prowess, whose name was Ohudlerk, I asked:

"Do we go fishing to-morrow?"

Ohudlerk nodded. *"Her-kin-nerk mi-ki-luk,"* he answered. "When the sun is low." (They all spoke a kind of pidgeon-Eskimo so that I might understand.) And Ohudlerk held out his hand at a certain distance from the ground, which is their fashion of indicating the hour.

It was long after four o'clock the next afternoon when we started for the river. Each of the five Eskimos at this camp carried a three-pronged harpoon, the wooden pole of which was about nine feet long and the prongs made of musk-ox horn. They had built a stone dam across the stream from bank to bank. Upstream of the dam, circular stone traps had been laid in the water, and into these traps the fish swam

through slits left in the dam. When the traps were full of
fish, the booted Eskimos stepped into them and speared the
fish. One of them passed me his harpoon, but the fish I
aimed at shot so swiftly into the trap in which I stood that
I missed them again and again, to the great glee of the
onlookers. After my exhibition of the white man's ineptitude, they leapt together into their traps and began to spear
fish to right and left with incredible aim, driving their forks
so furiously and repeatedly that sometimes they would stab
the same fish several times. Each time that a fish was speared,
the fisherman hooked a bone needle through its gill, and
ran it along a cord until it hung at his waist; but if he was
in a hurry, he would simply grip the fish in his teeth and
go on spearing. (The teeth of the Eskimos, incidentally,
serve them as a third and most powerful hand. When Utak's
wife was unable to pull off my soaking sealskin boots with
her hands, she would tug with her teeth and they would
slip off without trouble.) The spearing went on for about
ten minutes in a sort of frenzy of spurting water and splash-
ing men, and then it suddenly stopped. The traps were
empty now, except for a dozen stray fish taken from beneath the rocks. Back at camp the fish were slit open, their
precious oil was allowed to flow into sealskin bladders, and
the fish were hung up to dry.

It is an axiom of Eskimo life that men who have fished
or hunted deserve to eat, and the proper time to eat is as
soon as the game is in the hand. Three or four days' catch
was in the camp, and we gathered in the evening to feast
in Ohudlerk's tent. A great heap of dried Arctic trout lay
on the ground beside the host, its flesh blood red. Ohudlerk
took up a fish, sliced it from head down to the tail, and set
his teeth into the first slice. With his circular Eskimo knife

he cut off the first slice at his lips and passed what remained
to me, who sat at his left. I bit into it and passed it on, and
so slice after slice made the round of the circle, always clock-

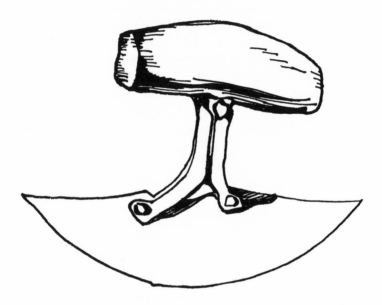

wise and with a speed such that each time I bit off as little as
I could in order not to disgrace myself by dropping out. Later,
and more especially in the igloo, I was to find it otherwise;
but here no one spoke, no one laughed, everyone gnawed
and swallowed and gulped with a kind of gloomy haste, a
dark gluttony, which I thought would never end and which
ended so suddenly that I was amazed. Abruptly, the sound
of the gripping jaws and smacking lips was gone. Their
appetite, like a fever, had fallen away. A kind of somnolent
appeasement filled the tent, and half these Eskimos were
already snoring in the places where a moment ago they had
been gulping and belching. Ohudlerk sat nodding and rum-

inating, and in this tranquillity my nerves relaxed and I myself began to doze.

For the first of many many times I looked at the seal-oil lamp, at the warm and gentle glow that rose from the wick floating in the blubber, and there descended into me an affection for this primitive utensil that I am sure will never leave me. This lamp is not a cruet but an open vessel hollowed out of soapstone and filled with seal blubber which melts as the flame heats it. The wick, made of a sort of cotton grown on the tundra, is shaped with the fingers into a sawtooth length and floats along the edge of the vessel just above the rim. For more light, you lengthen it; for less it is made shorter. When the lamp smokes the wick is of course too long: with a stick made of soapstone you crush it down. If

the lamp splutters, the vessel wants replenishing. You put your hand into a barrel of blubber, take out two or three chunks, and let them down into the vessel where they drop with a soft thud. No one who had not lived with this lamp within the confines of a small space, tent or igloo, can know the radiance it creates, the friendliness and intimacy that radiate from it. When you are alone with the seal-oil lamp, you are alone with your thoughts, and you have need of nobody. I was to owe it a great deal of consolation in the months to come.

Next day we left the fish camp and returned to Gjoa Haven. There was no canvas boat this time to convey me

across the river. There was not even a native in sight,
though all knew the night before that we were leaving.
Eskimos never say good-bye. Probably, I said to myself, because they are practical and insensitive. A newcomer means
many things: grub, tobacco, news. He is worth greeting.
But a man who leaves is no more than that, an advantage
to nobody. There were other things to be said than this, but
I could not know those other things in my first week among
the Netsilik.

We forded the creek, and when we reached the other
bank I turned, despite myself, hoping at least that some one
would wave a hand. All that I saw was a woman emerging
from a tent and going about her affairs.

Chapter III

It was in early October that for the first time in my life I saw the sea congeal, saw the moving waters freeze and petrify in waves, in ridges, and in hollows.

There are many people round the world who see this every year, but to me who grew up in a region where the temperature rarely falls to five below, where our peasants still talk of the winter of 1879-80 when the stream had frozen solid and bullock carts had crossed the ice from bank to bank, the sight was magical, legendary. Imagine, I said to myself, a man going from Cherbourg to Halifax by dog-team!

This self-evident exclamation summed up, almost by chance, what was significant about the freezing of the Glacial Ocean. For the sea here is the great winter highway that joins camp to camp, family to family. It is the hunting-ground that yields not only sustenance for a season but reserves of provisions against the lean months to come. It is the habitat of the Eskimo, the "land" on which his igloo is built, and he lives on the sea and not on the land through many months of the year. Highway, because the runners of the sled glide more smoothly and swiftly over the uniform ice at sea than over the humped and hollowed drifts of variable and uncertain snow on land. Hunting-ground—nay, pasture-land, wheat-field, orchard, in the figurative sense—because fish and seal are more plentiful and constant than caribou, and more to the Eskimo's taste; while the white fox is to him a mere article of commerce, a source of his "luxuries" and not fundamental to the Eskimo's life. Land, finally, for here by preference the igloo is built: since the water under the ice is warmer than the eternally frozen ground, the house built over the water is warmer than the house built on the ground.

The sea does not freeze solid in a single night. Day after day I watched it, and I saw how, helped by the shifting winds, the grainy-surfaced mirror would crack and break, the waters would flow free, and then the struggle would begin again. Something more powerful than the demonic power of the sea was vanquishing its impetuousness, curbing its restless spirit. Little by little it was forced to yield, and the waves flung by it against the already frozen shore would stop in mid-air, defeated, crystallized. One morning there was left only a small pool of water in the bay, of a green so dark that it was almost black. Out of it popped a seal, and then another seal. Next day this pool, too, was gone, and there remained only the different shades of green and grey and white to attest the phases of the struggle. I saw the Eskimos move cautiously out from shore, saw them strike the ice smartly with their heels to test its strength, and saw them cross the pack to mark the arrival of the greatest of seasons.

Gibson, meanwhile, had been making ready for the coming of winter. First, as much of the coal as could be stored had to be brought in from the mound that lay by the shore. Then the rest had to be carefully covered over, kept warm, as it were; for when coal freezes it will not burn, and in a land where coal, delivered, is worth one hundred and seventy dollars a ton, you do not willingly waste it. Everything that great cold could damage had to be cared for: electric batteries, for example, which lose half their efficiency when they freeze; the glass jars of tomatoes and of pickles, which would burst in this temperature if they were not insulated. Potatoes that freeze instantly can be thawed out and remain good; but if they are left to freeze gradually, they rot and are lost. In the out-building where the trading with the Eskimos went on, the Store, everything had to be got ready in advance, for the Store was desperately cold and damp and a wise man would arrange to work there as swiftly and briefly as possible. Therefore Gibson was sorting his stock, cutting up bolts of calico into three-yard lengths, putting closest at hand on the shelves those articles most in demand. I found him one day removing one of the planks that formed the steps of his warehouse.

"What are you doing?" I asked.

"Putting a rotten plank in the place of this sound one," he said. "A plank like this is worth fifteen dollars, delivered here."

The wind was high, and creek and ridge were swept by gusts that sent the powdered snow running over the plain. Land and sky were fused in the same grey unity; and as there was no horizon the clouds seemed to rise straight out of the earth and move like swollen puffs of smoke from an invisible fire. It is here at the Pole that nature makes up the weather which is served out to the rest of the northern hemisphere, and I have seen how the process goes on in this chemist's laboratory, this meteorological kitchen. Made up, and then made up anew, for the crucibles and retorts bubble without stopping, and change and caprice seem to be the only constant elements in the mixture. The wind here is a scene designer and it shifts its stage-settings in a night. You think yourself a valley, do you? it seems to say: I level you off in half a day, and creek and ridge are gone. I paint you a scene while you wait, transforming Gjoa Haven in an hour and making it vanish in a moment. There is no longer a Gjoa Haven, no longer one undulation of ridge and plain in an endless series of ridges and plains. There is left merely one little bit of the Arctic identifiable by its cloud-invested black beacons that rise like gibbets in a tale of horror or a treatise on mediaeval justice.

We went to bed one night amid clear frost and total calm. Towards one in the morning the wind rose suddenly like a man leaping out of bed and running through a darkened house. The Post groaned, the wireless mast quivered among the whistling antennae, the snow whipped against the house, and, like the brush of a painter, applied the first coat of the element in which the Post would be blanketed with a thickness of six feet. When day came I went out of doors wearing three layers of clothing, and in the blast that sent the snow now forward on a broad front like an army, now whirling and tossing like a band of dervishes, I seemed to be dressed in a sieve and was bewildered by an incomprehensible impression of nakedness. The snow swirled as do the leaves at home, only this blow was hostile, this was autumn at seventy degrees latitude north. In that vortex I saw from time to time a blurred form, a native running; but what I saw looked like a shadow running without its man.

Towards five in the evening, as night began to fall, we heard above the sound of the storm a kind of scratching in

the porch of the Post. Then silence. We read on, Paddy and
I. After a time he said:

"Funny, that noise a few minutes ago."

He went out to have a look, and there in the porch, where
the snow filtering through was stuck a foot deep to the wall,
we found two natives, Ohudlerk and his son.

"*Una-i-kto!*" they said. (It is not warm.)

They shook the snow from their clothes and came in. The
old man went over to the stove and warmed his hands.

"*Igloo-pak man-a-kto una-kto-alu!*" (The white man's
house is good, it is warm.)

Coughing and spitting as he talked, he told us that the
snow was of a good sort, travelling would be easy now, and
they had already built igloos on the big lake. The fishing?
Very good. Many big fish—*e-ka-luk*—in the lake. As a matter of fact, he had brought in a couple of sackfuls to trade
—handsome, red-fleshed, thick-lipped fish, frozen stiff.
Seals? His son had killed "three of the left hand," which is
to say, added to the fingers of the right hand, eight of them.
Again he pointed to the stove:

"*Una-i-kto-alu!*" (It is very cold.) And Ohudlerk and his
son stood motionless in the middle of the room, not daring
to sit down, a picture of the primitive in this last refuge of
civilization, their eyes staring upward full of interrogation,
of rumination, of mystery.

When the wind fell and the sun returned we went off to
the little lake to cut ice for our winter supply of drinking
water. The blocks of ice were brought up from the lake to
the Post and piled on a trestle made of a couple of long
planks placed across three empty barrels. (Left on the
ground they would be covered by the twelve-foot snowdrifts
that were on their way.) All winter long we should bring in

a block at a time and drop it into the water barrel where, the barrel standing less than two feet from the stove, it would melt readily and yet not melt too fast. Set three feet from the stove it would scarcely melt at all.

With an eight-foot crocodile-toothed saw, a breaking back, and aching muscles, we cut long strips of ice, about eighteen inches wide. The strip was then chopped into squares with an axe, after which we strove with hooks to raise the plunging, circling slippery blocks out of the water. That done, the block was trimmed and the load dragged up to the Post. Eventually we raised a high wall of pale green, translucent ice that glittered like crystal when the sun shone through it. But it was killing work. We cut thirty blocks the first day —less than a third of the winter's need. Next day the freeze was harder, the ice was twenty inches thick on the lake instead of the ten inches possible to work, and we had to put off the rest of the job until the clear water froze and we could cut again in the same channel as before.

Everything is like this in the Arctic, for this is preeminently the land of instability and change. Yesterday a thing was possible: to-day it cannot be done. The snow, for example. Yesterday it was too soft, too fresh for travelling: to-day it is firm and right: to-morrow fresh snow may fall again, and if you are not away to-day, who knows when you will be able to travel?

It was a little later, towards the end of the month, that the first sled of the season got away. A first sled is always an event, and every one gathers to see it off. It means that winter has come, that travelling is possible, that chill and squall and the season of drear and hideousness are past. Not that there was as yet much snow. It lay in patches still without covering the whole land, and to travel would mean endless meandering from drift to drift, sixty miles to do where the crow flew twenty-five. But Eskimos have no need to think of time, and effort is of the essence of their existence.

Ohudlerk and his family were going inland. Their dogs were harnessed each to his own lead, and as they moved they spread fanwise, each lead buckled to a long central strap. His wife had gone on ahead of the sled some fifty yards. There she stopped, turned, called and waved to the dogs, and they broke abruptly out, barking as they ran. Alongside the sled ran Ohudlerk, braking now and then by clinging to a rope tied to the rear of the sled, digging his heels into the snow and dragging with all his strength. They were bound across the creek and had not made a hundred yards when two dogs began to fight. Ohudlerk ran up, beat the dogs, and they went on. At the foot of a rise on the far side of the creek there was still so little snow that the terrain had to be carefully explored before they could advance. Just then they saw that a puppy had leapt off the sled and was making back for the shack. Black as a bowling-ball, he ran with his tail between his legs, weeping hot tears; and when he reached the shack he flattened out, slipped under it, turned round, and peered out with only the end of his nose showing like a shiny truffle. The woman came up and hauled him out by the nose. He played dead. She dragged him and then beat him. He fought, choked, strangled; then, seeing that the game was up, half rose to his feet. When she got him back to the sled there was fresh trouble. Impossible to break it out. Ohudlerk swore, the dogs barked and tugged—nothing happened. Snow had to be scooped up and placed under the runners, and after another ten minutes they had made thirty yards—and they had thirty miles to go!

The wind was whistling through me, and I went back inside. Half an hour later I thought of them idly and looked out of the window. They were still there. I had a cup of tea and looked again. This time they had disappeared over the ridge.

All this was useful to me as a foretaste of what I was to go through, for it had been arranged that Utak would, for the value in trade of one white fox, take me inland again with his wife and child, I to provide my own grub, and, of course, carry with me the usual small gifts for the camp. By the time we were ready to leave snow was plentiful and round the Post the drifts were ten feet high. We had to go to the Store to get my effects together, and to cover those seventy-five yards we were fitted out cap-a-pie, exactly as for a long trek. Standing in the outer porch, we drew a deep breath like sailors about to dive into the sea. Paddy opened the door and a gust of snow blinded us as, head lowered, we literally flung ourselves forth. Before me was a wall of snow six feet high and over its crest the storm was blowing. I put up my hands and felt my way, sightless, until I reached a point where the drift seemed as hard as iron. There I grappled with it, trying to climb over it. Suddenly I was in it up to the hips, held in place by it, my equilibrum gone so that, had it not been for the ludicrous position in which I found myself, I should have been rolled over and over by the wind. How I got to the Store I cannot say; but when I got there, Paddy was kicking steps into a drift before it, and over those steps we reached the door.

The shelves of the Store were covered with snow, blown in through every slight interstice in the wooden building. "A pocket knife you want, is it? Under that heap of snow, there, in the corner. There's a box of them."

At this time I was still eating white man's grub. "Tell you what you do," said Paddy. "You make a thick soup of salt pork, beans, rice and whatever else we have that's filling. After it's cooked you spread it on a plank, like a poultice, put it out in the porch, and it will freeze instantly. Then you take a hammer and break it up into chunks and put the pieces in a sack. Leave the sack out where the stuff will stay frozen, and take it along when you go out on the trail. When you get to an igloo you warm up one of these paving blocks and your dinner is served."

I was learning incidentally that when a thing really freezes it does not like to thaw out again. One evening I opened a tin of peas and put the peas, tin and all, into a pot of water on the stove. The water boiled and bubbled for ten minutes, after which I took the tin out, thinking there would be nothing left in it. The tin was strictly intact, an absolute block. I broke the block into three pieces and put them back into the boiling water. The result was no better. Finally I had to chop the frozen mass into tiny bits before it would even begin to melt.

An Eskimo sled varies in length between a dozen and eighteen feet and stands no more than six or eight inches off the ground. Its runners are of steel, but steel will not do. Steel sticks: snow clings to it, freezes in lumps and impedes smooth running. The Eskimos have their own way of overcoming this. During the summer they bring up mud from the lake-bottoms and heap it up on land, where it freezes. When winter comes they hack off great chunks of the mud and boil it in a cauldron over a seal-oil lamp. Once the mud is thawed completely out, they smear it, boiling, on the runners where it freezes again, instantly though roughly. Then they borrow a carpenter's plane, if they are near the Post, or take an iron file if no plane is to be had, and they trim and dress the mud coating into perfect shape. The last step in the process is taken with the aid of a jug of water and a square of bearskin, *nanu-rak*. The Eskimo fills his mouth with water (which warms the water), sprays the bearskin with it, and runs rapidly the length of the overturned sled, spraying and rubbing the soaked bearskin over the mud-coated runners. This race up and down the runners—as I watched Utak perform it in preparation for our departure—is comical, but it allows an even coating of ice to form, for the water freezes instantly; and when this is done you can send the sled gliding with the slightest touch of your little finger. No Eskimo takes the trail without this preparation, and often the sled is re-iced in mid-trail because the veneer of ice will have cracked and broken off.

When the runners have been iced, the sled is loaded, and the procedure followed never varies. First come the caribou skins on which we sleep in the igloo. They are folded in three, exactly the width of the sled and always in the same folds. The heavy articles are piled on next—wooden cases curiously bound round with straps made of the skin of the great seal. The heaviest case goes in the middle of the sled; the highest is placed up forward to serve the driver as his box. Then comes what remains—frozen seal and frozen fish, for example, serving both as food for men and feed for dogs. Here again there is an example of primitive astuteness. Much of this food has been stored in caches at different points along the trail, each cache marked by a heap of stones. The fish are so placed in the cache that the frozen block which they form is the precise width of the sled. The Eskimo has only to hack off with his axe a section of this solid mass, and it is ready for loading. After the fish are stowed, the smaller paraphernalia go on—my sleeping-bag, the Primus stove, the box in which are my cameras, my grub, the articles I have bought for gifts and trading—plugs of tobacco

for the men, triangular skin-needles for the women. Utak's
riches come last, and they are made up in the main of the
white man's discards—a broken file, a bit of rope picked
up from the ground, three nails, and so on.

Eskimos have very definite ideas about how things should
be done, and Utak showed a little of the temper I had heard
about when I was imprudent enough—more properly, igno-
rant enough—to suggest a change. There is only one way to
do anything, and that is their way. When I intervened, Utak
growled. Yet as he had built his load with extreme haste,
with that haste born of a previous delay, he stood back,
looked sharply at his work, and began suddenly to fling
everything off the sled and start over again. When he had
re-packed, we covered the load with a canvas sled-cover, and
it rested on the snow like a great corpse while the dogs were
hitched, each in its place. The dogs, incidentally, are very
jealous of their place in the line, and if they are moved they
will either fight savagely or refuse to stir.

When everything seemed to be ready, it was suddenly discovered that the snow-knife was still in the shack. This in-
dispensable article that serves for eating, for building the
igloo, for attacking the polar bear, was fetched and slipped
under the sled-cover within reach of the driver. Then it was
seen that the harpoon, without which there is no sealing,
had been left on the ground beside the sled. This was
packed, and Utak, looking carefully up and down the sled,
was satisfied. One moment. The tea-pot! How could we
have forgotten it? Dug up out of the snow at her feet, Utak's
wife, Unarnak, displayed a rusted and dented utensil which
had certainly come out of Gibson's dust-bin and was still
to have a long and triumphant life in the igloo.

The loading had taken a good hour, and I was standing
by, all thought of departure driven out of my mind by the

length of the preparations, when suddenly the sled was off
and I found myself running after it, stumbling in the snow,
trying to catch up with Utak as he ran alongside whipping
his dogs. When I was quite out of breath he stopped the
dogs and grinned as I came panting up, happy to have put
the white man in a ridiculous posture. This time we were
off. We crossed the bay, rose up the ridge, I turned and
waved to an indifferent Gibson, and that for which I had
travelled ten thousand miles was at hand. We were a mere
two hundred yards from the Post when already it seemed
to me that I had been transported to another planet.

This was the trail, the far-off wilderness, and as I looked
round it seemed to me there was nothing to say about it.
Nothing happened, really, and yet we on the trail were always at work. Watch that dog! She is getting ready to squat
and stop, and if she does, give her the whip as the sled passes
her (for her lead is long enough to allow the passage of the
sled). Mind that stone! If the runner strikes it, the coating
of ice may break. Sit forward on the sled, Utak signs to me,
and he lets me know that by shifting my weight I can move
the sled from side to side so that the stones in the road will
pass between the runners. It is like sailing a boat: nothing
happens at sea in fair weather, yet if you said so to a sailor
he would look at you pityingly. A sailor is always busy, and
seems to be making work when there isn't any. Let him
doze off for an hour or two: on waking, he has a hundred
things to do.

Here it is the same. The plain is wide and empty. One
ridge looks for all the world exactly like the last. I do what I
can, go through the motions, for I am still far from forming
an integral part of this sled, this family, this landscape. But
there was one thing I could not do that Utak did constantly,

and that was to talk to the dogs. He chattered to them and swore at them, when he was not telling them tales, as if, were the sound of his voice to die down, they would stop stock still. I had so few words of Eskimo that we could not talk together; but he was a sociable fellow, obliging enough when in good humor, and he taught me the names of the dogs. He would point with his whip and say: "Nulia-y-uk." Then, "Ar-luk." And so he went through them all while I forgot each name as fast as he pronounced the next. To him, of course, these names meant a great deal: Nulia-y-uk was the spirit of the waters to whom the Eskimos prayed for good sealing. Ar-luk had been the name of his grandfather, and the spirits of the dead had been propitiated by the handsome transfer of his name to one of the dogs. Meanwhile, the very fact of talking about his dogs filled Utak with pride and dropped within him a germ of friendliness, for nothing surpasses the vainglory of the Eskimo in his dogs, his sled, his people. I felt that I ought to learn these names, and he, apparently, felt this even more than I did, for he would repeat them with the greatest patience, again and again.

"And this one?" I would ask, pointing.

"Ki-na-tam-na," he would answer, separating the syllables with care.

By this time I was off the box, trotting beside him. We would wait for the sled to come alongside, grab the tobacco tin, roll cigarettes as we trudged on, and—I still emulating Utak, striving by mimicry to become part of this life—scrutinize our world. Here was a strap loose, and if I did not tighten it as the sled glided on, half the load might slip off. Was that a little cloud we saw forward on the left? No, nothing to worry about. We sat down on the sled to rest, back to the wind, smoked for a bit, and then, after Utak had hummed to himself a while, both sprang down from

the sled, he on his side and I on mine, to lighten the load
and encourage the dogs.

Strangest of all was the absence of color in this landscape.
This world of the North, when it was not brown was grey.
Snow, I discovered, is not white!

For you Outside snow is an enchanting thing that comes
in the night and brings to you of a sudden a white and
beautiful world lying in silence out of the window when
you wake in the morning. You shave and dress in fairyland,
and you are cheerful as you go in to breakfast. Your children
make snowmen and stick pipes in their faces. The picture
flashes across your mind of grand dukes wrapped in furs,
wafted away in curving troikas behind jingling bells to call
on a ballerina on one of the islands round St. Petersburg.
For men in the Arctic snow is a thing of endless labor, always either too soft or too hard; a thing that drifts in
through the chinks of the igloo and fills one's clothing; a
thing that comes down for the express purpose of burying
your dogs and harpoons and whatever else you have had
the ill-luck to forget out of doors. Being uneven in its fall,
now here and now gone, it makes the trail a laborious thing.
In spring the careless are blinded by it. It buries the Arctic
and levels it off with such uniformity that you have to dig
with your heel to find out whether you are on sea or on
land. It is something you have constantly to clear away with
a shovel, cut with a snow-knife, melt for drinking water—
and that is a chore by itself, for the snow remains for hours
like sodden blotting paper. It is the danger against which
you are endlessly on guard, for it hides your trapline, undoes
your world and your plans, imprisons you in its anonymity.
A week of snow is beautiful: ten months of it is drudgery.

I speak, of course, as a tenderfoot, neglecting the fact that for Utak snow was the long-awaited gift of the gods, the magical element that made travelling possible, that furnished him a rampart against the wind when he spent hours on the frozen sea waiting for the seal to rise, that formed the handsome blocks of which he built his house. And yet much of what I have said is as true for him as for the man come from Outside.

For Utak, meanwhile, this landscape was the most beautiful scene in the world. For me it was grey, undefined, a world without proportion, without dimension, above all without color. Never did the horizon draw its comforting line to divide earth from sky: the two were of the same substance. There was no middle distance, no perspective, no outline, nothing the eye could cling to except the thousands of smoky plumes of snow running along the ground before the wind. The North, in winter, is a shallow cauldron without bottom or edge in which every day several times a day the winds rise and fall, the weather is this and that. You move on in a calm, saying to yourself that the next few hours, at least, will be easy. You look up, and the squall is on the way. It is rising, it looks as if it will pass you by; and at the moment when you are saying to yourself that it has passed you by, down upon you it comes on the bias. You have not had time to prepare for it, and when you have come to yourself it is gone, far away, whirling elsewhere— and you have a little time in which to repair its damage before the next squall strikes.

The moment came when we lost our way in this grey cotton-wool through which we were moving. The air was dense with swirling powder; from the sled itself the dogs were visible only as so many shadowy forms; and Utak left me on my box and disappeared on the run, ahead of the dogs. First I would lose him entirely, then he would reappear abruptly and I would see him nose to the ground, staring, peering, moving with extraordinary rapidity. When the Eskimo wants to bestir himself, he can move very swiftly. I watched Utak that day weaving from right to left and back again, floating as if uplifted by the wind, and that fusion of man with nature was an absorbing spectacle. Suddenly he swerved rearward as birds do when, ceasing to struggle against the wind, they let themselves be borne upon it. Again I saw him, this time running ahead of us while the dogs tugged furiously in order not to lose sight of him. A great stone rose in our path and stopped the sled. There was scarcely time to shake it loose when the dogs were off again as fast as they could trot.

Now and then the leader would turn round and stare at me as if in astonishment. He could not understand why his Eskimo should be floating in the void like this. (The normal relation of man and beast was reversed: this time it was the dog who was saying, "I've got a first-rate Eskimo, but there is something erratic about him to-day.") Utak was hunting sled tracks in a storm. Sled tracks are about two inches wide, and I said to myself again and again, trying to make it clear to myself: Tracks two inches wide, eighteen inches apart, going from New York to Boston, and *nothing else*—no railway, no motor road, no foot path, 'no landmarks. A world blank in all its breadth, and somewhere a pair of tracks the only trace of its length. Now the astonishing thing is that he found them. Digging with his heel into the fresh snow, he had found tracks; and directly he found them he was off again on the run like a leaf in a storm.

Alone on the sled, I let myself go, shut my eyes and pressed down my eyelids as if my purpose were to solder them together. Of course it was cowardly of me, but when the wind is cutting your face into ribbons there is nothing else you can do. Certain parts of me—cheeks and chin, particularly—had begun to burn as if seared with a hot iron, and where the burning took place I felt the flesh suddenly harden. I was shrivelling up. I tried to lower my head, to turn sidewise away from the wind, to roll up in a tense and miserable ball. I was ready to give up, and for a word I should have broken into sobs. My soul was shaken. Nature here was too strong, there was no resisting her. I was not even a straw; and all the inventions of civilization were no proof against this. I thought of those steel runners, and how inferior they were to the whale-bone runners that no season could defeat.

Utak had come back and signalled me to stop the sled and wait where I was. Then he disappeared again. I have no notion how long he was gone. The seconds went by like hours, and as each second dropped, I wondered what would happen if he failed to find us again. He had gone off to see if, on the right, there might not be a rock he could identify. These were their landmarks, and they knew them as well as the peasants at home knew "the broken branch" or "the oak that was struck by lightning." A while ago he had been running straight south, and I, who travelled only by the compass or the stars, had said to myself that he was mad. But here, within one hundred and fifty miles of the Magnetic Pole, the compass went crazy, and there were no stars. He was looking for a sign known to himself, and there were times when—to my anguish—we turned round and went back half an hour in search of that sign.

Night was falling when of a sudden three glimmering points too faint to be called lights pricked the grey scene. The igloos! Through the translucent snow of which these houses are built the feeble gleam of seal-oil lamps was visible, bespeaking the breath of life and the presence of man on this pallid ocean of ice. I crept through a winding tunnel so low that I went on all fours and knocked in the dark against wet and wriggling hairy bodies. These were the dogs. They had taken shelter in the freezing porch against the greater cold outside. Not for an empire would they have stirred out of my path, and over and among them I crawled until I emerged into the igloo.

But was this an igloo? This witch's cave black on one side with the smoke of the lamp and sweating out on the other the damp exudation caused by the warmth of lamp and human bodies! Within, nothing was white save an occasional line that marked the fitting of block to block; and the odor was inconceivable. In the vague light of the lamp shapeless things, men and women, were stirring obscurely. If you wanted a hierarchy of light you might say that before electricity there was the gas-jet, before the gas-jet the lamp, before the lamp the wax taper, before the wax taper the tallow candle, and before the tallow candle the seal-oil vessel. I was in a brown bear's lair, a troglodyte's cave. What would elsewhere be the stone age was here the ice age.

I was too newly come from Outside to see in the igloo anything but filth: the charnel heap of frozen meat piled on the ground behind the lamp; the gnawed fish-heads strewn everywhere; the sordid rags on the lumpish flesh, as if these Eskimos had worn their party clothes to the Post and were here revealing their true selves, the maculate bodies they covered with skin and fur to hide the truth from the White. And to heighten the horror of the scene, one of these Eskimos would fling himself from time to time into the porch—as the tunnel is called through which I had crawled

—to drive out the dogs; and a howling would resound as of murder committed in a subterranean chamber.

Even to-day, as I write, it is still difficult for me to explain how it happened that I was able to accustom myself to this life, so that within a month a description like this would seem to me stupid, would seem a recital of non-essentials and a neglect of everything consequent in Eskimo existence.

Fortunately, I was too overcome with weariness to be able to think. Details met my eye and offended it, but they could not reach as far as my brain. My box had been dragged in, and like an automaton I opened it in order to find something to eat, something "white" that would preserve me from all this. My soup was not there! Had I forgotten it? Probably; and for the reason that I had thought about it too much not to forget it. What was the Eskimo word for "soup"? I thumbed through my dictionary without a thought that the Eskimo might never eat soup, and there might be no word for it. Instead, I cursed the dictionary with the curse usual the world over—that a dictionary never contains the words we need. I could not explain to Utak what was missing; but as he saw me hunting, turning my effects over and over, he too—and this was the only comic note of the evening—he too began to hunt, though he knew not what he was hunting. What was I to eat? That frozen fish? That repellent snow-covered thing I could hear grating in their teeth as they chewed?

The household stared at me, and I needed no word of Eskimo to understand what they were thinking: not only had this white man no titbits to offer to them, he had not even brought his own grub. They said nothing, but their disapproval was unmistakable. Sick at heart, I crept into my bag and fell asleep without a morsel of food.

We slept six in a row, squeezed together in an igloo

built to hold three, our heads turned towards the porch.
The men lay naked in their caribou sleeping-bags. I kept
my clothes on, and it was as if I were sleeping in a cage
with wild beasts. All night long something dripped from
the ceiling upon my face, and though each drop sent a
twinge of pain through me, I could not evade it because
we were squeezed too tightly together. All night long, too,
my neighbor, Utak's brother, made use of the tin that served
as chamber-pot, and each time he would hold it out at
arm's length without stirring, and empty it under my nose.
In a corner an old woman spat the whole night through,
and between the one and the other, in a spirit of the deep-
est gloom of heart, through which the two or three images
of warmth and comfort that I summoned were unable to
make their way, I fell finally asleep.

When I awoke the igloo was empty except for the old
woman: the men had gone fishing.

I crawled out of doors and had a look round. It wanted
almost an effort to identify the igloos in this landscape.
There were four in all, four molehills made of snow; and
had it not been for the harpoons and other accoutrements
sticking up like vertical black lines drawn on white paper,
I should not have seen them. These strokes were the only
signs of the existence of a camp in this white infinity.

The camp was deserted. Nothing stirred. Here and there
a puppy lay half buried in the snow. The men had gone
with their sleds and their dogs. Every day was for them a
day of work and travel: every morning they awoke to the
same seasonal chores: ice the runners, harness the dogs, un-
leash the 40-foot serpentine whip with its 12-inch handle,
and go off to the fishing or the hunt.

The camp was built on the flank of a ridge, doubtless

because the snow here was more plentiful. Below me I
could see a wide flat surface which was a lake. Three out
of the five men in the camp had gone ice-fishing on this
lake; the other two had preferred to go off to another lake,
twenty-five miles distant, on pretext that the fish there were
bigger. At this time of year the ice was only two feet thick,
and fishing was still easy.

Utak came up from the lake before the rest in order to
build me an igloo. It was not to be separated altogether from
his own, but would be a sort of lean-to opening into his
igloo, and through this opening he and his wife would be
able to keep an eye on my tin of biscuits. However, I should
at least sleep alone this night.

One hour sufficed Utak for the erection of my spiral
shelter, and it was no sooner finished than soiled. The dogs
climbed and ran all over it on the outside, as is their habit,
and yellowed its dome and sides. Ohudlerk hastened to
pay me a visit as soon as I had installed myself. With a
great deal of hawking and spitting he explained to me that
the igloo was perfect—from which I was to understand
how great was my debt to Utak. And Utak himself, by way
of creating a fitting atmosphere, came in with the gift of a
heap of rotted fish.

An igloo is very pretty when it is new, when it has just
been finished and the *iglerk,* the flat couch of snow that
rises about fifteen inches from the floor, has been smoothed
down. It is so pretty, so white, so pure with its little heaps
of powdered snow at the base of the meeting of the blocks,
that one is afraid to move in it for fear of soiling it. But
the miraculous industry of the Eskimo soon removes this
sense of caution and daintiness. In less than a day the igloo
is made cosy and homelike: everything is spattered and

maculated; the heaps of objects brought inside create great black spots where they lie; the ground is strewn with the débris of fish spat forth in the course of eating; everywhere there are stains of seal blood and droppings of puppies (puppies are allowed indoors).

I am told that there are Eskimos who keep their igloos clean, scraping the floor daily and sprinkling fresh snow over it to cover the stains. This is not the case with the Netsilik of King William Land, who seem to feel the most profound indifference, indeed contempt, for cleanliness. As for my igloo, they invaded it as if in conquered territory; and after all, it was their igloo, I was their guest, they had doubtless the right to treat it as their own. There they sat on my *iglerk,* belching and laughing, picking out a morsel of the fish that lay on the ground—our food and the dogs' as well—as if they had come each time upon something particularly savory, and spitting the bones out straight in front of them.

I say again that I was too green to have any notion of Eskimo values. Every instinct in me prompted resistance, impelled me to throw these men out,—to do things which would have been stupid since they would have astonished my Eskimos fully as much as they might have angered them. I knew nothing, for example, of the variant of communism they practised, and which I later learned was the explanation of their taking possession of me, their shameless sharing among themselves of my goods, which on this occasion made me think of them as inconceivably impudent, filled with effrontery, and of myself as helpless and in a hopeless situation. They were the masters, I the captive, I said to myself. You wanted to live with the Eskimos, did you? I said. Well, here you are, you silly ass.

Thus, my beginnings went very badly. Worse than the pillage was the fact that two days later my hands froze.

"Una-i-kto!"—It is cold, Utak had said on waking that morning. But we had gone off together on his sled to fish on the great lake whose name I had by now learned. It was called Kakivok-tar-vik, "the place where we fish with the three-pronged harpoon."

Half a mile out from shore Utak began by clearing the snow off the surface of the lake with his native shovel in a circle about twelve feet in diameter. Then he knelt down, a hand shading his eyes, his nose to the ice, and tried to judge whether or not the depth of the lake here was what it should be. I did as he did, and could see the bottom of the lake perfectly, the grasses waving and the fish moving past in their tranquil world. As soon as he spied the fish, Utak became feverish. He ran to the sled, which with the dogs had been left a hundred feet off, came back with an ice chisel, and now the ice was flying in an upward rain of chips. He was cutting out a hole, and it was incredible with what speed and precision he worked. I have seen Eskimos go through five feet of ice with one of these chisels in ten minutes. He would stop at every four or five inches, send down a sort of ladle made of bone, and slowly and cautiously bring up the chips.

When the hole had been pierced through, the water flowed in and brought to the surface the odd chips that still remained, which were carefully ladled off. Then, on the far side of the hole, Utak built a wind-screen of three snow blocks, one set straight ahead of him and each of the others serving as wings. This done, he spread a caribou skin, and knelt on it. With his left hand he unrolled a long cord at the end of which hung a small fish made of bone, with two fins. He let the decoy down into the water, and

when he jigged, or pulled on the cord, which he did with
the regularity of a clock, the fins beat. The little bone fish
was like a water-bug swimming. In his right hand, held
very near the hole, was the *kakivok,* the great three-pronged
harpoon. When the fish, lured by the decoy, came swimming beneath Utak, he would lower his harpoon gently
into the hole, and at the proper moment he would strike,
and the fish would be speared.

Nothing was more comical than the silhouette of Utak,
his bottom in the air, his nose literally scraping the ice, his
eyes fixed on the moving water, his whole being as motionless as a deer at the moment when it takes fright and is
about to run. At first I had knelt beside him. Then, my
hands freezing and my muscles stiff, I stood up to stretch.
He became furious, for a man walking round the hole
frightens away the fish. But one could hum as much as one
pleased without disturbing them, and as Utak peered into
the hole he kept up a monotonous humming. I came back
to where he crouched, for I was fascinated by what he was
doing. This seemed to please him, and undoubtedly it did.
The Eskimo is very proud of everything that he does, and
to see a white man imitating him is for him the highest
flattery.

With what patience that left hand, as regular as a metro-
nome, rose and fell while the hours went by! And what
passion the Eskimo put into this form of the chase! What
intensity was in his gaze! The tiniest fish that passed drew
from him muttered words, and it was clear that the game
absorbed him, that time and space had fled leaving him
only this hole in the ice over which he would peer for days
if necessary. As far as the eye could see in every direction
the scene was void of life; and in the midst of this immensity a single man, who might have been alone in the

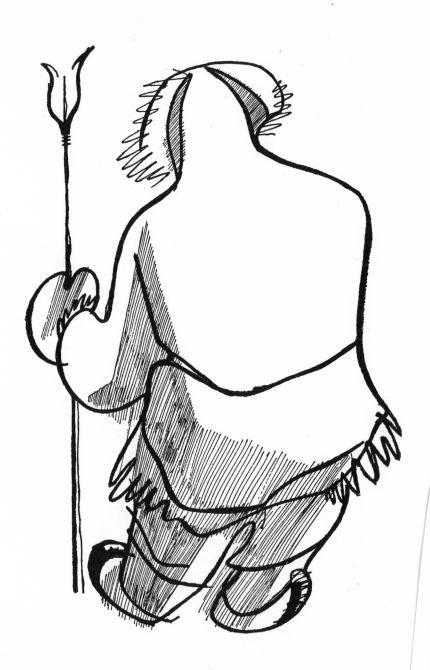

world, was absorbed with a scientist's concentration upon . . . upon what? Upon the art of filling his belly.

Had I not been tortured by the cold, I should have been content to watch for hours this admirable adjustment of primitive man to his element. But, although it could not have been more than fifteen degrees below zero, I was freezing. Doubtless my skin had not yet become adapted to this climate. My fingers burned in my gloves, and I was too vain to speak of it. But while I knelt there, thinking of nothing else, suddenly—a fish! Utak's right hand was closing over the handle of the *kakivok,* and before I could see what had happened, the thing was done, the fish was gasping on the ice, had flung itself twice in the air and then lay still, frozen almost on the spot. And Utak was back in the same posture, absorbed again in his chase.

We had been out several hours, and the pain in my fingers became so unbearable that I could have screamed. The heel of my hands also had begun to harden. When, finally, we stood up, I took off my gloves to have a look and saw that my fingers were waxen. I had frozen my eight fingertips.

Three days later my fingers were still useless: hard as wood, very painful, whenever I touched anything with them they burned, and I could not so much as roll my-self a cigarette. Rubbing them with snow did no good. Dipping them in coal-oil merely produced in them a sen-sation of cold. There was no remedy, and the best I could do was to hope they were not permanently frozen. Mean-while, I was chained to the igloo like a hospital patient to his bed.

From my *iglerk,* my couch, I watched the life of the women through the opening in the wall between our igloos.

Unarnak, Utak's wife, was industriously at work with her
kumak-sheun, her louse-catcher, a long caribou bone with
a tuft of polar-bear hair glued to the end. The hairs must
have had an extraordinary attraction for the lice, for this
species of hunting was always successful. It was a treat—
though I agree, of a special kind—to see Unarnak pull
three lice in succession off the hairs and crack them in her
teeth.

On the skins that covered their *iglerk* the little boy was
naked at play. He strutted, grimaced, chattered, and held
behind him a looking-glass while he peered round to see
in it the reflection of his bottom.

When the child forgot himself on the caribou skin his
mother put out a casual hand and scooped the brine off
the couch. The hand of the Eskimo is always busy, and it
serves him in a thousand ways: for example, to pick the
nose and then carefully place the catch in the mouth—a
detail for which I beg to be excused, but nothing is more
typically Eskimo than this. It is with her hand that Unarnak
trims the wick of the seal oil lamp; and when she has
finished she sucks the oil from her fingers, or else wipes
her fingers in her hair—though the latter means a less
thorough job. I have never yearned to find myself lord of
a harem of native mistresses; but the sight of Unarnak
would deprive any white man of the temptation to make
her dishonorable proposals.

At the other end of the *iglerk* Utak's mother, Niakognaluk, sat in her habitual seat. Squatting beside the completely shapeless old woman was a yellow bitch with flopping
ears, rendered equally shapeless by the fact that she was
heavy with a coming litter. The old woman sat all day long
scraping skins—a task that never ends in the life of the
Eskimo, for weather, snow, and water are constantly soaking

and hardening the clothes he wears and the skins he lies on, and it is only by this process of continual scraping that the hides can be softened again and made wearable and usable.

Niakognaluk is the only completely bald woman I have ever seen. She sat in her corner wearing an old woollen bonnet, dressed in hides so worn that all fur and hair was long gone out of them and they were as black and shiny as a blacksmith's leather apron. Bowed over the lamp, working with misshapen hands, her feet folded beneath her, she scraped and scraped; and as she worked tirelessly on she would murmur words which for all I knew might have been addressed to the lamp, to the dog, to herself. When a skin was finished she flung it against the igloo wall with an air of weariness and indifference and got up to get another, holding up her caribou trousers with both hands—the dress of these men and women is much alike—as she staggered across to the pile of skins, bent stiffly down, fumbled in the heap, and reeled back to her corner to squat again over her work.

She had two or three different scrapers to work with, but the real softening was done with her teeth. I have said before, I believe, that the Eskimo's teeth serve him as a third hand, and though I had demonstrations of this again and again, yet each time it was as marvellous in my eyes as a turn at the circus. The miracle was that when Niakognaluk had finished a skin it was really white and as supple as a glove.

Among the Eskimos as with the humble of every land, the Old Woman seemed to express the sum of experience, of hardship, of wisdom. She was symbolic; she was permanence; she was She Who Stays Behind. The others leave or die: she is always there. Each death, each winter, adds its burden to her load of life, bends and bows her a little more, but it does not achieve the breaking of her, and she goes on living. She mutters and seems to grumble, merely because she is old; but because she is old, also, her heart is kind. She makes no demands, and when you make her a little gift she sends forth a worn smile that is warm with friendliness.

Utak's mother was like this. She mumbled constantly over her work. She pretended endlessly that the child, who lived part of the day in the deep hood that hung down her back, would never leave her in peace. Tyrannical as are all Eskimo children, he rode her as if she were a spavined old mare, shook her as if she were a plum-tree; and while she complained her patience was limitless.

Generally the child was out with his mother, and the old woman sat alone with her dog. There was a sort of resemblance between the two. Two slanting slits were all the eyes one saw in the old woman's face, and the same was true of the dog. The bitch's coat and the old woman's covering were of the same color and the same state of decrepitude. Both were worn out by life, neither had any strength left; and when the old woman took up a whip-handle and beat the dog to drive her away, it was feebly and without conviction that she did so. The old dog would moan, but it would not stir. "You see," the dog seemed to say; "you try to beat me, but at bottom you don't even want to. And I don't want to go away. We belong here together." They would sit motionless, looking at each other, the dog with its flopping ears and bowed legs, the old woman with her rounded back and her misshapen hands. I could imagine their dialogue.

"You ought to be ashamed of yourself!" the old woman seemed to say. "To go on having puppies at your age! Will you never stop? And I'm sure their father is that Arluk, that useless hound who howls in harness before you've even laid a whip to him. Kigiarna, aren't you ashamed?"

The bitch would flatten herself out, cringing.

"And of course you intend to drop your litter in the warmth of the igloo. Naturally. I'll find the puppies one of these days in my sleeping-bag, and I'll be the one to bring them up. Not for the first time, either. You weren't so concerned about these things when you were younger. Time was when your puppies were born in the porch; out in the snow, even."

And Kigiarna would approve every word, pitiably.

Among these Netsilik Eskimos, these *Inuit* or "men, preeminently," as they boasted themselves, the routine upon waking in the igloo never varied. It went like this.

First, hawk and spit for at least half an hour.

Second, grumble and mutter until your wife, having crawled out of the *krepik*, the deerskin bag, has taken up the circular knife and cut off a great piece of the frozen fish that lies on the ground.

Third, eat the fish, panting and grumbling meanwhile because wife and child are stirring in the *krepik* and getting into the way of your free arm.

Fourth, between each bite, suck your fingers noisily and tell a story or recount your dream, a satisfied appetite having put you in a good humor.

Fifth, with great deal of puffing and snorting, light the Primus stove. If it refuses to go, fling it across the igloo and slide down growling into the *krepik*, after which silence is restored in the igloo. If the Primus should catch with little trouble,

sixth, brew tea, gulp down two or three mugs, and say *"Una-i-kto,"*—"It is cold,"—so that the Kabloona (the white man) may be seized with compassion and get up to prepare his grub for you. After each mug of tea, wipe up the leaves with your fingers and eat them.

Finally, having eaten and drunk and woken the entire household, come up out of your *krepik*, ready to be off fishing.

The men came in from their jigging and the silent igloo was suddenly filled with stampings, threshings and snortings as of beasts in a stable. Voices and laughter broke forth; the constant and horrible coughing and spitting began that seems always to attack the Eskimo indoors. The tea, which had been boiling all day long above the seal-oil lamp, was poured into mugs and bowls and its steam rose from between their hands in an odor of seal while the air of the igloo became a vapor in which the bodies were seen as shapeless blurs.

Almost immediately an incident took place that gave me a great fright.

Ohudlerk's son, Kakokto, who had been away fishing on the distant lake, had come back to visit his father. He and his wife were standing before me in my igloo, and as it was time to eat and they seemed to be expecting something, I fed them. Whether it was jealousy or not I do not know, but while I was talking to the young couple, Unarnak came in, picked up my sack of flour, and took it into her igloo. There she proceeded to bake an impressive quantity of *baneks*—a sort of flat bread—which she distributed to everybody present. I watched her out of the corner of my eye and observed that she had been lacking in the first article of courtesy, which was to offer the *baneks* first to me. I waited a moment; then, seeing that the sack was not restored to its place, I told her quietly to put it back where she had found it.

Up to that moment everybody had been in splendid humor—those in my igloo because they had supped handsomely, those in Utak's because they had received an unexpected offering. As soon as I had spoken—in the hearing of every one—silence fell. Unarnak, knowing that I considered her at fault, gathered together all the *baneks* and placed them without a word on my *iglerk,* with an air of complete disinterestedness. But her husband would not take it thus. Like a true Asiatic, this Eskimo conceived his finest vengeance to lie in ridicule. Refusing contemptuously the tea I offered him, he let himself back on his couch and then, the igloo being full of people, smoke, and laughter, lying back, and with an almost casual air, he began to tell them how I had frozen my fingers. It was not hard to guess his story.

"And there was the Kabloona," he said sarcastically, "walking in a circle and stamping his feet, blowing on his fingers, making noise enough to frighten away all the fish in the lake, and saying, *'Aiie! Aiie!* My fingers are frozen!' till he looked like an unhappy fish, like the littlest fish in the world."

All of them roared with laughter, for a game of this sort is always played collectively. Besides, they knew that if they laughed the wonderful story would go on. And it did. I could feel the tone of its rise, could see that Utak had become excited from the very fact of having a tale to tell, and was making it as daring and as cutting as he could.

"Finally we started back," he went on. "It was all he could do to drag himself back to his couch, and there he's been lying these three days past, whimpering and showing his fingers and moaning: *'Una-i-kto!'* "

And Utak, with wonderful mimicry, counterfeited not only my gestures but the very timbre of my voice.

"And to-night, finally, for a couple of grains of flour . . ."

The rest found all this very funny, and each time that a burst of laughter greeted one of his sallies Utak would turn towards me to see how I was taking it. Some of the others, indeed, rose from their places and came round to have a good look at me as I sat there, ill and half stupefied with fever,—for it was curious that my frozen fingers had raised my temperature.

I went on talking to Kakokto and his wife as if I had no notion what was towards, but at bottom I was extremely upset by the sudden turn which things had taken. And they did not entirely stop there. For when Utak had finished, he and his wife got up and went triumphantly out to tell their story in the next igloo.

Remembering what Paddy Gibson had said to me about Utak, I slept with one eye open. This fellow is subject to fits of temper, I thought. He killed his stepfather. He had to leave his own family and come to live on this side of the island because of it. I was uneasy. Never before had I heard that word for white man—Kabloona—pronounced with such contempt; and I suspected that this contempt came into an Eskimo's mouth only when he felt positively aggressive. I seemed to myself imprisoned in a disquieting atmosphere and had no notion what might come of this. I knew only one thing—that I could not retreat from the position of indifference and dignity which I had adopted.

I dropped off to sleep, and suddenly I awoke. I had no notion of the time and could hear the child crying. Utak was standing smoking a cigarette, his wife was stirring about, and all three were clothed. Unarnak came into my igloo and, thinking me asleep, picked up swiftly a pile of skins which belonged to them and had been stored with me for want of room in their igloo. They are going to strike camp and desert me, I said to myself, still with my eye on them. They seemed to be consulting each other, to hesitate. Finally they went to bed. Weariness sent me back to sleep—and in the morning it was all over. The first thing I saw on opening my eyes was Utak bending over me, grinning and offering me a mug of tea, a peace token.

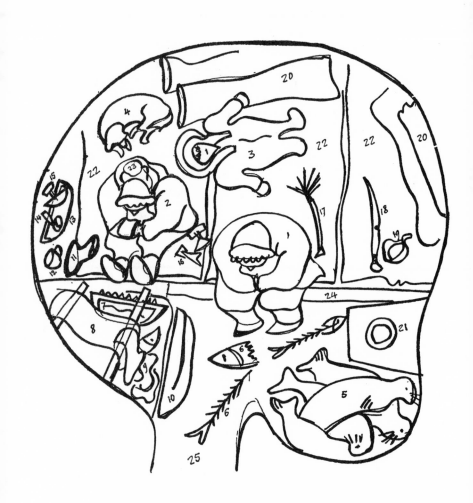

AN IGLOO SEEN FROM ABOVE

1. **Old man sitting on** the couch (made of snow) and talking to himself while nobody listens. He repeats the same thing ten times over, explaining how he saw the polar bear on the pack.
2. Wife sitting, holding the baby in the hood. Sometimes she bends forward, trims the seal-oil lamp or starts scraping skins.
3. Elder child, fast asleep on the couch, arms outstretched. His deerskin suit is a one-piece suit.
4. Old bitch asleep. Dogs are generally not admitted inside the igloo, except a bitch when she is going to have pups, or the pups themselves when they are young. The rest of the dogs sleep outside, or if too cold, in the porch.
5. Heap of frozen seals, stored for meat. If hungry, you just bend forward, cut yourself a slice, throw the rest back on the heap.
6. Parts of fish, half eaten up. Some of these fish, especially lake trout, are of tremendous size (up to 55 lbs.)
7. Seal-oil lamp. Made of soapstone, with blubber in it, slowly melting. The wick is made of a sort of cotton which grows on the tundra in summer. The lamp has to be trimmed all the time and the wick kept in proper shape.
8. Drying rack above the lamp. Generally made by sticking 2 poles in the wall of the igloo. The rack is always filled with clothes, socks, mitts, etc. When a skin is wet, it has to be dried and re-scraped every time to regain its softness.
9. Chunks of meat ready to be eaten (raw of course).
10. Snow block used to seal the entrance of the igloo at night. The same block lasts sometimes several nights in succession.
11. A caribou sock about to be scraped or mended.
12. A mug—bought at the store from the white man.
13. Little seal-oil lamp—handy for travelling. The other, too heavy, is left somewhere in the snow or on a rock.
14. The soapstone pipe of the lady. The bowl is made of soapstone, the tube of driftwood and the mouthpiece of musk-ox horn.
15. Eskimo circular knife. The only workable shape, given the position of the Eskimos on the couch, since it requires only a movement of the wrist and not of the elbow.
16. One of the various skin-scrapers. Their shape varies according to the kind of scraping required.
17. Louse-catcher. The handle is made of deer bone, the tuft of polar bear hair.
18. Eskimo snow-knife, originally made of stone or caribou bone. Nowadays the handle alone is of caribou bone, the blade is made of steel from the store.
19. Bowl carved in the musk-ox's skull, used to drink seal-blood.
20. Spare deerskins or rags—generally rolled or piled up in the back of the couch for some indefinite use.
21. Stone bowl—for meals.
22. Caribou skins spread on the snow-couch, to sleep on.
23. Baby inside the mother's hood—naked.
24. Wall of the sleeping bench, about one foot high above the ground.
25. Entrance to the igloo from the porch.

Chapter IV

It goes without saying that this tundra is barren of vegetation. No tree flourishes here, no bush is to be seen, the land is without pasture, without oases; neither the camel nor the wild ass could survive here where man is able to live. The Eskimo, preeminently a nomad and a sea-hunter, is driven by the need to feed his family from point to point round an irregular circle, and it is the revolution of the seasons that directs his march. When the run of Arctic salmon in the river is over, he goes down to the lakes to jig through the ice. Meanwhile, he has begun also to trap the white fox. As the winter advances, as the ice thickens too deep for jigging and the big fish lie on the lake bottom refusing to be lured up, the Eskimo is forced to move on, for his family and his dogs consume about fifty pounds of food a day, an average terribly hard to maintain. The next curve on his circle is sealing and polar-bear hunting on the frozen sea. Then with the spring the caribou pass through on their way north; the great season of visiting opens; and in the autumn the river fish return. Thus the Eskimo is constantly on the march, driven by hunger through a cycle of peregrination whose signal characteristic is hardship and whose highest reward is not possession, nor leisure, but a full belly.

This cycle has its grandeur. Nowhere in the world have I known the seasons to speak so commandingly, ordain so precisely and inescapably what man must do to survive. And yet this imperious voice, if I am to judge by the cheerfulness with which the Eskimos listen to it, the serenity with which they set about obeying it, is full of solicitude, too. The Eskimos do not look upon their country as a harsh land, and among the variety of reasons for this I should put first the reason that it is their own, their unchallenged kingdom. Not only are they the undisputed owners of this land, but they are alone in it. All the caribou of the plains are theirs; theirs all the fish in the lakes, all the seal in the sea. No man disputes their prizes with them. No marauders burst in to steal their poor possessions and enslave their children, as among certain peoples of Africa. No armies, as in Europe, invade them to deprive them of their dominion over the snows. Because theft is unknown in this quasi-communist community, because their poverty is unenvied, and they have no neighbors to hate them, they are able to do as they did when we left the lake one morning to go out on the sea —store in their igloos what will not be needed for sealing, plant their fishing tackle upright on the round boss of the snowhouses as landmarks, and start down the trail without so much as turning their heads to see if all is safe,—the front door, as it were, locked, the windows all shut, the gate pulled to.

Looking at them as they loaded their sleds, seeing how each was helped by the rest, how all labored in common with no hint of selfishness as they ran from igloo to igloo, from sled to sled, with what smiles and laughter they chatted and drank their final mugs of tea before the great whips whistled in the air that a moment before had been coiled like lassos on the snow, it came to me that here was indeed the communal life, the Biblical clan which hitherto I had imagined only against a background of sand and date-palm. I watched the procession move out on the lake and into the valley that lay beyond the opposite shore, and though from tip to end the sleds stretched out half a mile, in the perspective lent by distance they formed a common being, a black caterpillar whose rings moved in response to a close and unified life and instinct.

The departure itself was a wonderful sight—sleds piled high, dogs barking and choking as they tugged at the heavy loads and had to be helped by the shoulders of the men at the rear, the excited cries and calls of the wives gesticulating ahead, while the old women, tied high in place on the loads, moaned as their ancient bones were shaken. Once away, there was a ceaseless bustling. Men and women ran alongside, the long whip flashed out at one or another of the dogs: here was a crone who complained and was given a word of comfort, there an old pot swinging loose that had to be retied; and of a sudden a sled would sway, guided so that the runners would not meet the fresh dog-droppings whose momentary warmth would melt the carefully spread coat of ice.

And with all this, we seemed hardly to advance through the wide and monotonous expanse. Our first stop was near a fish camp, where each man had his cache and provisions were to be taken on. The stones were removed, the cache opened, a great chunk of frozen fish hacked off with an axe; and this was to be their food pending the catching of the first seal. Whenever we stopped like this, the driver would stand off to right or left of the dogs, and with a long slow flick of the whip caress each husky that remained standing. At that gentle stroke, the dog would lie down; but indeed most were so trained and habituated to this, that as

soon as they stopped they lay down in their tracks. Then
there were a hundred things to do: unload the old woman,
for her muscles ached; give suck to the baby; disentangle
the crossed harness of the dogs; drink tea; after which the
men would stand apart with their pipes and talk shop. The
Eskimo is never at a loss for reasons to linger by the way.
Because his life is hard, his leisure is precious; and except
among peasants and common laborers, there is no such
pleasure taken from an hour's idleness in our civilized
world. I was learning, besides, that the Eskimo always does
what he wants to do the moment the notion comes to him
of doing it. This day was the first on which I began to see
in the Eskimo something attractive, and in his existence
something that a civilized man might envy.

Utak's family, and I with them, were not bound immediately for the seal camp, but as Eskimo etiquette demanded
that we escort the others a little distance, we spent two
hours in their company before stopping to watch them out
of sight and then go back. We were "home" again, well in
sight of the igloos, when suddenly Utak pulled up sharp and
the dogs stopped. He had spied a ptarmigan running in the
wind. Generally you spot this snow-colored bird only when
you are fairly near it, and it is the dark beak and the
smudge of black on its tail that reveal its presence. A man
from Outside would raise his gun immediately, but the
Eskimo runs after it, knowing that the bird will not fly off.
It trots, then flies, then trots again; and as Utak ran towards
it I saw the ptarmigan trotting on its hairy—not feathered
—feet until the moment when, being within fifteen yards
of it, Utak raised his rifle. Crack! The bird flew off un-
harmed and Utak came back with a wide grin.

Three days later, though they continued to sting, I felt pretty sure that my fingers were not going to drop off. I decided to chance it and let Utak take me sealing with the others instead of back to the Post. There was, besides, a serious reason why he should join the others. We had gone jigging daily, and the fish had been so small that no catch would suffice to feed us all.

It was now November, and when we woke after two days on the trail, in a hastily built night shelter, the igloo was in total darkness. The cold was intense, and I was not alone to feel it, for Utak had been muttering all night long the familiar words, "Una-i-kto!"—it is cold. Why certain igloos are almost cosy and certain others, like this one, never anything but glacial, I never learned. The quality of the snow had something to do with it; the care taken in building was an explanation; the way in which it, and in particular the porch, was oriented in respect of the wind, played a part. And of course an igloo built for the night only was not to be compared to the "permanent" snowhouse in which the seal-oil lamp burns all day long, the tea is steaming on the Primus at every instant, the space is warmed by the constant presence of women and children and puppies. But even between temporary igloos there was a difference.

It was so cold that all of us had slept in our clothes, and when we woke in the morning and fumbled for the Primus stove, we were puffing like seals. The early morning tea drunk, we lay listening. Out of doors the wind smacked the igloo. This was not travelling weather, and yet it was eight o'clock, and we should have been on the move.

We crawled out and made ready to leave. I dug the harness out of the snow while Utak loaded the sled. It was still dark when we started, and as I ran alongside I clung to the sled with one hand, in part because I could not see where I was going.

Stopping in a blizzard meant nothing to these people if they decided suddenly that they wanted a cup of tea. One might be within two hours of camp, the stop might mean another night in a hastily built igloo,—it made no difference. The sled would glide to a halt, an empty box would be turned on its side, a Primus stove set within, and tea would be brewed. The wind was cutting you to ribbons, but what of that? It did not prevent Unarnak and her mother-in-law from enjoying a tranquil chat together, nor Utak from amusing himself peacefully by pulling his son round and round on a tiny sled while the child squealed with joy. On shipboard in a heavy sea you watch the porpoises at play and wonder that they can take it so easily: the Eskimos are like those porpoises.

That night our igloo was built in total darkness, and while Utak laid block on block I stumbled round outside with a native shovel, tamping the snow down into fine powder and tossing it against the sides of the igloo, after which I smoothed it down to fill the chinks between the blocks. The igloo was about three-quarters built when I crawled in with my flashlight and lit up Utak's finishing touches.

When Utak was in a good temper and we had been friends all day, he took a bit more care with the igloo in order to make me more comfortable. Whether it was well built or not meant relatively little to him, for the cold was his element. And I soon learnt that if I awoke to hear him moaning it was not because of the cold, really, but in order to persuade me to make tea for him instantly.

Late on the third day out we left the inlet through which we had been going and found ourselves on the open ice-bound sea. We had been winding and bumping along for two hours. Day was dying. No camp was in sight, but we were undoubtedly on the track of the camp, for our leader, trotting nose to the ground, smelled its traces and was hurrying forward. She would raise her head from time to time, look to right and left, and then run nose down again as if she had found what she was looking for. The wind stung my face and the blow was so hard that it seemed to me we had no time to lose.

I was blessing the thought of the near-by camp, when at a word from Utak the dogs stopped in their tracks and Unarnak sprang down from the sled. We could easily have reached the camp that night; but hunger and thirst had suddenly assailed them, and there was of course no arguing with them. Utak began to cut out blocks of snow of which he built a shelter for the night. I was so upset that at first I refused to do my part and stamped round and round with stinging fingers, waiting for this igloo to go up. I was violating all the rules of their communal life, and I knew it; yet it was too much for me, I could not help myself.

The women looked at me in astonishment. "What is the matter with the Kabloona?" they seemed to say. The dogs, buried in the snow, were sleeping peacefully. The child was playing with his little sled. Utak worked steadily on. Finally, the igloo was finished and we were inside. We drank tea—to punish me I had been served last—and I asked Utak, chiefly in order to learn what mood he was in:

"Shall we reach camp to-night?"

"Na-una,"—"I don't know"—he answered with a smile.

The Eskimo is always non-committal; but added to that, this time, was the reflection, "What a nuisance this Kabloona is, always wanting to get somewhere, always asking useless questions! What a barbarian!"

I had learnt by now what my share of the work of installation was: bring in blocks of snow for water; unpack the boxes; start the Primus stove going; set up the drying rack over the stove; lay out mugs, biscuits, and the tobacco tin on the *iglerk*; replenish the water bucket with snow; see that the candle stays upright; keep the Primus from clogging and going out. You stop the sled at six in the evening, say, and it is not far from eleven o'clock before everything needed has been done and you are finally able to lie back on your skins and enjoy the bliss of a cigarette. And the next morning it has all to be undone again.

Next day it was Utak who was the first to sight the camp, and out of his belly rumbled the word "Igloo!" that word so magical that its very sound in these spaces suffices to efface all fretting and weariness. After a camp is sighted, the intervening time falls into two periods. You see it in the distance and are half an hour away from it. You leap on to the sled and sit humming because you are in sight of port. Five minutes before you make port, this beatific peace drops away, a tremor of excitation runs through dogs and men, and the sled begins to fly as if burdenless over the ice until with a flourish you pull up and the dogs stop dead in their tracks.

The seal camp was built in the shelter of a sort of bluff that fell sheer into the sea. What was now the ridge of this bluff had once been the seashore, but with the passage of time the land here had risen to a considerable height. Ourselves travelling on the sea, we had come upon the camp round a small peninsula, seeing it first from the right, and only the dark spots made by the dogs, and the harpoons standing like penstrokes in the air, had been visible as we advanced. The drift here was so heavy that the blocks of the igloos were buried beneath it, and what we knew to be men coming towards us looked at first like so many shapeless dark forms.

Strange faces, these were, for wherever the snow had fallen upon their clothes and faces it had instantly frozen, and behind those white patches of frost it was hard to discern the human visage. Ice hung from the eyebrows of these men as from crossbars on an iron fence, hiding three quarters of the eye. It turned their moustaches into Venetian glass and came down from their fur collars over their chests to lend them the beards of Jewish prophets. Who, I said to myself, is this Eskimo Santa Claus coming towards me? It was Tutiak.

"*Pollak-pak-tu-tin?*" he said with a grin. (Have you come to visit?)

Ohudlerk came in from the sea to greet me, and I stepped towards him. My hand was still in my glove, but he drew off his mitt ceremoniously, for Eskimos do not shake gloved hands. When you arrive at a camp you must shake the hand of every one without exception. It may be that one of the women, her child slung in the deep hood hanging at her back, will, out of shyness, not offer her hand. You must approach her and take her hand. Her eyes will flash with pleasure and she will lower one shoulder, jerk herself slightly; half out from the hood will tumble the child; and this white bewildered little figure will hold forth its hand. If it does not, the mother will take it and place it in yours.

The Eskimos learnt the hand-shake from the white men,

but they have, if I may say so, transformed it into something Asiatic. It is no longer a hand-shake but a slow ceremonious elevation of the hand to the height of the face, and once arrived there, it is accompanied by a charming grin. I have never seen it without thinking of two mandarins greeting one another at the entrance to a pagoda.

Remembering that I had not a great deal of grub left, I considered that I should be safer if I had my own igloo. All the men lent a hand in building it, and it was scarcely finished before it was invaded by the whole camp. The number was not great—a seal camp never embraces more than four or five igloos, and here there were only three—but they were all present, standing, seated, waiting, stretching forth their hands to the tobacco tin. Half my provisions went in two hours, and while I was desperate they were enchanted. They could not have been gayer had they been pirates dividing the loot of a newly captured prize. Utak was the happiest of them all. He had put himself in charge of the pillage, and everything he could lay hands on was being distributed—his own grub, I must own, as freely as mine; for the important thing was hospitality, ownership was nothing. The assault became ferocious, and the free and easy manner with which they took charge almost gave me pleasure. They would nudge me without the slightest embarrassment, and say: "Look here, give the child something. You can see that he wants some jam. Where do you keep it hidden?" Or: "Is this all the tobacco you have? For a white man, you haven't much." One of them turned up my tin of butter, and as the butter was frozen they would cut into it with a spoon, dip the spoon for a moment into their tea, and lick the spoon clean at one gulp.

I am not a very methodical man, but I had had some notion of rationing my grub according to the number of

days I should be out. This was not a procedure compatible
with Eskimo life. I could never make them understand the
principle of rationing. In the same way, when they saw me
make a note of what, in the course of bartering for primitive
objects, I had paid for a seal-oil vessel or a native knife, they
would roar with laughter.

I must describe Ohudlerk's igloo. It might be called
"Stench and Family Life." You crawled through the usual
porch—the *tor-sho,* or neck, of the igloo—and when you
put your head inside the body of the snowhouse you were
assailed by a warm stink that all but strangled you. This
noble aroma came from a niche to the right of the entrance
which Rembrandt might have been delighted to paint. It
was heaped with the carcasses of skinned and frozen foxes,
with quarters of polar bear and seal, all stiff and smeared
with frozen blood. This niche has a name: *Ne-ke angi-y-uk*
it is called,—or in the parlance of the North, "The Big
Feed." When any one at all is hungry—whether a member
of the family or another—he has only to bend down from
the *iglerk* beside which the treasure is piled, put out his
hand, and having filled his mouth with what he can cram
into it, fling back the rest.

Odor, but warmth, too, the gentle warmth of the seal-oil
lamp kept trimmed by Ohudlerk's wife; odor, and above all
collective life visible in its variety and simultaneity. Ohudlerk would be sitting in the middle of the *iglerk,* staring
straight ahead with a concentrated gaze while he spun out
long sentences, explanations in which he became entangled
and lost, concerning his day's hunting. Nobody would listen
to him, yet everybody formed his audience. It is hard to
convey the impression of a scene in which every one was
decidedly present and forming part of a whole, yet each

sat in a kind of solitude in which he was free to act, to move, to ruminate at will. The old woman crouching beside her lamp would scrape and scrape, seemingly not listening and yet hearing all that was said, for from time to time she would put in a word of comment.

In a niche on the left sat Kakokto and his young wife: he with a broad Roman face, good features but a little bovine with his low forehead and his hair cut in bangs forming a sort of skull-cap on his head; she gentle, obviously in love with him although he gave no sign of response to her feeling. Neither of them spoke. She sat sewing hides, plying the strong triangular needle, while he, his hands on his knees, stared into the void.

At the deep end of the igloo the children were at play, naked on the caribou skins and like all children inhabiting a world of their own. The Eskimo young have prodigious vitality, never display the slightest fatigue, and like slum children in our cities, go to bed only when their elders do. In Ohudlerk's igloo they would knock against their grandmother, roll over and over, and when the old woman grumbled they stopped playing, stared at her a moment, and resumed as if she were not there.

From time to time the lamp spluttered. The old woman leant forward and with her misshapen hands fished round in the blubber for the bits of cotton used as wick, brought them up to the edge, shaped them in her fingers, and then in the silence went on scraping her skins.

I was unlucky at this camp, for the sealing was poor, and when Utak proposed to go north for polar bear I jumped at the chance of activity. Tutiak and Kakokto had gone up earlier in the day, and we expected to catch up with them. By mid-afternoon we saw two black dots far ahead, forced our dogs, and came up with our friends. As evening fell, they ahead and we following, we reached what seemed to be the end of the world, *finis terrae*. Before us rose a high bluff sloping down to the surface of the sea at either side; behind this small and hilly island lay the gigantic world of pack ice that is driven down here by the wind from McClintock Channel to pile up, miles wide, on this promontory of King William Land.

We camped, built a single igloo for the four of us, and disposed ourselves in it. I had got into my sleeping-bag, when Tutiak came through the porch into the opening of the igloo, on all fours, pushing before him an enormous basin filled to the rim with great hunks of seal.

We made the usual tea, and then . . . I do not know what the hour was, but I who had dozed off woke up. Under my eye were the three Eskimos, three silhouettes lit up from behind by the uncertain glow of a candle that threw on the walls of the igloo a mural of fantastically magnified shadows. All three men were down on the floor in the same posture,—on their knees, torsos bent forward with bottoms in air and faces near the ground, motionless except for their greedy hands and their greedier chaps. They were eating, and whether it was that the smell of the seal had been irresistible, or that the idea of the hunt had stimulated their appetites, they had embarked upon a feast. Each had a huge chunk of meat in his hands and mouth, and by the soundless flitting of their arms made immeasurably long in the shadows on the wall, I could see that even before one piece had been wholly gobbled their hands were fumbling in the basin for the next quarter. The smell in the igloo was of seal and of savages hot and gulping. From where I lay their faces appeared to me in profile glistening with fat and running with blood; and with their flattened crania, their hair covering their foreheads, their moustaches hanging low over their mouths,—at least Tutiak's moustache,—their enormous jaws, they inspired in me so ineradicable a notion of the stone age that I think always of this scene when I read or hear of pre-historic man.

I have seen astonishing things, in remote places and not merely in circuses. In the New Hebrides, for example, I have unpacked my own meat in a circle of cannibals and have seen in their eyes a gleam that was perhaps more interesting than comforting. Here, in this igloo, all that I had seen before was now surpassed. There were three men, and there must have been fifty pounds of meat. The three men attacked that meat with the rumblings and growlings of animals warning their kind away from their private prey. They ground their teeth and their jaws cracked as they ate, and they belched—Tutiak most wonderfully of all—with long canvernous fatty belchings as of brutes drowned in contentment. The walls of the igloo were horrid with the ruddy dripping of bloody spittle. And still they ate on, and still they put out simian arms and turned over with indescribable hands morsels in the beginning disdained and now become dainties greedily swallowed. And still, like beasts, they picked up chunks and flung them almost instantly down again in order to put their teeth into other and perhaps more succulent bits. They had long since stopped cutting the meat with their circular knives: their teeth sufficed, and the very bones of the seal crackled and splintered in their faces. What those teeth could do, I already knew. When the cover of a gasoline drum could not be pried off with the fingers, an Eskimo would take it between his teeth and it would come easily away. When a strap made of sealskin freezes hard—and I know nothing tougher than sealskin—an Eskimo will put it in his mouth and chew it soft again. And those teeth were hardly to be called teeth. Worn down to the gums, they were sunken and unbreakable stumps of bone. If I were to fight with an Eskimo, my greatest fear would be lest he crack my skull with his teeth.

But on this evening their hands were even more fantastic than their teeth. I can still see Tutiak, in a moment of respite, licking the palms of his hands, then sucking each of his fingers, and finally scraping between the fingers with his snow-knife, slowly, with that concentrated air of a thoughtful animal,—and then beginning over again to eat of the seal. Their capacity of itself was fascinating to observe, and it was clear that like animals they were capable of absorbing amazing quantities of food, quite ready to take their chances with hunger a few days later. It is this, of course, that explains the swollen cannibal bellies of these otherwise powerful primitive men.

The pack over which we were hunting the polar bear was like nothing I had ever seen in a picture. There was no majesty here, no huge impressive ice floes, no icebergs resting like high men-o'-war on the water and clearly outlined against a blue sky. Here there was no water, there was nothing but pack ice,—a jumble pale blue and green at the base, built up by a distant and crazy giant and filling all space with its grotesque shapes. This was the surface of the moon, a limitless chaos through which we moved, tiny figures with our toy sleds lighted from the horizon by but half a sun,—for already the season had come when only half the sun appeared above the horizon, swollen, bloated, enormous, and almost entirely decorative, for the light was fast dying out of this source of earthly life. Repeatedly, we would have to cut out a breach in the pack, a passage as through a jungle. The harness of the dogs would catch on the jagged points, the beasts would howl with fear as they were almost impaled, and again and again a sled would hang suspended, like a motor car over the edge of a bridge, while we dragged and bumped our way through this broken and craggy landscape. You tried to break the point on which the sled hung, and of a sudden the whole thing would give way and down would come the sled, the runners losing each time a little more of their mud, the straps straining and cracking, and the dogs howling with all their lungs. And we ourselves, when the huskies flew off, having smelled the tracks of bear, would run and stumble after, cursing and too breathed to be able to call out and halt the dogs. We were pygmies attempting the labor of giants and coming to nothing but grief. Twice I had slipped with my knee wedged so tightly between blocks of ice that I thought the bones must crack, and I went limping on.

And still no bear! Tracks, yes, as wide as my two hands; but that was all. I was not made for this sort of chase. I was completely fagged out. Weariness and absence of physical control and equilibrium induced in me a surge of foul temper, and as I stumbled and limped on I thought of the absurdity of continuing to look for bear in this stupid, petrified, and undoubtedly endless and fantastical chaos.

But my Eskimos would not give up. They would pile up blocks of ice against an iceberg, dig their way to the top with the help of their knives, and there, pulling out telescopes bartered at the Hudson's Bay post, would stare long and carefully in every direction. Baboons with telescopes, I said scornfully to myself; and in a way I was not too unjust, for the seriousness with which they gazed had something exceedingly comic. But the comedy was not rich enough to amuse me (what comedy would have been?). I was concerned for my knee, my fingers were still frost-bitten, and

I was drowning with weariness. All the strength that was left in me I put into cursing the Eskimos and calling out to them, who were beyond the carrying power of my voice, in my language, which they could not understand,—shouting that I did not give a fig for their polar bear, that they were hunting a needle in a haystack, that if they went on instead of back we should have no sleds to return on, for already the sleds had been battered and damaged by this terrain. (This last was so true that I had to sling my two cameras round my neck, front and back, for safety.) As well plead with the wind. It was a long time before they came down from their perch muttering to one another, and we continued a trail on which I felt we were dwarfs in an African veldt until, night beginning to fall, they decided to turn back.

That journey homeward in darkness was an unrelieved agony. I was cold; I was freezing; not only in the flesh, but my soul was frozen. As I sat on the swaying and creaking sled the cold became an obsession, almost an hallucination, and soon I was in a delirium of cold. I was haunted by a single image: before me was a wall, immense and blank, like a wall in a film. I was walking along that wall and looking for a door into it which I could not find. It was The Wall of Cold. If I could collect my thoughts, and remember the *Open, Seasame!* I should be saved, for beyond that wall was warmth.

My brain had shrunk to the dimensions of a dried raisin. Stubbornly, painfully, almost maliciously, it clung to a single thought, made room for no other image: "I am cold!" I was not cold as people Outside are cold. I was not shivering. I was *in* the cold, dipped into a trough where the temperature was thirty degrees below zero and where I turned and rolled over and over in search of a non-existent issue. And from time to time I would shake with anger: "If it is written that I shall see a fire again, I shall warm myself, *I shall warm myself!*" The four words filled my mind; I whispered and muttered them again and again, like an oath of vengeance. "It's no good arguing with me," I mumbled. "I won't listen to any one: I shall warm myself, warm myself with fury. I shall put my legs into the flames, and if they sizzle I shall not draw them out. That will teach them!"

On we went. I had become something other than a human body. I was a lump, a thing shrivelled up and inert. The sled bumped and quivered, and in my mind there was no question but that we should never make camp. I am sure that if any one had said we should, I should have argued with him hotly: "Don't talk nonsense. Of course we are not going anywhere. Besides, we're all mad." Rage and cold were the two pillars of my delirium, supported now and then by a vain sarcasm. "And what was it you were going to do out on that ice pack, you idiot!" At one moment I felt that I could beat myself with anger; and in another moment I burst out laughing at my own imbecility. Then a glimmer of hope would enter: "If only I can concentrate hard enough, I am sure I can wipe out this cold simply by ceasing to think of it."

How long this went on, I cannot say. Time had fled, and for me there was no difference between a minute and an aeon. I went out of my head, probably. Then, of a sudden, without transition, even I could see the lights of the camp a hundred yards away. Like a ghost, I stepped into reality.

Part Two
The Post

Chapter I

TWENTY-FIVE men, women, and children made up the entire population of King William Land, a territory ten thousand miles in extent. A Texan or an Australian would not think it at all remarkable, perhaps, but for a European the notion of this sparsity was hard to get used to.

I had now seen more than half the inhabitants of the island, and here at the Post I should see them all before my frost-bitten fingers were sound again and I could once more take the trail. Not only they, but Eskimos from the mainland and from other islands, too, would come through the Post in time, for this rude and none too spacious shack, with its little stove, its wash-basin standing on the corner of a table, its box of tools rusting in the porch; this Post cut off from all the world, with no sending wireless, no boat, no sled nor dogs of its own, where twelve pencils formed part of the annual re-stocking and there was not even a flint for my pocket lighter; this outpost set down in the remotest corner of desolation, represented to the Eskimos of the whole Central Arctic the sum of the white man's civilization —a storehouse of wealth, a seat of luxury, the capital not only of their world but of his.

All of these Eskimos came to the Post at least once a year,

and some came a good deal oftener, though it cost them a
month on the trail to come and go again. Mostly, they came
to trade; but there were many who arrived only in order
to visit. Probably because of their isolation, perhaps because
the difficulty of life in this harsh land lends especial price
to conviviality, the Spirit of Visiting is a goddess more
highly esteemed among the Eskimos than among any other
people I know. They need no reason to start out: that the
impulse to visit has suddenly come over them is reason
enough. In a moment they have lashed their sled, they are
off in a blizzard; they travel ten days, fishing and hunting
on the way to keep themselves alive; and on the evening
of the tenth day, when night has long since fallen and the
Post Manager is huddling by the stove and thinking "what
filthy weather!" they pull in with a great barking of dogs
and swishing of whips, having pushed the loaded sled
desperately with all their strength up the slope of the ridge
upon which the Post is built. Snorting and puffing in the
darkness, they shuffle into the Post and sit down in the
outer room reserved for them.

The Post Manager, torn from his musings or his magazine, goes out to speak to them.

"Have you brought many foxes?" he asks the head of the
family.

"No fox," the Eskimo answers.

"And what have you come for?"

"*Pollak-pak-tunga,*" says the Eskimo with a wide grin. (I
am visiting.)

Of course they will have said to themselves that there will
be other Eskimos round the Post; and the prospect of a
feast in another man's igloo will have been enough to persuade them to drop what they were doing—fishing or
trapping—and be off instantly in obedience to this strongest

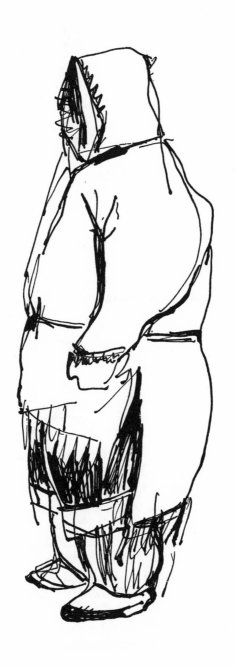

impulse in their existence—visiting. Let the fox be as plentiful as it may, let the fish run as never river has seen fish
run; once the idea of visiting has entered the Eskimo consciousness, nothing can displace it. And great as the adventure is for those who visit, it is no less an event for the
visited. In summer the newcomer plants his tent, in winter
he builds his igloo; and in the morning, when the Post
Manager looks out, the lonely shack has become a camp,
the sole igloo has been surrounded by three more of these
white mushrooms; and the trotting between tent and tent,
between igloo and igloo, the feasting here or there, is one of
the very deep sources of Eskimo joy.

In May or June, when, though winter is not over and the
sea is still frozen solid, the air is clear and one can see for
miles, the arrival of a sled provides a spectacle that goes on
for two hours. Everybody is out to watch its progress, and
never Breton sailor nor Nantucket widow stared at incoming ship with a gaze more intense. For one thing, a sled on
the frozen sea is the smallest object in the world, smaller
even than a boat seen from the air as it crosses the ocean. It
is microscopic, and I mean by this that it is not related to
anything human. Its movements, its changes of position, are
perceptible only *by the half-hour*. Its load may be two or
three feet high; its length will be, say, fourteen feet: what
are such dimensions against a sweep of fifty miles? The
Eskimo standing on shore beside you has seen it, of course,
long before you have seen it. He speaks of it, you raise your
telescope, and you whisper to yourself, "By Jove! He may be
right." "A sled?" you say to him; and the rumbling assent
comes up out of his belly, *"A-oo-dlar!"* (Coming!), with an
emphasis of conviction which itself comes out of his very
being. As animals are guided by the scent, so he knows

unquestioningly, intuitively, that this is a sled. There is an inner quiver of recognition, invisible to the white man but unmistakable for the man who feels it. You are free to go back indoors, for that dot will not have grown bigger in less than half an hour, and it may be two hours before it takes recognizable shape and is finally discernible as a sled.

With the passing of time you can make out that it is a thing on the move, a black object being pulled by an invisible thread, first across the horizon and then down from horizon towards where you stand. Probably there are three or four sleds, but as they all run in the same track, what you see is a single undulating ribbon of black. Now they pick up speed, they are close enough for the sharp-eyed natives to tell who the drivers are; and before you are aware of it they are only two hundred yards off and have made port.

Of a sudden the camp comes alive. There is a scurrying as if a giant foot had come down on a human ant-hill. Had Gjoa Haven been suddenly attacked by an enemy, the agitation would not be greater. Out of every igloo, like rabbits out of their holes, tumble and fly children and women. The women look like animated Christmas trees with the little fur tails bobbing all over their costumes as they run. In no time at all the bay is black with people.

The Eskimos have this extraordinary characteristic—twenty of them give you the impression of a hundred, lending magnificent confirmation to the words of Degas in criticism of another painter: "You make a crowd with five heads, not with fifty." I have arrived in seal camps at night and seen Eskimos swarming in every direction, crawling into and out of igloo porches, putting out hands and more hands to be shaken, crowding into my igloo in such numbers that there was scarcely room to raise a mug of tea to one's lips;—and counting them the next morning I have discovered that this populous cantonment number eighteen souls.

Here by the Post they were as many and as agitated as insects. There a sled is being unloaded, yonder is another being escorted in. Here are men standing before the harnessed dogs, calling to them to pull up to a given point, and before that has been done the same men have run to greet the sled behind. It is like an army parade in Paris on the Fourteenth of July: you have not seen the Dragoons past your post of observation before the Tanks have arrived, or the Marines, and you cannot make up your mind to which to give your attention. Most remarkable of all is the attitude of the newcomers, for all this aid and enthusiasm is received by them with cold impassive faces.

If you are an Eskimo, possessed of the Eskimo's self-respect, you will be concerned to arrive with dignity. There is an etiquette of arrival which you will not fail to observe. Like all etiquette, these forms deceive nobody, but it is necessary to go through them. You may be—and every one will know it—the veriest ne'er-do-well. Your dogs may be scrawny and mangey, and you may have had all the trouble in the world, puffing and lashing them with the whip, to get them to pull you into camp. No matter: you must make your entrance seated unconcernedly on the sled, driving your team as if you had never left the box from the time you started. Another thing. You must have stopped behind the ridge, and there, out of regard for form, have effected a transformation. Your sled must look ship-shape when you pull in,—sled-cover smooth and tightly relashed; and you yourself, your rough and practical boots stowed away and handsome impractical ones pulled on in their place, must drive in, nonchalantly smoking a cigarette and look-ing neither to right nor to left. Even when you are in, you must display no pleasure at the sight of your friends, no im-patience to shake their hands, exchange smiles with them, call out to them. Your sled is surrounded; friends are push-ing it forward from behind while others are leading your dogs on ahead; but you must wear a sober and concen-trated air. And once you have got down from the sled, you must rush immediately over to your dogs and chain them up, as if they were ferocious beasts, without appearing to notice anyone. Then, when all this has been done, you may turn round, lower your eyes like a modest conqueror, and condescend to smile and shake hands.

It was one of these spring arrivals that stirred up an ef-fervescence round the Post such as I had hitherto not seen. Two sleds had been sighted and a third was said to have broken down some distance way. In due time the visitors pulled in; and Utak and Ohudlerk constituted them-selves a committee of welcome—Utak because ever since that murder he had been making a special effort to dis-play himself a genuinely helpful and sociable fellow, and Ohudlerk for the simpler reason that he smelled caribou and was looking forward to a feast. They came and went, snorted and puffed, guided the dogs and helped unload; and in a few minutes the whole transient population of Gjoa Haven, surrounding the newcomers, had trooped into the Post and were standing round like children at a party, grinning and chattering and laughing. It is the custom that on their arrival at the Post newcomers are always given a "mug up,"—generally a thick soup, biscuits, and as much tea as they will drink. As a meal the thing is a joke to the Eskimo appetite; but it is flattering to eat in the white man's

house, and it would be impolitic to complain of the hospitality of a man out of whom one expected to get great things
shortly, in exchange for a few fox-skins. There we were,
Gibson and I, transformed into café waiters; and when it
was over we said to each other with a laugh, "The restau-
rant did good business to-day."

All of them, I say, had crowded in. Some were eating,
others looking on; but those who merely stood and looked
on were as gay as those who ate, for there are few joys to
the Eskimo heart as great as welcoming visitors. They filled
the benches and sat on the floor, and each time that one
of the guests sent forth a happy and rumbling regurgita-
tion, the others laughed delightedly and pronounced the
Eskimo syllable of assent and affirmation—a long drawn
out *eh-eh-eh!*—that was like a cheer, like applause. Tutiak
stood in their midst, and until two o'clock in the morning
he went on talking, most of the time to himself, for it is an
Eskimo habit to soliloquize endlessly in the presence of
others.

Finally they all got up, grinned, and were off, leaving the
air and the teacups filled with caribou hair.

"Off to bed, are they?" I said to Paddy.

"Not at all," he said; "they are going to eat."

I went out of doors, and saw that Paddy was right. At
three o'clock in the morning they were unpacking rotted
fish from their sleds in preparation for a feast.

Next day Utak went out to pull in the sled that had
broken down, while Ohudlerk, with his more practical
sense, had offered to go after the caribou meat which the
newcomers admitted having cached a few miles away.

The visitors were staying with Utak upon his repeated
insistence. In three days Utak would have no grub left and
would come whining to the Post Manager for a little tea

or coal oil. *"Miki-luk,"*—"Just a little," he would beg. But to-day this meant nothing to Utak. The social sense was stronger than the sense of self preservation, and among these Eskimos the man who distributed the greatest largesse was the man held in highest esteem.

Tutiak had this article of the Eskimo code constantly in mind—but from the receiving end. He was down on the bay, tom-codding in the wind in a temperature of thirty-five degrees below zero,—the tom-cod is a wretched fish, all mouth, and a man had to be poor indeed to want it,— when he saw the file of Eskimos walking towards the Store, the *Niu-va-vik*. Up the ridge he came on the run, and here he was in the Store, lecturing to the newcomers on each article and explaining its use. On and on he went without drawing breath, saliva drooling from his mouth, his chuckles drawing laughter from the others, pointing with his coarse finger to this and putting a hand on that as he spoke, and stressing each time, with a *"tam-na-lo"*—"this thing here"—the object he was talking about. At the Post, Tutiak's instinct always told him when food was coming, and nothing in the world could have made him leave before he was given a bowl of soup and a mug or two of tea. Having gulped these down, he wiped his moustache with the back of his hand and vanished,—as always among the Eskimos, without a word of thanks.

Trading at a Hudson's Bay Post is a struggle in which two mentalities, the White and the Eskimo, meet and lock. In the end each is persuaded that he has won the match— the white man because in this barter he has got his "price," and the Eskimo because he is convinced of having got something for nothing.

Your Eskimos turn up with sacks of foxes and signify

that they want to trade. The trading is done at the Store, which stands some forty yards off from the Post proper. You lead them out, and as they troop over the snow there is a good deal of strangled laughter. What a great farce this is! Once again they are going to do the white man in the eye, and once again the white man is not going to know what has happened to him. All those wonderful things that fill the Store are to be theirs for a few foxes. What can the white man want with foxes? In the igloo, a fox-skin will do as a clout, but even to wipe things with, the ptarmigan makes a better rag. It isn't possible that the white man should have so many things that need wiping!

One by one, like Arabs into a mosque, they file into the Store, wives and children at their heels. And though they have been inside before, each time that they see these treasures they stand stock still, silent, stunned. The Manager's house, the *igloo-pak,* is wonderful enough; but it is nothing beside the Store. To people for whom a rusted file is a treasure—Amundsen speaks of Eskimos travelling six hundred miles to get a few nails—this is the holy of holies. Here are whole boxes of nails, whole rows of iron files. They raise their heads and see fifty tea-kettles hanging from the ceiling almost within reach. Dazed, excited, they look at one another. The notion that thanks to a few tufts of frozen fur they are going to possess these gleaming treasures is too much for them. It sends them off into brief gusts of nervous laughter. And what an amazing being this white man is! Not only does he have all these pots and kettles that you see, but every year a new lot arrives. He must have, buried in his distant country, immense caches of pots and kettles. And the calico! And the tins of tobacco standing in rows on the shelves like divinities, motionless and magnificent!

Meanwhile the white man has gone round back of the counter and is examining his books. Virtually all of these Eskimos are in debt to him, and he smiles from his side the counter as if he expected that old debts were now about to be paid off and new ones contracted.

The first Eskimo, the most important among them, comes forward. He is impressed. He had forgotten the magnificence of the Store, and although it had been discussed again and again in the igloo, the reality is much more dazzling than all that had been remembered or imagined. He sets down a sack upon the floor, and as he unties the knot the room is filled with murmured commentaries. He opens the sack, hauls out something vaguely white and shapeless, and sets it on the counter where it knocks hollowly with the sound of wood. This is a fox. I do not believe that most women in Paris or New York would give very much for a fox as it looks when it is put down on the counter of an Arctic store—grimy, yellowy white, covered with frozen blood.

The white man stands smiling while the Eskimo hunts round in his mind. Finally, in a firm voice the Eskimo announces:

"*Ot-chor-lo!*" (Coal-oil.)

"*Ta-mar-mik?*" the White Man asks. (A whole fox worth?)

"*Eh-eh!*" says the Eskimo, signifying yes.

The white man disappears for a moment and returns with one or two tins of fuel, which he passes over the counter. He disposes of the first fox, and the Eskimo brings forth another. All this has been carefully planned in advance. The poorest foxes are presented first; for if the white man should take it into his head to insist upon the payment of an old debt, it will not be the best skins that will be lost.

But the white man seems not to be thinking of the debt and is still smiling across the counter.

"*Ti-pa-ko*," says the Eskimo this time. (Tobacco.)

"*Ta-mar-mik?*" the white man repeats.

This repetition of "the whole fox worth" bothers the Eskimo. He is seized by a vague fear, dares no longer affirm himself, and says finally in a meek voice:

"*Napi-dlu-go*." (Cut in two.)

Here is a problem he had not foreseen. What is he going to take for the other half of the fox? He looks at the ceiling and murmurs:

"*Na-una*." (I don't know.)

Suddenly an object on a shelf brings something to mind, and he points:

"*Tam-na-lo!*" (That thing there.)

The trading goes on, and each time that the white man shoves a fox under the counter the Eskimo learns that that fox has been exhausted. So long as it remains on the counter, it continues to possess purchasing power.

The first three or four foxes are easily bartered. There are the things the Eskimo cannot do without—coal-oil, tea, tobacco, rice, flour. But by the time they have reached the fifth fox, the Eskimo is lost. Not for want of rehearsal, Heaven knows. He and his wife have talked over this trading twenty times in their igloo, have exhausted every inch of every fox; but he cannot remember. He has forgotten, and you feel the void in his mind.

Fortunately, his wife is there, the toes of her boots at his heels, murmuring to him and nudging him. Awkward and undecided, he turns towards her, and she, her eyes shrewd and provocative in a face framed by the furry wolf-skin hood, prompts him.

"Calico!" she says. "A cooking pot!" Her eyes gleam as only the eyes of primitive women can gleam.

Ah, yes, he had forgotten. The pot. Two plates. A mug for the child. Three packages of needles. How could he have forgotten! And with this, ideas come to him. "This! And this! And that!" He points everywhere at once, fearful lest these new ideas suddenly escape him.

In the end he has gone too far, and when he leaves the Store, dragging behind him a wooden box filled with treasures, he senses vaguely that many of these shining objects are of no use to him. Oftener, however, it is simply that he no longer wants those things which, a moment ago, he was unable to resist. And then a second stage of trading begins —that between the natives themselves. And since in their eyes nothing possesses intrinsic value, but the value of an object is great or small accordingly as they desire or disdain it, a handsome dog-collar may be swapped for a clay pipe, or a half sack of flour for a red pencil. A needle thus becomes worth a whole fox, a worn strip of leather has the value of a lamp. And what is most curious is that no Eskimo will ever say to you that he has been had in a trade. It is not that his vanity forbids such a confession, but that this can never occur to him. He wanted what he got in the trade; soon after, perhaps, he ceased to want it; but between the two his primitive intellect will not allow him to establish any relationship. Nor is this phenomenon peculiar to Eskimos. In the South Sea islands I have known natives to do sixty miles through the bush and across rivers in order to trade for matches they furiously desired because the matches had red heads.

Everything about the Eskimo astonishes the white man, and everything about the white man is a subject of bewilderment for the Eskimo. Our least gesture seems to him pure madness, and our most casual and insignificant act may have incalculable results for him. Let but a Post Manager say to an Eskimo, "Here is a package of needles for your wife," and he will have started in that obscure consciousness which I hesitate to call a mind, a train of questions and ruminations that may lead anywhere. The free gift is unknown among the Eskimos: better yet, it is incomprehensible to them. Had the white man said, "Lend me your wife in exchange," the Eskimo would have understood. An exchange is normal; a gift passes his understanding. It sets his thoughts going. It is amoral. He will not thank the white man. He will go back to his igloo and ruminate. "Since the white man has given me these needles," he will in effect say to himself, "it must be that he does not want them; and if he does not want his treasures, why should not I have them?" From that day forth, this Eskimo will be a different man. He will begin by despising the white man, and soon he will plan cunningly to exploit him. Since the white man has proved himself a fool, why not? So the Eskimo becomes a liar and a cheat. A single generous impulse on the part of the white man has started the moral disintegration of a native.

There is no learning to know the Eskimo through an exchange of ideas. Properly speaking, the Eskimo does not think at all. He has no capacity for generalization. He cannot explain himself to you nor can he explain his people. When you have lived with his people you discover that each incident observed, each event in which you have participated, adds something to your knowledge of them; and if you do not end by knowing them through and through, it is because time is not long enough and chance has not put in your way all the significant gestures of their primitive, yet extremely ceremonious existence.

One day, for example, Utak brought another Eskimo into the Post, a slack and shiftless ne'er-do-well, a man perpetually destitute. He had arrived from ten days off to trade— a single fox. We were in mid-December and the man had not yet got round to mudding his runners, so that his wretched sled was next to useless. One mile out from the Post he had dropped a caribou-skin, had not missed it (proving he could not count up to four); and when, later, I told him that I had picked it up, he forgot to come to my quarters to fetch it. Each year this man and his wife had a

child; and as his wretched wife had no milk, each year without fail the child died. But they, the man and his wife, did not die. There was always an Eskimo to lend them a snow-knife, another to repair their sled for them on the trail, a third to house them because the man could not build a possible igloo. And never—it was this that was so admirable—never would you have heard a single impatient or angry word spoken about these two. Of course they were teased a bit at night in the igloo, and great tales were told of the man's comical futility; but they were unfailingly taken care of. The others would say, "He couldn't get here because of his sled": they would never say, "The man doesn't know how to get over a trail." When tools were lent him and he broke them, nobody complained. He spent a couple of days at the Post and was about to start out again when, at the last minute, Utak arrived running. Could the Post Manager "lend" Utak a snow-knife? The ne'er-do-well had just broken the one Utak had let him have. And this was said without bitterness, indeed with a laugh that showed all Utak's teeth. It was too bad! Of course he hadn't done it on purpose, so no one could hold it against him.

There were Eskimos who had no food. No one said of such a man, "He was too lazy to do any trapping." What people said was, "He did not trap this season." Why he should not have trapped was nobody's affair. I remember the case of a native who had an ample cache of fish and was well provided against the winter. While he was at the Post, two Eskimo families camped at his cache. Being without grub, they opened it and lived on it; and when he arrived, the cache was empty. Pity! But it couldn't be helped.

Many people imagine that the sun is necessary to human happiness and that the South Sea islanders must be the gayest, most leisurely and most contented folk on earth. No notion could be more falsely romantic, for happiness has nothing to do with climate: these Eskimos afforded me decisive proof that happiness is a disposition of the spirit. Here was a people living in the most rigorous climate in the world, in the most depressing surroundings imaginable, haunted by famine in a grey and sombre landscape sullen with the absence of life; shivering in their tents in the autumn, fighting the recurrent blizzard in the winter, toiling and moiling fifteen hours a day merely in order to get food and stay alive. Huddling and motionless in their igloos through this interminable night, they ought to have been melancholy men, men despondent and suicidal; instead, they were a cheerful people, always laughing, never weary of laughter.

A man is happy, in sum, when he is leading the life that suits him; and neither warmth nor comfort has anything to do with it. I watched these Eskimos at the Post. This house, you would say, ought to mean to them the zenith of well-being and relaxation: they had warmth, they had biscuits, they had tea, and no one asked them to work or pay for these blessings. But look at them! They are dull, sullen, miserable. Physically, they seem shrunken, their personalities diminished and extinguished. Instead of laughing, they brood; and you see them come in, take their seats on the bench and remain like sleepwalkers, expressionless and spiritless, waking just barely enough, when you pass, to give you a polite smile and then relapse into blankness. But open wide the door, fling them into the blizzard, and they come to. They wake up suddenly; they whistle; their women scurry about, their children crack the triumphant whip, their dogs bark like mad: an impression of joy, of life, fills the environs of the Post. In no time at all they have disappeared: the tempest—their cherished tempest of the Arctic—has blown them over the ridge like so many leaves.

For the white man, who knows other skies and other climates, this land is more often than not lugubrious. He lives here shut out of his lost Paradise, waiting and hoping to be transported back to what seems to him, now that he is here, an Eden. But the Eskimo, it goes without saying, knows nothing better to hope for. All this is normal to him; and indeed everything in his existence is normal. What will come will come: he knows pretty well in advance what it is that will come, and nothing either astonishes or saddens him. "It is cold!" he will say to you; but he will say it with a grin, out of politeness, because you are a white man and this is not your country. Utak repeated that *Una-i-kto* in my igloo, less because it was cold than because there was something shameful for him in staying with the white man instead of going off to hunt with the others.

It had seemed to me for some days that Kakokto's wife had been looking sulky. I mentioned it to Paddy at supper one evening, and a moment later I said to him:

"That fellow from Adelaide Peninsula, Kukshun: what's he hanging round here so long for?"

Paddy smiled. "You know," he said, "you've hit on something. She's upset because of him. Kakokto and Kukshun have been exchanging wives, and as usual the wives were not consulted. Lady Kakokto does not find Kukshun to her taste; a little briny, shall we say? It's put her out of sorts. She's one of the few women round here who is in love with her husband. Kakokto doesn't care specially about her, and he'll lend her to anybody who asks for her. For one thing, it's a tradition that has to be observed; for another, friendship has its obligations."

He went on to explain that the exchange of wives was common among the Eskimos. It is not, as with certain other primitive peoples, a token of hospitality. I myself had been received in the South Seas by chiefs who, in the way of welcome, had offered me a daughter or had begged me to choose a companion among the women of the village. This was different, was a simple matter of sociability, a courtesy not to be refused between friends or visitors. Among hunting partners—the Eskimos often hunt in pairs—it was automatic, a relief from the monotony of existence.

Between husbands, meanwhile, there was never any question of compensation. On the other hand, a "well-bred" bachelor whose friend accorded him this courtesy would expect to make his friend a little gift as a token of appreciation. The lady, the object of the courtesy, was as little compensated as consulted. Among other articles of the code there was one that was absolutely rigorous: the privilege of disposing of the lady belonged exclusively to the husband. The man who made his request directly of the wife committed a grave infraction of the code and serious trouble would certainly ensue.

To ask an Eskimo to lend you his wife is a thing so natural that no one will hesitate to put the question in a crowded igloo within hearing of half a dozen others. It does not so much as break the thread of conversation, and the husband will say yes or no, according to his momentary mood, with entire casualness.

The rest takes place as casually as the demand itself. Evening comes, conversation in the igloo will be running on about the usual topics—hunting, fishing, dogs, sleds. There will be tea and laughter; and when the moment arrives to go to bed—a moment indicated by certain signs such as the dying of the candle, the exhaustion of the tobacco tin, the prodigious jaw-cracking yawns, a happy digestion—the husband will slip peacefully into his *krepik,* his deerskin bag, while his wife lets herself down into yours. And the presence of the husband in the same igloo need not intimidate you: he knows nothing of jealousy and is asleep before you have settled yourself in the company of his wife.

It is inconceivable to the Eskimo that we do not do the same. One of my friends, a Hudson's Bay Post Manager, was about to be married; his fiancée was on her way to join him at his Post. He was very popular among the Eskimos, and his forthcoming marriage was a great subject of comment among them. A native said to him:

"When your wife is here, will you trade her with the other white men?"

"We don't do that," the Post Manager said with a laugh.

"Why not?" asked the astonished Eskimo. "There's no harm in it. A wife doesn't wear out. When I get mine back she is always as good as she was before."

It might seem from this that the native woman lived altogether in a state of abject inferiority to the male Eskimo, but this is not the case. What she loses in authority, as compared to the white woman, she makes up, by superior cunning, in many other ways. Native women are very shrewd, and they almost never fail to get what they want. Take Utak's wife, for example. It was because of her that we always got away late on the trail. It was because of her that, instead of going off sealing with the others, Utak came down to build his igloo near the Post where she might cajole us who were white men into making her little presents. When Utak went to the Store to trade, Unarnak was always at his heels, and it was comical to see that crab-like pigeon-toed shuffle of hers as she stood never at his side but only behind him, turning as he turned, backing up as he backed up, coming forward as he came forward, hidden behind her man until the moment when she put her head round and murmured to him those calculated suggestions which in the end always made her share of the barter greater than he had intended. And it was only after they had got back to the igloo, that, each time, Utak saw he had once again been done in the eye by his wife.

It was a perpetual joy to watch this comedy, this almost wordless struggle in which the wife—and by no means Utak's alone, but all of them—inevitably got the better of the husband. With the skill of actresses, the wives played their parts; and with the candour of provincial audiences, the husbands were taken in. There does not exist an Eskimo woman untrained in the art of wheedling, not one unable to repeat with tireless and yet insinuating insistence the mention of what she wants, until the husband, worn down by her persistence, gives way. Heaven knows, there was nothing subtle about the manoeuvre, and I marvelled each time that men so clever in the rest of their existence—an almost strictly material existence, it is true—should be so dull of wit, so definitely idiotic in the matter of handling their women.

Women were behind everything in this Eskimo world. If one native abandoned a given group in order to go off and live with another, you could be sure it was done at the instigation of his wife. If a couple suddenly grew into a triangular household, you were virtually certain that it was the wife and not the husband who had dictated the choice of the permanent friend. And if, one day, that triangle was reduced to a couple again as the result of a murder, there was never any doubt but that it was the wife who had plotted and prompted the murder. But I have a story to tell you . . .

My story is of Ekaluk who came out of the porch of the igloo one morning and looked round.

Little plumes of snow were running before the wind over the plain and powdering the earth with a fine layer of

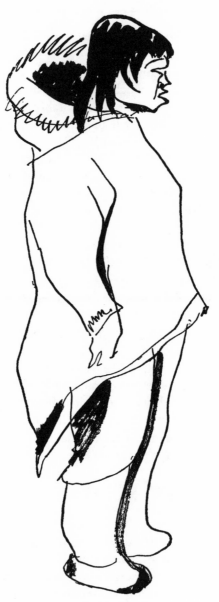

EKALUK

white. Nothing else stirred. Near by, two puppies lay asleep on the snow. The igloos were hushed and seemingly deserted. The men had gone off to fish through the ice of a lake whose unbroken surface stretched into infinity. All these things the young man saw with an eye quick to seize details in this vast landscape. And he saw, too, receding in the distance, a dark form that he knew to be Ohokto, hurrying on foot to his fishing. Watching him, there dropped into Ekaluk's mind the words spoken a half hour before by Kanaiok, his mistress and Ohokto's wife: "Why don't you do it? Now is the time!"

This was not the first time that Kanaiok had urged him to do it. In the beginning, Ekaluk had taken her into his sleeping-bag as a matter of desire and convention, in the common way of neighboring Eskimos. Ohokto had of course not taken it amiss; and besides, he was no longer young. But things had not stopped there: Ekaluk had ended by taking a fancy to the young woman—in Eskimo fashion, naturally; not out of love, but simply because he wanted a woman to himself. And he had come to live in their igloo. Still Ohokto had said nothing. He had merely grown more silent. Now Ekaluk had got it into his head that Kanaiok would make him a proper wife. He liked her. She could sew skins wonderfully. She was an excellent housewife, for there was always tea and *baneks* in her igloo. And Kanaiok, for her part, found Ekaluk's body more agreeable than her husband's. It was less intelligent, but it was younger, warmer.

Like most Eskimo women, Kanaiok was both clever and persistent, and she soon achieved a complete ascendancy over this young, simple-minded, and violent lover. "Why not?" she would urge. "Do away with Ohokto, and we'll go off to another camp and live together. I'll sew you the handsomest

clothes in the world, and your igloo will be the one that all
men will most willingly visit."

Ekaluk was not bright. He had no words to say what he
felt. But these things troubled his mind. More and more
violently he desired this woman for himself alone. And
Kanaiok gave him no peace, harassed him ceaselessly; and
when Ekaluk, angered by her persistence, flew into a rage
and beat her, she would be silent for several days. Then she
would begin again: Doubtless Ekaluk was a coward; she
had thought him a man. Since this was how he was, she
would say no more. As a matter of fact, if you wanted a
man, a real one, there was Ohokto; and indeed she was
lucky to be his wife.

This sort of mockery worked on Ekaluk. It was a spur in
the side of the young animal (he might have been twenty-
two years old). And this morning he had made up his mind
to do the thing as soon as he got the chance—for an Eskimo
never kills face to face, but always from behind. He would
stab Ohokto from behind. Already he could see himself
doing it. Kanaiok knew what was going through his mind.
She had been quick to flatter him, to cajole him this morning; and when Ohokto had left, she, snuffing with elaborate
casualness the wick of the seal-oil lamp, had whispered a
quantity of things into Ekaluk's ear.

All this was stirring confusedly in Ekaluk's mind as he
went forward to his sled, turned it right side up, and harnessed his dogs. Ohokto had not been out of sight ten minutes when Ekaluk's sled was gliding down the declivity that
led to the lake.

He knew he was going to kill, but he knew not how. A
mind like his could make no plans in advance. He knew
merely that when the occasion offered itself, he, a hunter
and an Eskimo, would seize it. All that he was sure of was

that this was the day when the thing would be done. Kanaiok's voice rang in his ears, and of a sudden his blood began
to beat in his chest. He whipped up the dogs, and they, seeming to understand, trotted rapidly through the grey air. Already a silhouette was visible on the ice. It was Ohokto.

Ohokto was on his knees over a hole in the ice, in the customary posture. In front of him three heavy blocks of snow
formed a rampart against the wind. He was kneeling on a
bed of crushed ice over which he had spread his caribou-
skin. Ohokto was motionless, a statue of immobility. Eskimos are able to kneel like this for hours without the slightest
movement, without the least fatigue, watching the fish pass
slowly to and fro under the ice as in a dream. Only the left
hand is in motion, the hand that does the jigging and rises
and falls with the regularity of the tick-tock of a clock while
five or six feet under the ice the decoy—fins made of bone—
flutters in the same rhythm. Within reach of the right hand
lies the great three-pronged harpoon, ready for the kill.

Ohokto is motionless. The wind may veer, the blizzard
may come, nothing will budge Ohokto. His is the patience
of the hunter, and his concern with the kill is so concentrated that nothing can distract him from it. He does not so
much as turn his head when Ekaluk draws near.

The easiest thing in the world to do is to stop one's dogs:
they seem always ready to rest. A whispered "Hoo!" will cut
them short and turn their heads towards the driver. Ekaluk
has stopped his team at about fifty yards from the hole, instinctively concerned not to frighten the fish. He strokes
them with his whip, and they lie down. The whip is then
slipped under the straps along the sled.

For an Eskimo, there is nothing so automatic as to pick
up one's snow-knife at the moment of getting off a sled.
Ekaluk's knife is in his hand as he goes towards Ohokto. A

blizzard has come up, and Ekaluk moves at the center of a whirling wall of snow through which he can see a bare hundred feet. Probably there are other natives out on the lake, but in this wall of snow Ekaluk is as good as invisible to them—and besides, what he is up to is his own affair.

As he walks slowly forward towards his still motionless friend, a gleam of consciousness pierces his brain. He is about to kill Ohokto from behind. Two strokes of a spear in the ice will make a hole down which he can send Ohokto; and if ever the police come—they never come in the winter —clever the man who can find a body under eight feet of ice!

Now the thing is very clear in Ekaluk's mind. But at the moment when he stands over his friend, Ohokto straightens up and murmurs mysteriously:

"Angi-y-uk." (Big ones.)

Big fish! After days of harpooning fish so small that they were not worth bringing in, so that Ekaluk had preferred to spend his hours with Kanaiok in the igloo! And now the big fish are back! It must have been the new moon last night that brought them.

It was at this moment that Ekaluk forgot the purpose of his coming and forgot the murderous knife in his hand. He knelt without a word beside Ohokto, who had returned to his knees as soon as he had spoken, and side by side the man who had been about to kill and the man who had been about to die peered together above the hole. One after another they speared great fish, violently red of flesh; and it was as if the fish had been sent to save Ohokto from murder.

Ekaluk had forgotten; for Ekaluk was first of all a hunter, and fish or seal spoke louder to his instinct than woman or murder. Frozen instantly, hard as wood, the fish were piled on Ekaluk's sled, the dogs were on their feet, and the sled was away.

Neither man spoke. The Spirit of Fishing filled them both, each for himself. From time to time Ekaluk would call out to his dogs, or Ohokto would jump down from the sled to release a tangled trace and quickly remount again. They had crossed the great lake called Kakivok-tar-vik and were nearing the camp when by one of the recurrent miracles of the Arctic the wind suddenly shifted, the grey veil vanished from the air, and the sinking sun was revealed—a sun of mercy.

And then Ekaluk remembered. Two hundred yards ahead, Kanaiok was waiting for him, prepared to leave with him. His dogs were already slowing down; and at the moment when they stopped dead he stepped behind Ohokto and sank the snow-knife into his back. Ohokto toppled over like a sack of grain. Lying in his heavy overcoat on the ground, his short arms motionless, he looked like a grotesque dead doll. Ekaluk ran past the dogs, struck his harpoon into the snow, and crawled on all fours into the porch.

I said to Gibson one day, "What would happen if I asked one of these Eskimos for his wife?"

"Very likely he'd let you have her."

"Without a word? Without any—er—bargaining about it?"

"Oh, quite! In the first place, it's done. And then, you see, it's something of an honor. The fact that out of them all you, a white man, picked her, would make the rest think more highly of her. And so far as the husband goes, of course he'd expect something in exchange. These people never actually

give anything to anybody. They lend things, they help one
another along; but whether it's a wife or a dog or a pocket

knife, it's always either a direct swap or a claim on the
other fellow in the future."

"And suppose I asked for
her several days running?"

"That wouldn't upset him.
He might say to you, 'To-
morrow: I want her myself
to-night.' But the chances are
that you could have her. And
her husband and the rest
would sit round in the igloo,
laughing and chatting about
you. The husband would be
congratulated upon having
made a rich friend. Prob-
ably he would let the others
talk on while he dreamt of
the things he'd get out of
you."

"As a matter of fact," Paddy went on, "I've known Eskimo women to come and ask to sleep with white men off
their own bat. There were three of us at the post one night,
a trapper called Dave, a Major who had stopped by on an
inspection tour, and me. We were all abed in the same room,
towards midnight, the Major and I reading by candlelight
and Dave dozing off in his corner, when suddenly the door
opened and a woman came in. She and her husband were
working for me round the post. She shut the door, squatted
down, and just sat. Nobody said anything for a while, and I
was wondering vaguely what she was up to, when Dave,

who had been woken out of his doze, said rather peevishly, 'Ask her what the devil she wants!' I was the only one who could make himself understood, so I said, 'What do you want?' She pointed to Dave in his corner, and said, 'This one.'

"Dave's father was a Scotch dominie and he didn't go in much for that kind of thing. When I explained, he yelled, 'Tell her to get out of here! I shan't have anything to do with the slut!' and he got up, grabbed a tin of tobacco, handed it to her, shoved her out of the door, and went back to bed muttering I don't know what.

"The Major and I jollied him about his sex appeal, asked him what his secret was, and that was all there was to that.

"Next night, at about the same hour, the door opened again, the woman came in, and again she just squatted down and stared. This time it was me she was after. I let her know that the thing was impossible, and she left without saying anything.

"In the morning, as I started out to the Store, her husband came up to me and asked what the matter was? What was wrong with the Kabloona? His wife had twice proposed herself and twice been turned down. Maybe she was too old? Well, he had a daughter. Too bad she was three hundred miles off, but later in the season she'd be along. He was sorry his wife didn't appeal to us."

Now I began to understand. Utak had paid me a visit the day of Paddy's story. I had thought he had come to beg a length of rope, but I saw now that he was scratching round for a way to propose his wife to me. I hadn't caught on, and he had slipped out as soundless as a mouse. And he wasn't the only one. All the Eskimos had been low in grub for

about a week past. One after the other, they had been coming into the Post, sitting on the bench in the outer room just
where they could be seen through the open doorway from
our inner room, saying nothing but waiting to be spoken to.
Each had sat out his hour or two with characteristic patience
and immobility, and, seeing that nothing was coming of it,
had left. Probably each had said to himself, on leaving,
"Next time, perhaps."

My curiosity was aroused. I began to wonder. I reminded
myself virtuously that I was in a sense shirking my duty. If
not the primary, then at least the secondary reason for my being here was to study the nature of the Eskimo. All the
anthropologists that I had read seemed to attach prodigious
importance to the sexual life of primitive peoples (perhaps
because the sexual relations of the civilized peoples yielded a
greater fund of psychological than of biological data). Was
this not a legitimate department of investigation for me? But
my difficulty was a curious one: it was not to resist temptation, but to be tempted.

I said as much to Paddy, and he smiled.

"Not very dainty, these Eskimo women, are they?" he
agreed. And he added with the noble simplicity that builds
empires: "It's that stink of caribou about them that I can't
go."

He was silent a moment. "What puzzles me, though, is
their husbands," he went on. "I remember—never mind who
and where it was—a chap came by once who had trapped
along the River too long to be bothered by these things, and
he traded one of these women. We had her to breakfast next
morning—."

But I had better tell the story in my own way, since it gave
rise to reflections in my mind with which it became rapidly
entangled.

The woman had been waiting in a corner like an animal, her eyes, as usual, fixed on the floor. The white man beckoned to her and she arrived at table with that crab-like, pigeon-toed walk—the most graceless and inhuman gait in the world. Once in her chair she crouched there, motionless until the white man encouraged her, urged her to eat and drink. Slowly she stretched forth a hand, picked up a spoon —and the spoon fell out of her hand. The white man had to pick it up for her.

A music-hall ape, one of those simians who unfold their napkin, eat, drink, smoke cigars, is infinitely more adroit than an Eskimo at a white man's table. Here was a human being that could not hold a spoon in its hand; therefore it must be that even to hold a spoon properly wants generations of heredity. Here was a creature as helpless at table as the white man was helpless in a blizzard. These hands that were so skilful with the circular Eskimo knife when a great fish was to be cut up; these hands that knew almost of themselves how to transform tough hides into comfortable clothes, that plied the needle with such swiftness and deftness, could not even butter a slice of bread.

As they sat at table, the husband came into the outer room, followed by a friend. The white man glanced at the husband through the open doorway: not a sign, not a gesture, betrayed his interest in the situation. The woman herself was unperturbed. She went peacefully on biting into her bread without so much as a nod to her husband. When the white man, putting the bread back in its box, passed the husband, the Eskimo smiled amiably, as always, and in his smile there was not the least reference to the situation. And when his wife rose from table and rolled herself a cigarette at the tobacco box, he did not throw her even the most furtive glance. She, for her part was still shy with the white man; and when his eyes met hers she smiled gently with that Eskimo smile which is not even amiability but urbanity.

Breakfast ended, she got up and joined her husband and his friend in the outer room. In a moment all three were laughing gaily, there was certainly not a word said about what had happened. The three natives had begun to play a game—two would hide something in the room, and the third would have to find it. They played like this for an hour, laughing and giggling like little children.

I went to bed that night still thinking of Gibson's story. What, I wondered, could have been the thoughts of that husband tranquilly sitting in the outer room? Was he indifferent? Was his mind totally blank? Was he cynical? Again and again I was to be baulked in my understanding by the 20,000 years of evolution—or is it more?—that separate the Eskimo and me. When I witnessed an event, when I participated in a fact, I, as a civilized, or at least evolved European, found it impossible not to dwell upon that fact, to attempt to interpret it. Doubtless the Eskimo never attempted to interpret, to understand. The thing was there—and that was all. The man of Neanderthal and the man of Rockefeller Center must of necessity view and value things each in his own way. Here sits a human being in one room while in another room sit his wife and a passive, a most casual, lover. And what does he do? He laughs. About what is going on in the other room? Not at all. He laughs because it is fun to play at hiding things with a friend.

He is not jealous, then? No. And the reason may be that jealousy is a function of the sense of individual property; and he has this sense, if at all, in the very faintest degree. You enjoy his wife? What harm can come to him of that? If what you intended was to take from him his wife, deprive him of this essential human and social factor (not property), that would be serious and he would not hesitate to kill you. But to lie with her? Not only is that no deprivation, but it allows him to lie with other women—and that is extremely agreeable.

It goes without saying that I am far from proposing that the sexual ethics of the Netsilik should be adopted by, or could be adapted to, western Christendom. Nor am I unaware that it is not necessary to be a feminist to ask, "But what of the status of Eskimo women?" Their status, parenthetically, suits them well enough; and I have indicated here and there in these pages that they are not only the mistresses of their households but also, in most Eskimo families, the shrewd prompters of their husband's decisions. However, it is not about this that I want to speak. What I believe worth saying is that Eskimo *mores* are the direct reflection of the material circumstances in which they live. Epithets like "cynical" and "indifferent" are here totally out of place. Eskimo life is materially the hardest life lived by any people on earth. Necessity certainly commands and probably explains every phase of Eskimo manners. Nature, such as it is in their world, permits no appreciable degree of refinement, and this because it allows no significant degree of leisure. The Eskimo eats enormously because he must eat enormously to keep warm. He knows no pleasures of the palate, unless it be an occasional bit of rotted meat, which he likes because it is a sort of condiment and tickles the palate. Having nothing else to do evenings in the igloo, his sexual life is intense— and it would be an error to imagine that cold slowed up this life. He is, again of necessity, communistic in his attitude to property, not precisely charitable but certainly ready to share all he has with his kind; and because there is never a time when he may not be the one to benefit by this singular economics, he is always ready to share with others his wife, his snow-knife, his cache of fish.

An apparition at the Post pulled me up one day with a shock of amazement. I am as well aware as the next man that sexual aberration knows no geography and no chronology, that inversion is a phenomenon observable in ancient as in modern times, in primitive as in civilized societies. Yet it was not in my thoughts that I should one day see a homosexual Eskimo; and if I put this man in my notebooks, and write about him now, it is not because of his aberration but because he was, in his repellent way, a singularly comic and glittering figure, at once loathsome and fascinating.

There was never such a master of pantomime as this infinitely strange, perpetually agitated, and yet extraordinarily self-possessed rogue who dropped in one afternoon from Back's River and was off again the next day. He seemed to take it for granted that neither Gibson nor I would understand his speech, for immediately on coming in he began to display his talent as mime, and he did it with obvious relish. He had no need of words: face and hands sufficed him to paint for us his four days on the trail. He had run out of tea on the second day, and he wrote in sign language a poem of the brewing and drinking of his last cup. He had started with only a little coal-oil; and in a moment he was coaxing the last drop of oil out of an invisible tin, aping marvellously— how he did it I do not know—the very tin itself, showing us with his hands what emptiness was. He simulated the mangey dogs trotting with lowered heads and flopping ears, their rumps convulsed and tense with fear of the whip. He acted out for us the sled bumping and scraping over the pack ice for want of mud on its runners. Forgetting himself momentarily, he would speak rapid words, but his pantomime went faster than his words, and he would fasten his eyes on your face with the shrewdness and the childish self-satisfaction of an old actor, as if saying, "Don't you admire the way I am doing this?"

Another thing: he looked exactly like portraits of Louis XIII; and not only did I sketch him, but fearing that my drawing might be the fruit of my imagination, I photographed him; and it was Louis XIII to the life who stared at me from the negative. A narrow strip of beard that looked half natural and half make-up, ran down his chin, and he was either all curtsies and scrapings, bowing forward with rounded back to leer at you while his hands went dismayingly over your person and he murmured over the beauty of your clothes, or he would straighten up abruptly, stick out his chest, and posture stiffly as if posing for his portrait.

In the South Seas I had come upon a cannibal who was the spit and image of Robespierre. Here, at the other end of the earth, I saw before me a rakish Louis XIII who fumbled disgustingly with your clothes, paid you a thousand compliments accompanied by a thousand bows, and then let you know without a chance of voice or visage that a little tin of solidified alcohol for his Primus stove was exactly what he needed. Each broadside of compliments was so much artillery preparation before the real attack, which spoke of three planks for his sled, a plug of tobacco, another mug of tea. The Kabloona seems not to be ripe? Let us try again. "How warm your house is, how solidly built this bench!" He aimed at random in every direction, and soon he ceased to take pains with his discourse of seduction. The window was *na-mak-to,* was very fine; everything became *na-mak-to,* as if the word must make wonderful music in the white man's ear.

And then he would sit stiffly down, motionless in a sort of

comical dignity while he watched you out of the corner of his eye. But his hands never ceased from fluttering, and even in the air they did not draw forms, they caressed them. His eyelids fell into folds when he shut his eyes, and there was something about them both pink and obscene. From where I sat, his eyes appeared to me like the eyes in a primitive drawing—one staring straight ahead and the other seen only in part, as in a face drawn in profile. It was absurd, grotesque: the crow's feet at the eyes, the sly little goat's beard, the hands fluttering at the end of arms too short; plump tiny hands that twitched, expressed impatience, were reaching out for you and trying to cajole you, and that in a skilfully graphic gesture were describing just what they wanted—a package of cigarette-paper. Thank you! He would put the paper right into his pocket. There! And the man would sit down again, and again he would fix you with those eyes, decide that you were growing cool towards him, and start up his pantomime. What a magnificent pipe that is you are smoking! What a pity that he had lost his own pipe some weeks ago. (His pipe was most certainly in his pocket.) Ah, how he loved to smoke a pipe!

To heighten the impression of inversion this man dragged along with him, behind him, a child whose features were no less astonishing than his own—a little Aiglon with romantic locks brushed across his forehead and immense, incredibly ringed eyes that were a little melancholy and rather protuberant. What was this? Was it a girl, a boy? A boy, yes, said our Louis XIII, turning round to stroke the passive forehead; and a very good trapper. He got two foxes the other day. The word "trapper" went very ill with the look of the boy, and I was sure that the man was lying about his minion. As the evening wore on, and the child began to droop with sleep, he refused to allow the boy to go off to the igloo alone, explaining with inconceivable gestures that they always slept together (gesture of rocking the child to sleep in his arms) and saying that the boy was never able to go to sleep without him.

Of what strange elements this scene was composed! Thirty below in a Post banked with six feet of snow; Louis XIII; l'Aiglon; the weaving of those lewd hands; the tin of alcohol on the table; the child's astonishing eyes and girlish face contrasting so strangely with the rough clothes; Gibson's manifest and uneasy disgust. The whole thing was beyond words disconcerting, and I said to myself that next day, when this man and the child had moved off over the sea, had vanished into the infinity of the North, I should be perfectly right to believe that the whole thing had been a dream.

Chapter II

ALTHOUGH I have so often referred to it, I have not yet described the Post. Since it was against this curiously changing setting that much of what I have to tell took place, I must paint it for you.

Banked for warmth with six feet of snow blocks all round (except where the drift had been carefully removed to allow the light to come in through the windows), its roof and eaves completely hidden under snow, this wooden house looked from outside, in winter, for all the world like a square igloo. The outermost door opened into a winter porch, a lean-to whose frame was of wood and its walls of snow. Here the coal was stored; here too a bitch and her puppies lived, sheltered both from the greater cold outside and—the pups at any rate—from the ravenous hunger of the other dogs. Through a second door you entered into an inner porch, itself a permanent part of the house. This porch was nearly as cold as the first, which was not a great deal warmer than the open air. Here, hanging from pegs, you would have seen our outer garments, made of caribou skin, the snow beaten from them before we took them off and hung them up. Our boots, too, stood in this porch. The primitive snow-beater (*a-na-oo-tak*), with which we beat our coats as if they were carpets, was here ready to hand. There was a a snow-knife, a shovel, a great broom with which the porch was dutifully swept after each wind that brought the drift seeping in. The kindling which I chopped nightly before going to bed was here. There was a box of rusted tools, there were fox-traps left by the natives, and that miraculous pea soup in the sack, ready to be taken out on my next journey. This porch was cheerless and dark, its black corners invisible in the feeble light of a single small window.

Next came the natives' room—a long table, benches round the wall, mugs on the table. Here Gibson and I became café waiters each time that a group of Eskimos arrived. Here too the Eskimos camped round the Post collected daily and sat interminably in silence or in laughter. Our immediate provisions were stored in this room—rice, bread, sugar, dried vegetables. At the far side of the room rose a partition built only to within a couple of feet of the ceiling in order that the warmth from the stove in the inner room might come over. Incidentally, that warmth prevented our jams and pickles from freezing and bursting their glass jars.

In the inner room Gibson and I had our living quarters. Here we ate, read, chatted, and mused for whole hours together, each sitting in his own corner while the wind sent the wireless mast swaying in the air and piled up the snow in great drifts. Paddy would go over his accounts and dream of a great day of trading. I would study the Eskimo language, write up my notes and, so long as the season permitted, light would come in through two windows placed opposite one another which, when snow banked the house, lent the effect of great loopholes in a fortress. At the back a second partition, cut by two doorways in each of which a curtain hung, separated this room from the cubicles where we slept, another partition between us.

Paddy had done wonders with his living room. It was warm and intimate and was the frame within which our life was lived. Here within a hundred miles of the Magnetic Pole there was a kind of bourgeois cosiness that was unbelievable. I used to say to myself that there were no bourgeois places, there were only domesticated souls. One could be an adventurer in New York, and one could also be an old maid in the polar regions.

I had only to raise my eyes to be justified in this reflection. The razor strop hung by the looking-glass, the broom stood behind the door, the pin-cushion rested on the window-sill. Nothing would have been present to remind one of the Arctic if a few white foxes, the "money" that paid for my excursions on the trail, had not been hanging from the ceiling. Scrambled eggs for breakfast? Do sit down, I beg you. The linoleum is stretched taut over the table and awaits your coming. We have a full line of tomato ketchups and fish-sauces.

Really, were it not for the snow bank it would be impossible to tell this house from an average suburban shanty. There were the biscuit-boxes standing in rows on the shelf. Here was the bread in its bread-box, carefully wrapped in a damp cloth to keep it from growing stale too quickly. Chromos hung on the walls, and there was even a vase of artificial flowers—which I would hide from time to time and Gibson would bring out again almost immediately. See the spoons lying in their drawer, and the row of hooks from which hang the skewer, the ladle, the strainer, and the corkscrew. Here is a wicker armchair—salvaged from Amundsen's boat—with its hospitable back and arms; if you saw me sitting in it beside the stove you would certainly say to yourself that I looked like a Paris concierge.

I used to think of all this and smile to myself. "Those

heroes of the North," indeed! Were I a Hudson's Bay manager I should not change with any shop assistant in the
world. What! Get up at seven in the morning, run like mad
to the underground, get a dressing-down each time I was
criminally late five minutes, lunch in half an hour, and
spend my life restless and worrying about my job! Not me!
As Post Manager, I should get up when I pleased, take my
time over my coffee, hear the natives cough in the outer
room, put my head out and say to them, *"Hila na-go-y-ok,"*
(nice weather) and shut the door without waiting for their
acknowledgment of my greeting. And what had I to worry
about? Coal enough for three years, yeast enough for fifteen,
so much jam that I didn't know what to do with it. Once a
month I wrote out a statement of my inventory, and it
reached headquarters six months after it was written. If I
found myself yawning after lunch, I took a nap. I couldn't
go to the films, it's true; but I was fond of reading, and there
was not a place in the world so peacefully suited to reading
as my Arctic.

The blizzard does not blow every day. Adventure has two
faces—one showing men at grips with the elements, the
other showing them darning their socks. It was in Gibson's
living-room that I saw a remarkable photograph of three
members of an Antarctic expedition. They were sitting in a
hut, one of them mending his pants, another smoking with
a faraway look in his eyes, the third writing a letter. Had
they the same peace in their own homes, I wondered?

I was just back from the trail, my fingers were still frost-
bitten, I was warm, and I felt as snug as a bacillus in a
cheese. I could not imagine a cosier existence.

December had come and the lamp was lighted all day
long. Hitherto, by cleaning the outermost windows (there

were three in each embrasure, set one inside the other) we
had still got a little daylight: now the season of light was
dying fast. Each evening was long, calm, and lamplit. I
had never imagined such tranquillity. The only sounds that
broke upon the silence were those familiar sounds that are
so precious in the domestic life of man—the suction of the
gas-lamp as it was pumped before being lighted; the crack-
ling of the block of ice as it melted in the water bucket by
the stove; the tick-tock of the Big Ben. And there was the
singing of the antennae of the wireless mast, a mysterious
drone that set me dreaming and never failed to bring to
mind the answer I used to get when, as a child, I asked why
the electric wires hummed along our highways: "Those are
calls going over the wire," I would invariably be told. The
precious coal died slowly in the stove while I sat with my
book, dozing and musing and telling myself without the
slightest anxiety, indeed with a sort of pleasure, that within
me, too, things were moving towards death. (As soon as
man is at peace, musing, he feels himself old.) Gibson and
I would sit face to face, speaking no word, each sunk deep
within himself, each at peace with the world, while only the
pulsing lamp gave off the impression of life. Now and then
one of us would rise and turn the knob of the radio: nothing
would come. Nothing would ever come again, and it was
well thus. Silence was better than sound.

It was a curious thing that however long these long evenings might be, we could not tear ourselves away from
them. We would sit on indefinitely in that room while the
hands of the clock turned, showing that it was one in the
morning, then two, then after two. And still we would not
go to bed. In the end, Gibson would stir out of his torpor,
and it was as if something very heavy had budged. He
would half rise out of his chair, put his finger on the per-

petual calendar, and the click that would sound in that silence was something almost fateful, made one truly conscious
that another day had been released into eternity. We would
come to. Gibson would go back and light his bedside lamp
while I waited until he called out, "All set!" Then I would
put out the big lamp. "Good night!" would float back and
forth over the partition between our cubicles, and each
would continue to read or ruminate in his sleeping-bag until
one lamp went out and then the other, and the only sign
of life that remained was the scuffing of a lone dog on the
snow-covered roof.

Is there another land in the world where the silence is so
total? There is no wind here in the leaves, for there are no
leaves. No bird screeches. No sound of running water is
heard. No beast is here to take fright and scurry in the darkness. There is not a stone to be loosened under a human
foot and roll down a bank, for all these stones are cemented
by frost and hidden under snow. Yet it is not that this world
is dead: it is merely that the beings who haunt this solitude
are soundless and invisible. The fox running through the
night over the tundra, the seal marauding in the sea, are as
if they were not. And if from time to time you did not see
a little white beast caught in a trap, seated and staring at
you, you would not know that life existed in this void.

Insensibly, nevertheless, things changed. They changed so
gradually that their alteration was imperceptible. Bit by bit
this silence that had been so remedial, that had soothed me
and laid to rest my frayed nerves, began to seem to me a
weight. The horizon was closing in round me. The prison,
once so radiantly peaceful, was now unveiling its true face.
The visits of the Eskimos grew more rare and the solitude
grew longer. But more than this, an almost physical opera-

tion of shrinking was going on. I who had come from Outside had first been enclosed by the Arctic. Then my horizon
had contracted to the limits of Gjoa Haven; from Gjoa
Haven the circle had been reduced to the dimensions of the
Post; and now, in the dead of the polar winter, the line I
hesitated to cross was drawn in a radius of five feet round
the stove. It seemed to me to be true as much of Gibson as
of me, that we were forced more and more to retire into
ourselves, to live spiritually upon our own resources; and the
flame of life within us withdrew farther and farther into a
secret hiding-place, our heartbeats grew slower and slower.
The day would come when we should have to shake ourselves to keep them from stopping altogether. Sunk deep in
this well of silence, we were being stifled by it, we were at
the bottom of a pit out of which it was inconceivably difficult to draw ourselves. And yet the re-emergence into the
air, into life, had to be attempted.

One hesitated to go out. Winter was really shutting us in.
And where go? One might venture out of doors for a bit,
but that was all. The whole day long, that "thing," as we
called it, had waxed and grown in intensity. The wind had
become squall, the squall storm. When you went out to
scrape the snow off the windows—not so much for the little
light that might come through, but because to see that pale
grey glow made breathing easier indoors—you lowered your
head and fought the violent air.

At night in bed I would lie listening to the storm. Except
for the absence of movement, it was exactly like being at sea,
and the swaying and creaking of a ship was easy enough to
imagine. The Post was pounded by muffled blows that
seemed to come up from a keel. This was a battle of one-
eyed giants, wind against wood, the one ceaselessly attacking,

the other passively on the defensive—like a ship at sea. The whistling of the wireless mast completed the illusion.

Emptying the slop bucket was a trial. As a matter of fact, whether your destination lay ten yards or ten miles off made no difference in your preparations; and the disproportion between those preparations and the aim of your errand was grotesque. The battle began while you were still in the porch. You put your shoulder against the door and pushed with all your strength, quite as at sea; and when, suddenly, it gave way, a packet of snow hit you so hard in the face that you stepped back to recover your breath. The walls of the porch were plastered with snow two feet thick, and if you were so unfortunate as to knock against a wall, your neck or boots were filled instantly with a great lump that landed with a soft thud. Of course, once the door was open it would not shut again, the doorway would begin to fill with snow, I would call out to Paddy, and between us we would shovel the snow away and pull the door to. Outside, the wind would cut like a knife right across your face. If you had been smoking a cigar it would have sliced the cigar off at your lips.

This is a corner of the world where weather has not yet been domesticated. Everywhere else than at the poles, it has been pacified, has taken a quasi-definitive form, has settled down. There are east winds and west winds; they bring rain or they do not, and you know that after the rain, fine days will follow. Your weather is more or less pigeon-holed. Not here. Weather up here still wanders free, uncaptured, lurks and roves in an irregular circle.

But indeed nothing up here is settled. Before you know it, the island is bare of foxes, there isn't a fox left. The Eskimos are gone in a wink, their igloos empty, although last night they were still about. The landscape itself changes as if manned by scene-shifters. You stare and say to yourself in bewilderment, "Am I mad, or is it this land that is out of its wits?" When you see igloos disappear suddenly before your eyes; when invisible dogs stir beneath the snow under your feet as you walk; when things rise suddenly out of the earth and vanish as if sucked up into the air, it is hard to think of life as normal. You knew very well what this landscape looked like; and where is it? The shack you saw yesterday is today but a roof lying on the surface of the snow. What is this, you wonder? Is it the prelude to Judgment Day? Our globe that we thought a solid turns out to be a mere soap-bubble blown into different shapes by the wind. In this sea of grey your heart quakes, your brain reels. You are enclosed in it like a rat in a box, and some one is there shaking the box with all his furious might. You stand speechless, childish, despairing; and in a moment you fly into a rage, you want to bite and tear the snow with your teeth, to do battle with the storm in a hand-to-hand encounter. And when you get back into the Post the change is stupefying. You have been whirling in an icy bacchanal, and this sudden peace is just as dramatic as that war. It is so overpowering that you sink down upon your bed and lie without stirring, completely undone.

Towards mid-December, the day—if our dim obscurity can be called day—begins to die at half past one in the afternoon. What is strange is that it is just before day dies that the wind falls and one can see farthest. Regularly at this hour the curtain of snow will rise—not to the south, where, somewhere, we know the sun to be, but to the west, where it reveals the shore line and lends us again the assurance that we are on earth. Except for this band of light we might easily believe ourselves to be living in a nebula, in something that had not yet hardened and through which one moved like a shade in slippers.

There is no dawdling out of doors round the Post. Once you are out, you scurry, you trot, and you stumble, fall, and pick yourself up again. You stumble constantly, and the reason is that this land is without shadow, without perspective; it is as if you had only one eye. Hollows and humps have no contour and are alike invisible. You take a step and are off ludicrously into space; another, and you are on your knees in a hummock of snow. You can see that beacon standing a quarter of a mile away, but you cannot see what is at your feet: open your eyes as wide as you please, stare as hard as you will, what is at your feet is invisible to you.

Often when I wandered alone in this silence, this infinite solitude, this dead infinity, I wondered if I were dreaming. Who was this man that seemed to be me and that stumbled in rude clothes over the snow, an Eskimo knife in his hand? If this was I, what was I doing here, floating like a phantom through this grey air? "You will be shut in, walled up, unable to stir, stupefied with boredom while you await the return of daylight." Who was it that had warned me thus? Bishop Fallaize, wasn't it? Forgive me, your Grace, but I had not a moment of boredom in the Arctic. Least of all, I swear, when I became lost in a blizzard. There was no time for boredom.

I was out trapping. It was an escape from the excessively oppressive atmosphere of the Post. But as white men are not allowed to trap here, I was watching certain traps for an Eskimo. He had set them, and I used to go out to visit them. One day, taking advantage of the couple of hours of dusk that remained to us, I went off in the wind, a sack of bait slung across my chest in Eskimo fashion. It was one of those

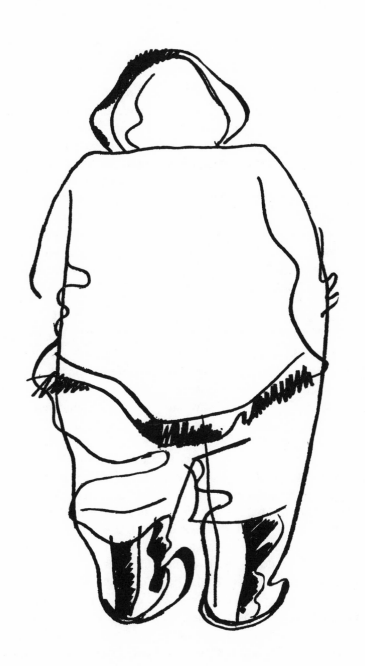

days when you look round and say to yourself, "Not too good, but it will do," and you chance it anyway. I was bound for a trap-line about half a mile from the Post. I reached it, reset two traps, stood up and looked round to make certain of my bearings. Behind me the wind was blowing harder. I was in a situation which makes people like me a bit nervous but in which also they say, invariably, "Just one more and I'll turn back." Already I was having trouble with the shavings of fish that constituted the bait. They would blow off the trap, and I would run after them to put them back where they belonged. I knew well enough that I was playing the fool, but I was stubborn, and I hummed a tune to let myself know that I was perfectly sure of being able to look after myself. I did turn back, though, and I came finally in sight of the cairn that marked my first trap. By this time the blow was stiff, I was worried, and I had stopped humming. I couldn't fool myself any longer. There was no comfort in this situation. I was fidgety, exasperated; and wherever I looked I saw snow-filled space and nothing else. I started to run, stumbled, panted as I ran, and then fell heavily, as if I had been tripped up. By the time I was on my feet again things looked really bad.

I got as far as the cairn and drew breath. Ahead of me, in the direction of the Post, was a bare patch of rock, and with my eyes riveted on it I went forward. I knew that if I took my eyes off it I should never in my life see it again. The thought bothered me. It is absurd, I said to myself, that a man's life should hang on a thing like this, on keeping his eyes glued to a black dot in a gray cloth. But I was less than half a mile from the Post, I knew where I was going, and in ten minutes all danger would be behind me.

It was ahead of me. Suddenly the snow was whirling round me, encircling me, and the whole landscape vanished.

I shouldn't have started to run. Running is the worst thing a man can do. It makes him perspire, and when he stops he freezes. But I ran nevertheless. I said to myself that my life was a matter of seconds, that each second was priceless, and that if I did not reach my objective immediately I was gone.

I ran back where I had come from. This is how men get lost, for they always arrive at a different point from that which they are running to. They think they have spotted a landmark. It is on the right. But it is not on the right; it is not on the left; it is nowhere. Then they go round and round in a circle, out of breath. Damn! There goes a glove! And it means that the hand—under an axe—will follow the glove. They stop, try to catch their breath, and feel that the end is near. Their *attige,* or inner coat, is frozen with sweat; and as they no longer know what to do, they do the maddest things. They strip to take off this coat of ice, and then freeze without it. They tramp backward and forward for two days in order not to freeze to death; and then they topple over. Not far from where I stood trembling, the grave of Luca was dug after he had been found gloveless and frozen stiff.

I did not want to become one of those men: it was too stupid. I wanted to be calm. But there were no landmarks. I had no notion where I was. The stones I had only just seen had disappeared as by enchantment. I was somebody's play-thing, and I knew now that Death had his own peculiar sense of humor.

Visibility was barely five yards. I sat down. This looks like the end, I thought. I am a dead man. An Eskimo would have built an igloo in this blizzard: I couldn't. I hadn't had enough practice. I thought of those men on Herschel Island who had been playing football just outside the settlement when a blizzard had sprung up. They had crawled into ice-houses to escape it. Five had frozen to death. I tried to dismiss the thought, saying to myself that I must keep my head. Still, here I was, ten minutes from the Post and already dead. A living dead man! The idea amused me and I thought, I must make a note of it. But how, being dead, could I make a note of it? This little humorous passage was useful: it furnished me momentary relief.

If you see a man in a blizzard bending over a rock you may be sure it is me and that I am lost. The shadow that I now am is scrutinizing that rock as soberly as it has ever stared at anything in the world. It is trying to remember, saying to itself: Have I ever seen this bit of rock before? A geologist would not look at it half as intently. Certainly I had seen it before, but where? When? Then, after a moment, I straightened up and said to myself as calmly as I could, No. I do not know this bit of stone.

Suddenly I thought I saw something and hurried towards it. A black dot. But no. A single swift gust of wind erased it from this grey blotting-paper. Death was playful. There are people with whom Death plays for three whole days.

I gave up the notion of direction. I began merely to roam. If there was a chance in a million that I should come out safe, I was taking it. I do not know what happens to the brain, or if eyes are capable of going mad, but every one who has been lost like this will tell you of extraordinary optical effects. You rush towards a landmark a quarter of a mile away, sure that it is one of the beacons round the Post: it is four yards off and is a tuft of blackened weed. This time I really saw a curiously black spot and my heart jumped as I recognized it. It was one of another set of traps I was serving. But how could it be? For it meant I was out at sea!

How could I, in a radius of half a mile, have wandered so far off my course?

The shore line. "I follow the shore line!" Stubbornly, afraid that if I did not cling to the word I should lose the thing, I repeated to myself, "The shore line!" It might easily have slipped away from me: I had already proof enough that things were as malicious as people. And I knew the shore line should curve: why was it not curving, confound it!

It curved, thank God! I was safe. Up there at the Post Gibson must have been thinking that I too would be good for five foxes a season. Not this time! There was the beacon straight ahead of me, and I was going straight towards it. A gust. The snow blinded me. I looked again. Where was that beacon? This was really too much! Fortunately, my retina if not my mind knew in what direction I should be going. I sprang forward . . . and a form emerged from the blizzard close enough to touch me. It was Gibson.

"Mm!" he said. "I was beginning to be worried."

We went back to the Post without a word. I dropped my sack in the outer porch, went in, and sat down. Then, by way of scolding me gently, Gibson muttered that he had been looking for me from the top of the knoll and had been quite sure that I was lost.

I scarcely heard what he said. I was dazed and inert. As in the blizzard, I wondered now if this man sitting by the stove was me. How could it be, if five minutes ago I had been dead? And if this was me, it was only half of me, for I still saw in the mind's eye that other me, wandering vainly in the storm. In this confusion, this soft cotton-wool nightmare, I remained for a little time, and then I came suddenly alive.

"Gibson!" I shouted. "Let's get drunk. Let's get a couple of Eskimo women." But there were no Eskimo women (Gibson would not have indulged himself in any case), and

as for getting drunk, our three bottles of rum were much
too precious to use in any but the greatest emergency. At half
past midnight we lay each in his bed, reading by lamplight.
We had never before retired so early.

Paddy was not the man to go out of doors. He had been
too long in the Arctic to find fascination in unnecessary trial
and struggle. Nothing could tarnish the glow of tranquillity
that lay over the surface of his existence. He had dug himself
out a hole, and in it he lived. Everything in the Post was set,
once and for always. Eggs, potatoes, potatoes, eggs: he never
changed his routine, and his stomach knew no other fare.
Scrupulously and meticulously, his life was ordered. All
his worries—whatever they might have been—had been
wrapped up in a bundle, carefully tied and sealed, and
shoved out of sight. He was the perfect Post Manager,
stripped for action.

When six o'clock came he would stir in his armchair.

"I guess we might as well have some supper," he would
say as if the thought had never before occurred to him. He
would peel his potatoes, boil three times as many as we could
eat, and thus be free of this chore for two more evenings. His
life was so efficiently organized that it went like an automaton and he never had any reason to think. He had one fear,
however, and nothing could be more natural: he was constantly afraid lest I upset his routine. Let me make but the
slightest suggestion, let me display the slightest evidence of
moodiness, and he would prick up his ears, would become
on the instant alert, and would spend the next twelve hours
smoothing my ruffled feathers. Really, I do much more than
my share! (It isn't true: I do nothing at all.) What must I
think of him, with his crusty old bachelor ways! (I think, in
fact, highly of him, and gratefully.) And when I had come

round and had begun to joke again, he would fall back with relief into his routine.

By way of distraction, and also because it was necessary, I spent a good deal of time compiling an Eskimo-English dictionary. Primitive languages have a directness which has long gone out of the subtle and metaphorical terminology of civilized speech. The Eskimo word for bishop, for example, is *ri-oo-mata,* "the man who thinks"; their word for polar bear is *tara-i-tua-luk,* "he who is without shadow" (though the polar bear is also called "the eternal vagabond"). There is a sort of poetry of the concrete in their speech that is very moving. Thus, *mi-kse,* the word for "reality" is literally translatable as "the thing turned towards you." When an object moans in the wind it is said to "grind its teeth." If two people have fallen out they are said to "drift away from one another," and if a man has not understood you, it is said that "you have missed him," *sil-la-ko-kto,* as if your words were a spear that had missed its mark. Our abstractions flatter the mind, but their concrete images go direct to the senses and tickle the palate, the sense of smell and of sight.

Now and then in the midst of my study Paddy would interrupt me with:
"Coppermine in five minutes!"
Coppermine talked to the North on Sundays at three in the afternoon, and we would drop everything and glue our ears to the radio.
At that moment, in the official wireless station at Coppermine, a bespectacled little man would have set down a needle on a worn gramophone record, grinding out an old-fashioned military march which always put me in mind of slightly pompous and yet very touching wooden soldiers in

uniforms of another age. Then the little man—I had seen
him at work many months before—would go to the micro-
phone, and in a chatty familiar voice would address himself
to the fifteen white trappers, the police, and the scattered
Hudson's Bay men. It was always very moving, for it was
not a broadcast but a greeting and a conversation between
members of a tiny but fervent family.

"Good afternoon, everybody," he would begin, "this is
VBK Coppermine."

"Good afternoon," fifteen solitary white men would murmur religiously under their breath with no possibility of
being heard.

"The temperature here is thirty-five below. Barometer,
29:40. Strong northeast wind . . ."

Ah! the warmth of that voice wandering over the ice and
through the polar wastes to the ears of the family!

"Hello, Angus Gavin, Perry River! We have mail here for
you, Angus. We'll try to get it to you sometime in the spring.
. . . Hello, Frank Milne, Cambridge Bay! I hear you have
no matches left, Frank. When the police sled comes up to
fetch the winter mail it will bring you a few boxes from the
Hudson's Bay man here; but his own stock is low."

All this was much more important than news of the great
world Outside. We got that news rarely, for one thing; and
for another, what could it mean to us? Whereas these little
things—the boxes of matches, the lighter flints, the question
whether or not caribou skins had been set aside for shipment
to you the following spring—these things were life itself.

Then, apart from helpful details, there was the life of the
community. Some posts, in particular the police, had their
sending as well as receiving sets, and conversations went on
that revealed the intense concern and affection that sub-
sisted between these men. What sort of winter were you hav-

ing? Had you been affected by the epidemic of dog-disease
that was thinning out the huskies in our part of the world?
How was your sealing going? Sometimes there were long
conversations about two puppies that one man had promised
another and was still unable to send up to him, the discussion stretching over a period of six months.

Coppermine's weekly chat hardly lasted ten minutes:

"That's about all there is," the voice would say; "but here
is Father Le Mer who wants to say a few words."

The voice would change, but the subject of conversation
hardly varied. Missionary or Hudson's Bay man, the strain
was always the same:

"Hello, Father Buliard, Walker Bay! I hope your dogs are
in good shape and seal are plentiful . . ."

The new voice would make its rounds, touching the Arctic
here and there; then it would cease and the first voice would
return:

"Well, that's all for today. This is VBK Coppermine sign-
ing off."

What ought to have been a comfort was more often than
not a torture to us, for the Post set was practically always out
of order. We would hear the fuzzy hollow sound of the
sender's voice, would cry out happily, "Here she is!" and
then, with nerves taut and ears strained, we would hear a
sort of exhalation of breath, a bark, a sound of scraping,
a few disconnected words—then silence. Stubbornly, we
would stand by; and the worst was that occasionally we got
something.

"Message for Paddy Gib . . ." Our hearts would jump
into our throats; and before the name Gibson could be pronounced the set was dead. What could that message have
been? Where was it from? We were never to know, and the

thought filled us both with anger. "I told you the con-
founded radio was no good!" I would storm, and for two
hours neither of us would say a word. Weeks went by with
no better reception than this. We swore each time that we
would not turn the radio on, and each time we broke our
oath to no avail.

"We'll try to get your mail up to you in the spring." I had
written letters and had given them to a native, Kernek, who
was to pass them on to an Eskimo on his way by sled to
Perry River. From Perry River, it might be, some one would
be able to take them down to Coppermine. If they caught
the winter plane out of Coppermine, the rest was easy. But
Kernek had not been able to find the man who was going
down to Perry River and had brought back my letters. Now
my family in France would have no news of me until the
spring, when I should somehow arrange with Perry River to
send off a cable. I had counted on seven months to get a
letter to France: it turned out that it would take twelve. To
amuse myself, I drew up a mail schedule.

Relay	Miles	Points	Transport
1	100	King William Land to Sherman Inlet	Eskimo sled
2	150	Sherman Inlet to Perry River	Eskimo sled
3	150	Perry River to Cambridge Bay	Eskimo sled
4	300	Cambridge Bay to Coppermine	Police sled
5	1,500	Coppermine to Edmonton	Airplane
6	1,900	Edmonton to Montreal	Railway
7	4,000	Montreal to Le Havre	Ship
8	250	Le Havre to my home	Railway

Total 8,350 miles, of which 700 miles by sled, 1,500 by plane, 4,000
by ship, and 2,150 miles by rail.

I have already said that a trading session was a duel between Post Manager and Eskimo, a duel that lasts for hours
and is repeated each time with the same conventions and for-
malities. The fewer the foxes a native has to trade, the longer
the duel goes on; because invariably he manoeuvres, stops,
takes inordinately long to make up his mind, moans and
whines—and when it is all over he perceives, or pretends to
perceive, that he has forgotten to get in trade what he most
needed, and he tries to wheedle more out of the Post Manager without payment.

Old Tutiak arrived one day with four foxes. The whole
colony followed him into the Store, and when we were all
present, and he had taken a good look round as if to ask,
"Is everybody ready?" Tutiak flung two foxes at once boldly
and magnanimously on the counter.

"My debt," he said simply; and he turned to left and right
as if to say, "That's the sort of man I am." Instinctively I
looked for applause, and certainly his audience were enormously impressed. Paddy, I must say, was no less impressed
than the others, for to find Tutiak out of debt was something new in his career. The remaining foxes were traded,
and when all was over, the foxes out of sight, and Paddy was
preparing to leave the Store, Tutiak began his little game.

He had not taken the necessaries of life in trade, because
he knew well enough that Paddy would be forced to give
them to him. Ah! he grunted suddenly. Tea! He had no tea!
How could a man take the trail in this season—brr!—without tea? It was unthinkable, wasn't it?

And he turned to his audience who nodded assent. Tutiak
was perfectly right. A man could not take the trail without
tea, and a Post Manager who let him take the trail without tea would be an evil man.

"And tobacco!" Tutiak added. How much had he left?

Mi-ki-luk, very little. His hands fell into the shape of a round tin containing less than an inch of tobacco.

There isn't much you can do about it. You cannot ignore it. The others are there, staring at you and drawing up from the depths of themselves that long Eskimo syllable of affirmation, *eh-eh-eh!* Regretfully, you put down on the counter a packet of tea and two tins of tobacco.

But the others have their eyes on Tutiak, too, and the star of this comedy must play his part for all it is worth. A pocket knife! He was forgetting that his son had lost his pocket knife. (*"Eh-eh-eh!"* from the chorus.) And a file, of course, a file. Ah! That's it. *Na-ma-kto:* very good. The Kabloona is a man of heart, a man who understands.

The Kabloona has meanwhile leant across the counter with a smile:

"And that will make one fox in debt."

What! In debt again! Tutiak is breathless with amazement. (Wonderful, these native faces when they are acting.) This was something that he had not looked for. He stands stock still, gathers all his strength and wits. With the rest watching him, his prestige is at stake. The brave words are flung forth:

"Oo-van-ga watt-i-ago." (I shall very soon . . .)

And with the help of his eloquent hands he embarks upon a speech. "I, when I come back"—the hand pulls an imaginary sled towards the Post—"I shall bring many foxes. The season is here. There will be many many foxes." (The hands sketch rapidly scores of foxes in their traps.) "Just now the moon . . ." He is watching the white man's face and sees that the moon does not take. Back he goes over his tracks. "I know all the fox-holes in the region. My traps . . ." This seems to be working well, and he goes all out, gestures and words flowing and tumbling in a happy swift-moving music-hall turn that enchants his audience and moves the actor to radiant smiles. He will be off to the great lake where he has the longest trap-line on the island. By the time he reaches the lake the days will be longer, and the moon . . . He veers off from the moon to remark that the foxes are now on the move, goes back to the moon, entangles himself in a long discussion of season, fox, and weather, half boastful and half pathetic; then turns and observes that he is being far too clever. The natives are listening, enraptured, but the Kabloona has turned his back and is straightening the stock on the shelves. Obviously, there is nothing more to be got out of him; but no matter. What we have got is now ours, and there is no further need to play a part. Tutiak bends down, picks up his treasures, and goes out, followed by the others. You can hear him talking loudly out of doors while the Post Manager, with freezing fingers, is rapidly entering the transaction in his books.

What goes on in the Eskimo's mind in the matter of trading is rudimentary but complex. It starts in the igloo before he embarks for the Post. There, swollen with pride, he drinks mug upon mug of tea and boasts to his wife and his visitors. He is the great hunter, the man who can do anything he sets his mind to; the man who could if he wished trap all foxes on the island. (All this because he has four foxes in a sack.) When he gets to the Store, he will show them all how to handle the Kabloona.

And what happens at the Store is that out of vanity he makes a fool of himself.

"I'll take two foxes worth of tobacco. No, not just half a fox worth, but two foxes worth! That's the kind of man I am!"

All this to make his friends sit up. For in the igloo it was not thus that he had planned to trade. Once he and his wife were alone, they had taken a sort of inventory, they had arrived at a notion of what they needed for their well-being. The wife (I have said this before) would get more or less what she wanted; but several things would intervene to land the husband with things worthless to him. First, his lack of memory. Secondly, his vanity. Finally, the deep social sense of all Eskimos, the magnanimity they never fail to display towards their kind, and which here in the Store leads them to take things in trade that will be rapidly bestowed upon others, like that excessive amount of tobacco.

Another thing that he must count with is his notion of the white man. The Kabloona is part old fox and part madman. The old fox in him has learnt all the Eskimo tricks, and when you stood on the other side of the counter from him, at the Store, you wanted to play your cards with care. There was almost always an audience of friends present: therefore, as a matter of face you had to do the Kabloona in the eye or lose caste. And the remarkable thing was that the Eskimo always believed, whatever he brought away from the Store, that he had done the white man in the eye; and for hours afterwards, in the igloo, the thought would continue to give him enormous pleasure.

As for the white man's madness, nothing could be more self-evident. The fox that he seemed to cherish was clearly a useless beast. The way in which he allowed you to go into debt to him was plain simplemindedness. And the disproportionately precious and beautiful things you were given in exchange for a fox-skin were the best proof in the world that the man had no intelligence.

The other Kabloona, the Post Manager's friend, was even madder than the Post Manager himself. You brought him a crudely carved bit of caribou bone, and what didn't you get for it! A pipe; a length of rope; a tin of tobacco. Yet you couldn't count on him. Yesterday he refused to trade for two fish needles.

That, indeed, was true: I had refused these bones with which they pierce the fish to carry it on a cord. And I had been amused to see the look of worry and suspicion that came into the Eskimo's eye when I refused them. It was as if he were saying to himself, "Can the Kabloona by chance have come to his senses?" But his face had cleared up again when he had seen me wrap up the caribou bone carefully in a bit of rag.

Another day Kakokto brought me in great triumph two bits of whale-bone.

"Niuvi-u-malerk-tu-tin?" (Do you want to trade these?)

I told him that they did not interest me, and he stared at me incredulously. Then he laughed and said:

"You never know what these white men want."

Next day he was off on the trail; and when I went out of doors I saw the two bits of bone lying on the snow outside his igloo. Since I had refused them, they must be valueless, and Kakokto had flung them away.

The white man being mad and irresponsible, he is a fit subject for exploitation. But the Eskimo being without consistency and perseverance, he is unable to exploit the white man systematically. I remember that Utak, one day, received a present of a sack of flour. Added to his small stock of provisions, the flour would have allowed him to go trapping and bring back two or three foxes to augment his supplies. Such a thought would never have occurred to him. He loitered round the Post, spent most of the hours asleep in his igloo, and when he awoke, pretty much all of that beautiful flour with which his wife baked those *baneks* that were like

the white man's bread, was gone. What was left of the flour
was consumed while he sat ruminating, pondering the in-
vention of another lie that would win him another sack of
flour. Since the white man has made one gift, why should he
not make another?

We used to keep at the Post a stock of frozen fish in the
event that a police sled turned up and was short of dog-feed.
During the summer, the Eskimos would sell the Post Manager a cache of this fish; and to make it more precious they
would add that it was "very heavy for the dogs." In mid-winter they were back. They were hungry; they had no fish left;
it didn't matter about themselves, but the kid had nothing to
eat. In a word, you gave them back the fish that you had
once bought from them.

For me who had no part in this, but was merely an ob-
server, the play of relationship between Post Manager and
Eskimo was endlessly interesting. But there were occasions
enough—some of them I have already related—when, on the
trail and in the igloo, I was myself the object of their spolia-
tion. The Eskimos had evolved a uniform technique for getting the better of the white man, and they employed it in
great things as in small, on the trail as at the Post. If I have
said it already, I shall say it again: theft was never in their
minds. What underlay the whole procedure was that article
of the Eskimo code which ruled that everything in the igloo
belonged to everybody in the igloo; or at any rate was to be
shared among all those present in the igloo. If the family
with which I was travelling had no tobacco, for example,
they had the right to dip into my tin. But I was a Kabloona.
I did not know of this right. Their language, meanwhile,
was concrete and not abstract, wherefore they could not explain such things as rights to me. Even had they tried halt-
ingly to do so,—and this would never have occurred to them

—I was still too unfamiliar with their language to understand. So, in the presence of my ignorance of their code, and given the limitations of their language (which is to say their mental processes), when they sought to share my tobacco they took one of three ways.

There was the direct attack. The Eskimo came into my igloo; and because he was acquainted with me, perhaps had been of service to me, he was relatively bold. His object was insignificant. He was out merely to pick up my tin and roll himself a cigarette. But he had scarcely straightened up on entering through the porch before the whole terrain was in his eye and a plan in his mind. Forward he came to my *iglerk,* but in the very act of coming forward he had his eye on me. If he saw that I was not in the mood to be imposed upon (from my point of view), he feinted, picked up a bit of fish, busied himself somehow. Then, with an absent-minded air he sat down beside me and talked vaguely in order to feel me out. For an Eskimo, the white man's face is an open book, a thing almost indecently unveiled. A contraction of your facial muscles, a certain tenseness in the hand with which you pick up a mug of tea, the way you turn suddenly on the *iglerk,* will tell him without fail that you are a bit on the nervous side and that he will do well to go slow. After a few words, therefore, my Eskimo sketched a gesture towards the tin—but a casual and feline gesture, for he was aware that a brusque movement would annoy me if I was jumpy, whereas a smooth and supple movement would stimulate no reflex in me. His arm came slowly up, his hand opened, his fingers closed round the tin. I, thinking, perhaps about something else, had not said a word. His purpose was achieved.

Of itself, nothing could seem more harmless. What is the value of a cigarette! Yet, a capital event has taken place.

Word has gone round all the igloos: here is a Kabloona whose tobacco box is easy to grab. A point has been scored against me.

Now suppose that you are a stranger. The Eskimo has never done you a service. You have met on the trail, at a camp. He and his wife are avid to smoke your tobacco. She suggests that he go straight for the tin. He objects. He does not know you; you will be offended; it is too risky. If she is one of the brighter and cheekier sort of Eskimo wives, she will cover him with ridicule.

"What!" she will exclaim. "Not dip into his tobacco tin! What a fool you are to be afraid. Watch me! I'll show you how it's done. I'll grab the box and be back with a handful of tobacco before he knows it is gone."

She will come into your igloo, move forward with her crafty pigeon-toed shuffle, fix you with a glittering and pro-vocative eye, put out a swift, cat-like paw, and her hand will be full of tobacco before you are aware of what has happened.

"Here!" you call as she starts out of the porch. "Put that back!"

Unless you have had experience, you hesitate to protest; but if experience has taught you that it is not safe to let these things pass, they never happen twice, whether it is the husband or the wife who has tried to get the better of you.

There is still a third mode of attack. If both husband and wife are afraid to try, they will send their child to do the job. Eskimo children are very attractive once they are out of the hood and running about. The white man finds them irresistible, and the parents know it. They groom the little fellow and send him along. These children, who are as shrewd as monkeys, know very well what is up, and they have great fun at it. Besides, there is no risk: no Eskimo has ever punished a child, and it is inconceivable that the white man should hurt the little boy.

To these three methods I may add a fourth, though here the scale is entirely different. There are Eskimos—by no means all of them—who will send a wife to propose herself to the white man in order that the family may profit from the arrangement. If the white man agrees, the woman will bag everything she can lay her hands on—not behind his back, indeed, for the Eskimos are not sneak-thieves, but by wheedling and cajolery. And when she leaves him, if there is a thing as small as a needle in her path on the way out, she will pick it up in full view of him and carry this treasure off.

Manœuvres like these are the easiest things in the world to explain. But what shall I say of the Eskimo mental process as such?

I remember that one day an Eskimo came into the Post with a troubled look on his face. Gibson and I stood before him and waited for him to speak. As no word came from him, Gibson asked him after a time what the matter was. Standing in the middle of the room, the Eskimo raised his eyes vaguely to the ceiling, pointed to his chest, and said, *"Hamane"* (here). That was where a pain was, we assumed. He remained standing, and it was clear that he had more to say, for he would wave a hand and let it fall; he would open his mouth, bring up the hand once more, and again his hand would drop. Finally he began to speak, lost the thread of his thought, and wandered in a mental labyrinth. Men like ourselves have some control over our thought: this primitive man had none. He began in the middle, pronouncing directly the most important word in his mind. Then he went back to the beginning of a phrase and started afresh. I re-

membered what a missionary had said to me about the
Eskimo: "He thinks; then he stops thinking; then he thinks
again. But he cannot pursue a train of thought from beginning to end." A word would come forth from this Eskimo.
Then nothing. Suddenly images would flow through his
mind, but so many that he could not reduce this chaos to
order. Disconnected words would tumble out of his mouth
as if he was afraid that unless he pronounced all of them
simultaneously, they would leave him and never return.
Then silence again.

Our Eskimo stood like this, pensive, pitiful, wondering
what he wanted to say. Finally he coughed; and this suddenly brought back to him what had been in his mind. And
so, with his finger, he drew great circles on his chest to
show where he was in pain, staring meanwhile at Paddy
and me as if we were accusing him of lying and needed to
be convinced.

There is no end to the examples I witnessed and heard of
the difference in mentality between the two races; and the
more instances I collected, the wider the gap between them
seemed to be.

One year, at Tree River, the police were taking a census
of the natives. They would interrogate them, write down
their names, father's names, and the rest, while the Eskimos
stood by mystified, wondering what the police could be
doing with these things we call paper and pencil. When it
was explained to them, they understood—that is, they decided that the white man possessed no memory and had
invented this curious practice in order to preserve what he
would otherwise forget.

Shortly afterwards, a young Eskimo arrived at this same
Post and installed himself on a bench opposite the sergeant

in charge. He sat and sat until the policeman, disgusted by the sight of his tranquil nose-picking, threw him out. Ten minutes later the door opened; the native came in with a broad grin and sat down again as if nothing had happened. The policeman, astonished, called an interpreter in to find out why the man had come back.

"You threw him out ten minutes ago," said the interpreter. "But as he knows that you have no memory, he merely waited a while and then came in again, quite sure you must have forgotten him."

The Eskimo, you will exclaim, has the mind of a child. Agreed: but is it not interesting that to the Eskimo it is we who seem like children? We are impatient; we ask a thousand useless questions; as soon as things go wrong we show our discontent without fear of losing face. The Eskimo feels himself constantly obliged to soothe us, placate us, as if we were children who would fly into a rage unless we had our way.

Besides, we are inept, incapable. What can we do? Build an igloo? No. Carry a really heavy pack? No. Spear fish? No. Not even women's work, for we are incapable of sewing hides or boots, and undoubtedly we would ruin a skin if we tried scraping it.

It is true that a part of this sense of superiority over the white man is affected. I remember that I took Utak's wife to the Store, to pick out of my stock of caribou hides a few to be sewn up into socks. I spread them on the floor, and immediately there came into her face a look half pity and half scorn. The reason was not that the skins were poor: they had been carefully chosen for me by the shrewdest woman in Coppermine. It was that she had seen me on the trail, where I had stumbled, where I had proved that I did not know how to tie their kind of knot in the strips of sealskin of which their lashings are made, and had in other ways displayed my ineptitude. As a matter of fact the Eskimo takes it for granted that the white man does everything badly. But he never interferes or gives advice, as we do. Instead, he waits until you have done the job—lashed the sled, for example; and when you have finished he comes calmly forward, undoes your work, and does it all over again.

Down she went on the floor, then, fumbling the skins, scratching them with her finger-nail to have a good look at the fur, folding them to see their thickness, chewing a corner to learn their texture and soundness—and flinging them back with an air of disgust as if to say, "How can a man own such awful hides!" Nevertheless, she went back over them again, condescended to pick out three, and carried them off to her igloo—but not before having extorted from me a beautiful caribou belly of the purest white, a chunk of seal-sinew (the nerves, drawn out one by one, are used as thread), and two packets of needles—enough for six months' sewing in her household.

In the course of a good many months in the North I came upon three types of Eskimo. There were those of the west, in the direction of Alaska, who had grown into the white man's way of life and might almost have been called "sophisticated." There were the Netsilik of King William Land who lived a primitive existence, but had sufficient occasional contact with the white man to be tainted by that contact. And there were the truly primitive Eskimos who, apart from a rare missionary priest, hardly knew what a white man looked like. The Eskimos of whom I have thus far written were of the second group; and though they had, as I have

said, been somewhat tainted, it was curious to see that they
had this in common with the primitive Eskimos whom I
was later to visit, that the lie with intent to do injury was
virtually unknown among them. Of course they lied to me,
again and again, when I was impatient on the trail, when
it seemed to them that I needed to be soothed. A white man
might have thought those lies redounded to his harm; but
this was not their view. What could not hurt them, they
seemed to reason, could not hurt me; and if a white lie
would pacify me—for example, if they told me we should
be two days reaching a given point, knowing full well that
we should be four or five—they told the white lie, the inoffensive lie, without blinking. But if, by chance, one of them
should lie to me with injurious intent, the rest would hasten
to warn me of it. This was the only infraction I ever saw of
one of the strongest articles of their code, the article com-
manding non-interference in a neighbor's affairs.

What was true of the Netsilik of King William Land was
even more true of the primitive Eskimos I visited at Pelly
Bay and saw elsewhere in these regions. And it came out
most clearly in their rare encounters with the Canadian
police.

There was an Eskimo whose wife had died and left him
with three children. Unable to bring them up alone, he
sought another wife. Finally, in the neighborhood of Sherman Inlet, he came upon Utak's sister and married her.

They lived in peace for a time, after which the wife, finding her husband too old for her taste, took a lover and
persuaded her lover to kill her husband. The younger man
shot the older man from behind and flung his body into a
lake. Somehow the police were informed, and an inquiry
was started. But the murder had been done and the informa-

tion laid during the summer. For the police to charter a vessel would have been expensive. They waited till winter, and came up on a sled. Necessarily, their first task was to find the *corpus delicti*. But the corpse was somewhere under six feet of ice in a lake two miles long, and the search was unavailing. Not for want of good will on the part of the murderer and his paramour, however. Both were on hand to help the police, and the murderer, standing by, said in a matter-of-fact tone:

"*Hamane*"—"here."

And the woman, chiming in, said, "Yes. It was here that you threw him into the lake."

The body was not found, and the murderers were not taken off to prison. No Eskimo understood, nor understands to this day, why the police came up.

But very likely these Eskimos will never understand the white man's notion of justice. There is a good deal of killing among them, but in their eyes it is always just and often an act of communal devotion.

Round Adelaide Peninsula there lived a great shaman. The man had been the best hunter of his clan, therefore the one most respectfully listened to (they have no chiefs nor formal leaders); and, as his influence grew and grew, he became a medicine man.

There are good and evil sorcerers: this one was evil. He took advantage of his power to abuse the wives of the clan and to oblige its members to bring him tribute of every sort. What was more, the natives said that he had seven deaths on his conscience—which did not mean that he had killed seven men himself, for the shaman is generally too clever to do his own killing. This could not go on, and yet no one knew how to stop it, for the Eskimos are superstitious: they feel the need of their shaman again and again as tempests rage or the seal grow scarce. In the end, however, the men talked it over, word went from igloo to igloo that this man must be killed; and although much time passed before the thing was done, it was finally done by a young hunter in the course of the chase. Again the police heard of the murder, and again a police sergeant came up by sled to apprehend the murderer.

On his way in, the sergeant came upon a group of Eskimos. As is habitual, he camped near by, passed his tobacco tin around, and as the evening of friendly tea-drinking and conversation proceeded, the sergeant said finally, "I am looking for such and such a man."

"But here he is!" the Eskimos cried out in chorus.

They pointed to the man who sat by, a wide smile on his face. Of course it was he! And very proud he was, too, of what he had done. He mounted the policeman's sled without a word of protest, and for an act of devotion to the clan, did his time in the prison at Aklavik. The only man who had any trouble with him was the lawyer appointed by the Court to defend him, for he insisted stubbornly upon telling the whole truth.

Among the Eskimos, meanwhile, the mystery of the white man's justice remained.

There was the case of Agil-hi-ak, "The Ptarmigan." This case was hardest of all to understand. For in the first place, Agil-hi-ak had merely killed a young man who had sought to run off with his wife. The fact that, in the way of hunting partners, the young man had enjoyed Agil-hi-ak's wife offended nobody; but to want to take her away, have her to himself, was criminal and deserved death. Secondly, what did they do by way of punishing Agil-hi-ak? They housed him warmly; they gave him clothes to wear; they fed him well and brought him all the tobacco he could smoke. Everybody was kind to him. They took him off on a long wonderful journey to Aklavik, over a thousand miles away, where he saw more white men's houses *(igloo-pak)* than could be imagined. Precisely because he had killed a man he was freed from every hardship. That was all very well, but what about his wife, meanwhile, and his two children? For a time the clan supported them, passing them along from igloo to igloo. Wherever she lodged, she was a burden, for Eskimo life is hard; men are few and mouths are many. Fortunately, a white trapper had taken a liking to her, and she and the children had finally left the clan.

It was four years before Agil-hi-ak came back. His wife and children were gone, his dogs were dead; and though he could not have put a name to it, he had tuberculosis, as have so many natives after living for a time in the white man's hamlets. And he had lost his taste for the open life, yearned to return to Aklavik, where the white man was through with him since he had "expiated his crime." Agil-hi-ak was not a better Eskimo for having submitted himself to the white man's justice.

Such stories as Agil-hi-ak's made the trip to Aklavik popular amongst the Eskimos. One or two might have been hanged there, but the most of them had merely been housed and fed. To think that one had only to kill a man in order to receive the gift of this great excursion! One day an Eskimo came to the police and told them that he had killed two Indians near Bear Lake. There had been no witnesses, unfortunately, but the Eskimo insisted, was positive that he had killed his Indians. His face was so filled with glee, he looked so much like a kid about to be fed his favorite candies, that the police were suspicious.

"Too easy!" they said. "He thinks he is going to get a round-trip ticket to Aklavik for this story; but you don't

catch us out, my lad. For once the police are not going
to be done in the eye. Clear out, now, and leave us be!"

A year went by, and a white trapper arrived at the police
post. He had come in from Bear Lake, and there, in a shack,
he had found two dead Indians.

One of the most impressive specimens of pure Eskimo,
a man I felt to be incapable of any sort of indignity, was
Angutjuk. He drove up to the Post alone from Sherman
Inlet and let himself quietly in. I was there when he
arrived, and to see the delicate fashion in which he took his
seat, and the air of authority with which he leaned back and
remained completely motionless, at once aloof and present,
gave me my first notion of Eskimo aristocracy. Here was a
man, not a troglodyte; and his glance as he looked at me
seemed to come from a great distance, from another world—
but still a world of men, not of primitive beings. Had you
seen him, you would have said to yourself that he came of
an old race; and it was clear to me that he belonged to the
blessed time when the natives had as yet had no contact
with the white man. He was exquisitely courteous; his
smile was not a grin; he was distant out of good breeding
and not out of jealousy or hatred. There was nothing he
envied the white man, and not envying him he could not
detest him. Nor did he seek to copy him. He was here and
the white man was there. "You are of one race, I am of
another," his face seemed to say as he sat motionless in the
chair. "I do not object to meeting you, but I shall be off as
soon as my business is done."

Our manners were not his. He belched, but with dignity,
with gravity, without departing from the impassivity that
lay over his face and half-shut eyes. He dozed, but he would
stir at my slightest movement—for the native, like an

animal, is always alert, never really asleep. His ancient face was framed in a fur collarette and the collarette was of three different colors of wolverene fur. Enshrined within the circle of fur was a sort of hieratic head, its cheekbones prominent and powerful, curved eyebrows advancing like promontories, nose long and polished as in a Florentine portrait. He had neither beard nor moustache, but the thin shoots of hair on his face gave him the vaguely comic look of an old actor. Remembering what gift they have for pantomime, what marvellous things their faces become when they are telling stories, I said to myself how much I regretted the insufficiency of my knowledge of his language, for Angutjuk must be a great story-teller.

He sat for the time being like a statue; not handsome, his face smooth, upper lip pricked with little blue points of embryo moustache, as if he had neglected to shave that morning. His eyes were rimmed with red, and although he told me they had always been like that, I put a few drops in them to soothe them. For this, the old man changed seats, so that the light shone full upon his face. He lay back his head as trustfully as a child, and after his eyes had absorbed the liquid he went back to his seat and was once more motionless.

The Post was warm, and the old man was clearly enjoying his stay. His eyes were almost shut. They were not alike, actually, for one opened in an arc while the other was a mere slit.

"Angutjuk," I said, "have you trapped many foxes?"

It is not good form to ask this question. It is an infraction of a man's individual rights, which is to say, it concerns nobody but himself. A shadow of ill-humor passed across his face and was gone. He waited a moment, smiled, and then said slowly:

"I am not much of a hunter."

What a lesson in good breeding! I did not need to wait until the next day to be sure that he would produce more foxes than all the others together.

His record is curious: two hundred and twenty-six foxes in one year; and nine in the next. Obviously, trapping had not interested him the second year.

I offered him a cigar. Angutjuk was the only Eskimo within many hundred miles who could smoke a cigar. The others were made ill by them; but of course they did not show it. Offered a cigar, they would grin and say, "*eh-eh-eh!*" and in two or three minutes they were out of doors. They always came back smiling bravely, but the cigar was gone.

Slowly Angutjuk stretched forth his arm, and the hand that took the cigar was, I saw, covered with snow-knife scars. The cigar went into his mouth with a kind of jerky haste that was an article of Eskimo manners and implied that the receiver thought himself in great luck, that this was a great treat. Back sank the head into its fur, the features became again stony and the human relapsed into his immobility of old wood.

Peacefully, Angutjuk took up a magazine, looked at the pictures upside down, and put the magazine back on the table. Eyes half shut, he seemed to be dreaming, and I imagined that behind that motionless face a series of hunting grounds was passing through his thoughts. He opened his eyes and spoke:

"*Inut-koak. Oo-van-ga.*" Slowly the syllables came out: "An old man, I." There again was Eskimo coquetry, put on to bring forth my protest. Or did he really mean it? For there must be grand old hunters like this man who with the coming of great age feel themselves no longer what they were and are ready for death. They die—I have seen it happen—simply because they have decided to give up the struggle; and once they have made up their minds not to go on living, the body ceases to do its work and life goes out of them in the simplest, the most inexplicable fashion.

I do not believe that I was inordinately slow to learn something of the Eskimo mentality, but I must say that the more I learnt the greater seemed to me the difficulty of penetrating it. Everything, presumably, has a logic of its own; and certainly if the Eskimo mind operated in accordance with a species of logic, that logic was not ours. The Eskimo did not appear to me to reason at all, but to brood, to ruminate, to grapple with something—perhaps not a thought but at any rate an image; and in grappling to become absorbed in that image to the point of obsession. And although what I have said elsewhere about the degree of pleasure he takes from his life is true, although I am able to say again that the Eskimos are, taken all in all, the most cheerful people I have yet lived among; nevertheless, in their moments of despondency they are capable of an intensity of moodiness and a readiness to surrender this life that is irreconcilable with their virtually constant and general cheerfulness.

I had not been a week at the Post when Tutiak, my first Eskimo acquaintance, came in one morning with his lower lip blown up, cracked and clotted like a half-grilled sausage, his tattered rags and unwashed person filling the air with the rancid odor of stale caribou, that pungent smell that no Eskimo is without. He was sick, and he was miserable.

Paddy took a look at the pus-filled lip.

"Blood-poisoning," he said, and he brought out a medical

handbook from which it appeared that hot compresses were
the only remedy we could apply.

Tutiak sat meanwhile slumped over in a chair. His eyes
were half shut; he was groggy, dazed with fever; and
though he moaned from time to time, even I could see that
nothing in this man was making the slightest struggle
against the spread of the infection. In his ragged *attige,* his
clotted hair hanging limp over the unresisting features, his
slack and shapeless body, I saw the despair of a hunter who
had given up the chase. What had happened to him was a
mystery to him, and this mystery portended the slow inva-
sion of a death he would not fight against. I stood in the
presence of a man out of whom the instinct of self-preservation had fled. The phagocytes in his blood that were fighting
to keep him alive received no encouragement from his soul;
the army, so to speak, were fighting without their general.
Even after Paddy and I had spent four or five hours a day
for several days changing hot compresses every few minutes,
feeding the old man bouillon to keep him going, cleaning
out the infection as best we could, his despondency continued, his mood grew blacker, his surrender more complete.
Finally the swelling went down, the lip was drying and
healing, and still there was no change in his state of mind.

In the middle of the night, his wife sent their little girl
to fetch us to the shack in which they were housed—the
season was autumn and the snow had not yet come. He lay
on a caribou skin on the ground, raving and muttering
incoherently, and his wife explained that it was because he
was not allowed to go off to join the others. (We had told
him he must stay at the Post.) He did not want to die at
the Post. He wanted to die in camp, with his own people.
His lip was clean and a scar had begun to form. There was

TUTIAK

nothing we could do that night; and after a bit we walked back to our quarters, very worried about Tutiak.

Next day we woke late and went immediately down to the shack. Tutiak and his family had just left. He had to leave. Every instinct told· him to go back to his hunting grounds, back to his own kind. With his dogs, his wife, and his child he was already moving up the rise on the far side of the creek, his patched and tattered clothes flying in the wind, and now, as we gazed, he vanished, becoming one with the colorless earth. It was well, thus; it is well that man return to his kind and to the earth from which he is sprung.

A group of Eskimos were sitting in an igloo. Night had fallen, and they sat laughing and smoking after a good day of sealing. Conversation was animated, but it was not general, as with us. Among the Eskimos each talks in turn, and often what each says sends the rest off into laughter. The women sat by over their work. Women take no part in a conversation, but they listen sharply to everything that is said and join in the laughter. Seal meat was boiling in the *katta*, the pot; the igloo was full of smoke; the idea of a coming feast excited the men, and the pitch of their conversation rose and became playfully crude. At that moment the word was spoken. Not an insulting word, not a direct slap, but a word mockingly flung forth and therefore more painful, a word that made a man lose face before the others, that crippled him if he had no retort. One of the younger men had spoken. Encouraged by the laughter of the rest he had gone further than he intended. Planted before an older man, who was lying back on the *iglerk*, he said to him scornfully, "When you don't miss a seal, you certainly strike him square. If we were all as accurate as you are, the clan would have to get along without eating."

The old man's blood rushed to his face, but except for a single flash of the eyes he remained impassive. He sat still, unable to reply. A white man, having no answer, would have stood up and fought. Not so an Eskimo. He got up after a moment and slipped out of the igloo. His igloo. This made it more unbearable.

Straightening up out of doors, he stood still. The night was black. He felt sick inside with an animal sickness. Something indescribable had happened. This world in which he had lived and hunted his whole life long, was tottering. He strode to the other end of the camp, and crawled into Akyak's igloo. There, without a word, he sat down. Akyak was alone. She looked at him and wondered what the old man was doing in her igloo when he had guests at home. But she asked no questions. Casually, she picked up the teapot and poured him out a mug of tea. He drank it at a gulp, and then said suddenly:

"*Inut-koak*"—"I am an old man."

Astonished, Akyak protested vaguely; but he was not listening. Already he was on his way out.

When, later, he got back to his igloo, his friends had gone. His wife sat alone, scraping hides.

Days went by, and life at the camp continued as before. The old man went sealing with the rest. But those words gnawed at him unbearably. Had he been able to reply to them instantly, he would have been delivered of this load on his heart; but the load of which he had not on the instant unburdened himself, he could not now shake off. Bowed over his hole in the ice, he brooded. If he had been able to kill several seals in a row, he would have resumed his place as the great hunter of the clan, and it would have been his privilege to speak mockingly to the younger man. But fate was against him. He missed seal after seal.

Bit by bit he changed. The burden was there, tormenting him, weighing him down, taking possession of him like a cancer. And there was nothing to do about it. He was afraid of the younger man now. Besides, he was an Eskimo, and his thoughts were not to be revealed.

The day came when he would no longer sit with the rest in another Eskimo's igloo. While they laughed and feasted, he remained at home, motionless on his *iglerk,* eyes shut, arms hanging loose, like a sick doll. He had stopped going with the others out on the ice. He was beginning to mutter to himself. He was forgetting to eat. His dogs would howl, and he would not so much as go out of doors to beat them.

All this the whole camp observed; and though the young man was blamed, nobody interfered. It was the old man's affair if he had found nothing to answer. Still, the others would come to see him, whether out of curiosity or malice it is hard to say. They would find him sitting at his end of the *iglerk,* saying over and over to himself:

"Inut-koak"—"I am an old man."

Some would try to cheer him up.

"Come, come!" they would say. "You have the best wife in the camp. There's nobody like you with a woman."

"Inut-koak!" he would repeat obstinately. Then he would send a sidelong glance at his wife, and she would smile faintly, having nothing to say, and fill the mugs with tea. What that smile meant he no longer knew. After all, he was an old man . . . His visitors would invent pretexts to leave after the second mug of tea.

Alone with his malady, the old man turned over and over in his mind that insolent sentence. Had he been able to retort straight off, ah! . . . But he had not done it. It must be true, then, that he was old. And nobody grew any younger, ever.

He was not thinking, but brooding. Like all his kind, a mental problem was to him not a subject for thought but for torment, and its end was obsession. He could not shake this one off. There was only one way to be rid of it, and that was death. But whose death? His, or the young man's?

It was going to be his, and he knew it. He was too old to kill. The thought invaded him, took possession of him, and as he never struggled against it, it undermined him.

Now the camp knew what was in his mind, and still nobody intervened. His friends continued to come round for their mug of tea as if they had no notion of his anguish.

One day he made up his mind. It was evening, his family were there, and the old man spoke.

"Prepare the rope," he said to his wife.

Nobody stirred. They were all like this, and it was true of all of them that once an Eskimo had made up his mind there was no dissuading him from his decision. Not a word was said. The dutiful wife came forward with a rope made of seal. A noose made in it never slips.

Two children crawled noiselessly out to spread the news through the camp.

In the igloo the old man fashioned a running noose. With a single jerk the thing was done. Seated on the edge of the *iglerk,* his face bent down to the ground, he had strangled himself, and his body lay slack. No one would touch it. They would leave it as it was, and strike camp to escape the evil spirit that had possessed this man. The next day they were gone and the igloos stood empty in the white expanse.

I was struck by two separate elements in this suicide. One was the element of mental ill-health, of neurosis, in these primitive men. The other was the element of individual liberty, the respect for personality displayed by the community.

The lengths to which this non-interference went, were, as
the story of the suicide indicates, total; but even in little
things it was surprising. For example, you asked an Eskimo
the name of his hunting partner, and he might very well
not tell it to you. What the hunting partner—a friend of
twenty years—chose to call himself in his relations with the
Kabloona was strictly his own affair. It might be a name
quite different from that by which his friends knew him.
Actually, each of these Eskimos had three names: the one
given him at birth, the name used by his friends, and the
name he gave to the white man. And he might take a
fourth name at any moment, for any reason, without notice.
(Incidentally, a man might bear a woman's name, or a
woman a man's: it made no difference, for an infant was
named less to identify it unmistakably than to placate the
spirit of the dead man or woman for whom the new-born
was named. And a dog would be named in the same
fashion.)

I recall an instance of non-interference which, from the
white man's point of view, was more comical than anything
else, although the subject of the story is serious enough.
Ohudlerk had a son-in-law who was a half-breed trapper.
One day he appeared at his son-in-law's igloo and informed
him that his mother had decided to hang herself: let him
therefore not be astonished when, on his next journey east,
he did not see her round the camp. The son-in-law had
enough of his Norwegian father in him to be shocked by the
story. Gibson was appealed to and took the half-breed's
side.

Two days later Ohudlerk came back to the Post with a
solution. He had been thinking the matter over. If the white
man did not want the old woman to hang herself, it must

be that the suicide would in some mysterious way embarrass him. Would it not be satisfactory, then, if Ohudlerk drove the old woman to the other side of the promontory, out of sight of the settlement, half a mile away, and let her hang herself there?

Paddy spoke very sternly to Ohudlerk, forbidding this reasonable arrangement, and the old fellow went off in a bad temper and deep bewilderment. The desires of the aged ought to be respected, he insisted. He was confoundedly annoyed.

Thereupon, the old woman suddenly died a natural death, and Ohudlerk was furious.

"You see," he said. "She died anyway. Why couldn't you have let her die the way she wanted to? Now we shall have trouble."

A soul that is thwarted in its manner of dying will create much mischief. And immediately Ohudlerk went through a variety of medicine-man rites in order to appease the assuredly wrathful soul of the half-breed's mother.

Again and again, that winter, I said to myself that I must write the story of two men at a Post. Two men anywhere else, I dare say, would furnish matter for the same story, provided they were alone together and the ring round them was sufficiently small and unbreakable.

I liked Gibson as soon as I saw him, and from the moment of my arrival we got on exceedingly well. He was a man of poise and order; he took life calmly and philosophically; he had an endless budget of good stories. In the beginning, we would sit for hours at table, discussing with warmth and friendliness every topic that suggested itself, and I soon felt a real affection for him. Probably he liked me, too, for his kindness to me was infinite, and almost every day I had occasion to thank him.

But as winter closed in round us, and week after week our world narrowed until it was reduced—in my mind, at any rate—to the dimensions of a trap, I went from impatience to restlessness, and from restlessness finally to monomania. I began to rage inwardly, and the very traits in my friend and host which had struck me in the beginning as admirable, ultimately seemed to me detestable. The time came when I could no longer bear the sight of this man who was unfailingly kind to me, whose suggestions were so valuable to me, who, each time that I was off on the trail, would run after my sled at the last minute with still another thoughtful little gift for me. That calm which I had once admired I now called laziness; that philosophic imperturbability became in my eyes insensitiveness. The meticulous organization of his existence was maniacal old-maidenliness and an insult to human dignity.

Naturally, it was the little things that exasperated me: it always is. Vice and virtue have no part in the irritation we feel against those with whom we live in intimate contact. I cannot tell you what a melodramatic object the stovepipe key represented for me. The key regulated the draft in the pipe, and therewith the degree of heat given off by the stove. Heat in a house in the Arctic is obviously of some importance. I always got up before Gibson did, started the stove with the kindling I had chopped the night before, and would let the draft run full blast so that the stove would draw and the room—frozen cold during the night—warm up quickly. This done, if I had been permitted, I should have reduced the draft.

Paddy did not see things as I did. All the time that I was building the fire, shovelling in the coal, setting the table for breakfast, there was silence from his cubicle. But the moment the stove was roaring and the pipe red, I would hear him stir. "Well, well," he would murmur; and having slipped on a pair of pants he would come into the living-room, go straight to the stove, and close the draft with a "We might as well . . . " that he never finished, so that I never knew whether "we might as well" save the pipe from burning out, or economize the coal, or what was in his mind. The man must have had his eye on the pipe all night, for he was out and at the stove the moment the pipe grew red.

I never said anything, for I knew that if I explained what I was up to, he would smile. I dare say you have seen a stubborn man smile and you know that it is like the smile of a deaf man, of a man who does not want to hear and will not listen. When you see that smile you wish instantly that a special kind of mallet existed for the cracking of such men's skulls.

Then there was the teapot. The teapot stood on a shelf. We drank tea in prodigious quantity and were always reaching for that pot. Now, as it stood habitually behind a tin of lard, I used to change the places of the two objects, putting the teapot in front and the lard behind. And each time, Paddy would put them back in their customary and in-efficient order. Whether it was stubbornness or force of habit I couldn't tell; for when I ventured a word he would say merely, "Oh, well . . . "

It seemed to me I should never, anywhere in the world, meet another such automaton. If you set down the salt-cellar in the wrong place on the table, it threw his whole existence out of gear and sent him into a panic. His life was so regulated that he went through each motion every day at the same moment and in the same order. When he got out of bed, he always began the day by saying to himself, "Well, well." Then, having drawn on his pants, he would go automatically to the stove. After that, he would raise the lid on the kettle to see if the water was ready to boil, and then return to his cubicle. He would come out with a towel, get a basinful of water from the bucket, and wash—always beginning at the same place on his face. That done, he would brush his teeth over the slop bucket. And for an empire, he would not have changed a single one of these motions.

What amuses me as I write is that I must myself have gone through a like routine at the Post, for I know that I do it at home. Each of us has his own way of taking his bath, for instance: some wash their faces in the bath, others not; some scrub their feet first, others last; and each man probably has a different way of tackling his back. But such, I say again, was the atmosphere of isolation and brooding in which we lived at that Post, that all sense of proportion had dropped away from me. I was grown inhuman; and yet I was sure it was Gibson who was inhuman, who was but a body furnished with mechanical reflexes, moving by reflexes, emitting sounds in response to automatic stimuli and without the intervention of mind. When one o'clock came, invariably he would say, "I guess we might have a mug-up." He would never say that it might be time to eat, to set the table: the word was always "mug-up." In the same way, whenever a voice on the radio bade us good night at the end of a broadcast, he always answered "Good night" and with the same little laugh.

In all of this there was something extremely important that I now blame myself for not seeing. I should have recognized that order, even automatism, was a necessary defense for survival, both mental and physical, at that Post. It was an essential adaptation to environment that Gibson had achieved and without which he might have gone mad. I say to myself now that Gibson was a methodical man, the contrary of a maniacal old maid; and that if he had not been, his exasperation with me might—from his length of stay in those parts—have been so much greater than mine with him, that he might actually have been a dangerous man to live with. But apart from the question of nerves there was the fact of giving life form, as a matter of material self-preservation. What I mean will be clear when I speak later of the routine of establishing oneself in an igloo where, without routine, a man would literally be killed by nature herself.

Meanwhile, there was the latch on the outer door. It was an iron latch, and if you were in a hurry to escape the cold and had not both hands free, it was very hard to work. Hard enough for us, it was almost impossible for the Eskimos, for though they are clever enough with their own tools on the trail or the hunt, they are all thumbs with the white man's tools. One day, speaking as casually as I was able, I said:

"We ought to change that lock, you know. It works very badly."

You should have seen the look of terror in Gibson's face. Recovering himself he said with an ineffably weary, suspicious and (I thought) superior smile:

"Oh, no! It's the best lock on the place."

This time, instead of dropping the subject, I went on to explain what was the matter with the lock; and his answer was that what I thought bad about it was what really made it a good lock.

"But look at the trouble the natives have with it," I insisted.

"Oh, the natives!" he said shrugging his shoulders. "They'll always have trouble with a lock."

It was true, but it annoyed me to hear him say so. At that moment, a native trying to get in was rattling the door. Gibson flushed.

"They'll end by breaking that lock, confound them," he said; and he went back to the magazine he was reading.

But my ingratitude was boundless. Here was a man who had taken me in, had permitted me to share his precious solitude, had guided me in my first fumbling acquaintance with a people strange to me. When I tried to buy a *kulaktik,* an outer coat, he insisted upon making me a gift of one. When I started off without glasses against the blinding snow of spring, he ran after me to press a pair upon me. When I came in from a long trek frost-bitten and hardly able to brew myself a pot of tea, he looked after me. And I, instead of thanking him for the tea I was drinking, would think of those pies he baked, and sit inwardly fuming.

I hate prunes. They always give you prunes in hospital. As a child, when I had to be punished, prunes were my punishment. Now that I was forty years old, I saw no reason why I should go on being punished. I was not in hospital: why should I go on eating prunes? Gibson never baked any pies but prune pies. As delicately as I could, and then as firmly as I could, I let him know that there was nothing I loved so much in the world as an apple pie. Do you think that could change him? Each time that he came back from the Store with materials for his pies, I would ask casually:

"What's it going to be?"

"Prunes," he would say; and then, fearful of an outburst, he would mumble his little joke in a low voice, as if to himself: "The humble prune."

I could have murdered him! When for the third time he

had pronounced those words, "The humble prune!" with
that smile which said the Arctic might sink into the sea and
still it would be prunes, my eyes went straight to the axe that
stood in a corner of the room. "I'll crack his skull with that
axe," I said to myself grinding my teeth. "And if he is still
alive when I bend over him, I'll look him in the eye and say
to him, 'The humble prune!' "

A day or two would pass, the detestation would die down,
and then it would flare up again. "Look at him," I would
mutter to myself, "He's getting fat. He wasn't like that when
I arrived. I ought to tell him about it. He's turning into a
domesticated animal, a fireside cat. His skin is sagging. His
eye is dead. His movements are lumbering and sluggish.
He's developing a paunch. It's stuffed with eggs and potatoes, potatoes and eggs. And those gestures! The way he sits
down to peel his spuds. The finicking fashion he has of setting the frying pan on the stove. And look at that pan!
Could there be a worse pan in the world to fry eggs in? But
try telling him so! You know what he'll say: 'No, really.
I've tried them all. This is the *only* pan to fry eggs in.' And
if I tell him the difference between one pan and another he
will go out of the room, I'll hear him grumbling in the next
room; and he'll be back a little later, having reflected with
considerable pride that he is master in this house and whatever I say can make no difference."

Even his serene good breeding got on my nerves. It seemed
to me mere obsequiousness. When he belched he always
said "Pardon me"; and I would say to myself, "You'd do better not to belch instead of sitting there smugly begging my
pardon." If, reaching for the sugar, he said, "Excuse me," I
would rebel and remember that he always said "Excuse me,"
even when he passed behind me. I had to get away from
him, away from the Post, or go mad.

It is no pleasure for me to be exhibiting myself in this particularly objectionable fashion, but I do not believe I am wrong to generalize from the experience and say—since I had never been seized like this before—that it is one of the things that happen in the polar regions to a man from Outside. Fortunately, mention of it leads me straight into a subject easier to write about.

I had made up my mind that somehow or other I would get to Pelly Bay, a point two hundred and fifty miles from Gjoa Haven, to the east of King William Land on another island. The natives there were true primitives, and apart from an Oblate priest, Father Henry, they never saw a white man except when one or two of them made the annual trading expedition to this Post. The difficulty was that there was not a dog-team on King William Land that could undertake such a trip; and I had reached the state of believing that Gibson did not want me to take it,—not so much because he thought it dangerously hard, but because he meant to block my every desire. He said to me one day:

"Hadn't you better begin arranging to get back to Perry River?"

"I can't do that," I said, "until I've had a little time with the Eskimos at Pelly Bay."

A troubled look came into his eyes. "I'm afraid," he said slowly, "that's going to be hard. It's really a problem, you know, getting to Pelly Bay. Nobody round here has any grub—"

"I know," I broke in. "I'll trade foxes when I get there. The Pelly Bay natives have all the seal anybody can want."

"I don't know," said Gibson dubiously; and I broke in again.

"Look here," I said. "I want very much to **go to Pelly**

Bay. If you know any reason why I shouldn't try it, please tell me what it is."

"Not at all, not at all. I just thought you might have some trouble getting there and back."

The more he objected, the stronger grew my determination to go to Pelly Bay. This Post life was beating me down, I was growing thinner and more fretful each day, and the trail, I thought, would cure me. Gibson, seeing my obstinacy, ceased to oppose me—or to warn me, as he must have felt he was doing. We were in January, and I should have to wait for the full moon,—there being as yet no sun to light the way in this month. The Pelly Bay Eskimos were long overdue, for they came ordinarily at Christmas time. I had made up my mind to get hold of Utak and pay him whatever he asked (in foxes) to take me there. Meanwhile, I roamed morosely round the Post, wondering when Utak would turn up and when I could get out of this cursed stifling atmosphere.

On the 15th of January, Gibson and I were sitting round the stove at ten in the evening, I more gloomy than ever. The wind was high and the night had been pitch black for hours. Suddenly Tutiak rushed in to report that a sled was coming up the ridge. Gibson went out, and in a moment he was back.

"You're in luck," he said. "It's the sled from Pelly Bay."

Dear old Paddy! In a flash all the rancour of weeks died out of my heart.

Part Three
Pelly Bay

Chapter I

ALGUNERK, a man originally from Pelly Bay, agreed to take me east with him for two foxes. He and his family were going back, it was his country, and he knew the trail by heart. Provided I let him have the value in trade of the two foxes immediately, we should be off next day. He swore it, and I began hastily to get my things together.

I cannot say whether the Eskimo deceives himself or whether he intends merely to deceive the Kabloona, but as soon as you begin to negotiate with him he displays a stolid pride, an unshakable confidence, that are magnificent. His dogs? He has the best leader ever bred in these parts—ask anybody. The route? You are not serious? Nobody in the world knows it better; and his eyebrows go up in an expression of offended dignity while the others, to whom he has meanwhile turned for confirmation, nod their heads sagely as if to say: "You ought to count yourself lucky to be travelling with such a man."

Thus, even before you have started, the Eskimo farce has begun; and all this for a couple of foxes, plus, of course, the things he hopes to cadge from you on the way. He has smelled riches, and already they seem to be his. The advantage that the primitive man has over you is that only

one thought at a time finds lodgment in his brain, and all
his energies converge upon that thought. To achieve what

is in his mind, he will say exactly what
is necessary. You have had a look at his
sled and you tell him you've seen better
sleds. His sled? Don't give it a thought.
Just the other side of the water he has
another one ready, a new one. (No
harm in saying so, at any rate.) Big?
An eighteen-footer; and as soon as we
get to it, he will himself transfer your
belongings. But what a lucky thing that
you mentioned that sled! It is so big
that he will need another length of rope
to lash it properly. And by the way:
what if the Kabloona ran out of coal-
oil on the trail? He, Algunerk, ought
to have a little coal-oil in reserve,
shouldn't he? There was no being too
careful on a hard trip like this.

How long would it take to reach
Pelly Bay? Let's see: how long had he been coming here? He
counts on his fingers. Two igloos, three igloos, four igloos
. . . an igloo equals a night on the road.—As he counts, he
watches your face. How many igloos may I say before the
white man begins to take fright? Eight nights, which is to
say nine days in all. Actually, we were to take seventeen.

When white men travel, they sit on the sled, and the
running alongside or ahead of the dogs is done by the Eskimos. At least, that was what the books told me, but I never
had the luck to travel in style. Out of fifteen hundred miles
of trail, I did well over fourteen hundred on foot. As for

those triumphal departures—dogs barking with joy, straining at their collars, bounding in the air with impatience to
be off; this was apparently not for me either. My Netsilik
never needed to use the sled anchor in order to keep their
sleds from flying off: their dogs were invariably on their
bellies whimpering in the snow when the signal came, and
it was a brutal kick in the side that started the leader on his
way. Meanwhile, Algunerk had only one thing in mind,
which was to delay the departure as long as possible while
he extorted as much as he could out of the Post Manager,
who, for my sake, would not refuse these last-minute pleas.

He spent two days at his little game. A dozen times a day
he would come into the Post with a troubled, overburdened,
bustling air (all in my interest, it goes without saying), roll
a cigarette out of my tobacco tin, and lower his head and
stare at me is if saying, "What a lucky thing for you to be
travelling with Algunerk. It was Providence that put me in
your path." Had his glance said that Providence had set the
Kabloona in Algunerk's path, this would have been not only
the truth, but it would have been what was in Algunerk's
mind and in the mind of all the natives who sat in his igloo,
gleefully drinking mug upon mug of tea—my tea! Good old
Algunerk! There was nobody like him to fall into this bit
of luck. Utak had never been able to get as much as this out
of the Kabloona. And Algunerk would lean back on the
iglerk, sipping his tea with half shut eyes. He was an important man; he deserved their flattery; he accepted it as his
due; and like the ex-shaman that he was, he watched the
others through his eyelashes to see the effect he was producing.

His sled was only a fourteen-footer and seemed to me to
be loaded as high as a house. We went through the usual
forms: at the last minute Algunerk perceived that he needed

another buckle for the dog harness, and that one of the collars was almost worn through. He was given a new collar, necessitating for poor Gibson a fourth trip to the Store. But just when the audience were telling themselves that Algunerk would get everything Gibson had, Paddy's face flushed with anger, the Eskimo took fright, the dogs were whipped up, and we were off.

We got away fairly well, but we had not gone half a mile before it became necessary for some one to run on ahead of the dogs, both by way of encouraging them and in order to keep them on the trail. I did the running, finding it less hard than plodding alongside the sled, because out in front I could trot at a uniform pace and free my mind of worry. I would turn round from time to time, so that Algunerk— sitting tranquilly on the sled with his family—might with a contented wave of his hand assure me of the direction.

Generally the Eskimos stop and make camp about two miles out from the Post. They are unable to resist the childish urge to unpack their riches, rip open the tins, and enjoy what is called in the Arctic a big feed. This time I was there to insist that they do at least a few miles more, and we went on till dark, the journey marked by the usual incidents. For example, the driver breaks his whip in his anger with the dogs. Having broken the whip, his anger redoubles, and he beats the dogs until they spread fanwise as far as they can go, like a flight of partridges, howling and running to hide one behind another until the harness is completely entangled, after which we have to stop and disentangle them.

It was dark when we built the igloo, and once inside I saw that Algunerk's wife—who had spent her time at the Post sending sidelong provocative glances at Gibson and me—was, to say the least of it, no housekeeper. Gibson had given them a handsome new Primus stove. She lit it. It went out. She spilled alcohol over everything, and finally, having tried to relight the stove with a sheaf of papers, she gave it up. There she stood, motionless, idiotic, helpless.

Already the igloo was an indescribable agglomeration of objects: burnt paper, old packing boxes, chewing-gum stuck to the side of the *iglerk,* the ground strewn with spoons, a hurricane lamp, and frozen fish. A seal stood against the wall looking on with its dead eye. Their little girl sat on the couch playing with a clock; and a cigarette-holder, Gibson's favorite cigarette-holder which Algunerk's wife had wheedled out of him, lay in the heap of fish. A moment before, Algunerk had grabbed the stubborn Primus stove and flung it angrily against the wall: it lay now on the ground, feet in the air. All that he had so much desired when at the Post, all those treasures won from the Post Manager by whining, cunning, and flattery, had been no more than the stage properties in a play the plot of which consisted simply in getting the better of the white man; and now these things won with delight had become broken and almost hated toys.

I was too accustomed to igloo odors to take any account of them, but igloo disorder was still something that I could see. It was symbolic. While the Eskimo was at the Post he was fascinated by the civilization it represented. As soon as he got his hands on these toys of civilization he found himself unable to play with them. They resisted his best efforts. The cigarette-holder slipped out of his wife's teeth and broke. The Primus stove refused obstinately to work. The Big Ben would not run, no matter how hard his child banged it on the couch. "We are not for you," these things seemed to say; and the Eskimo was vexed, felt himself an object of ridicule; and in the pride of his race he shook with anger. What was he, an Eskimo, doing, playing at being a white man? With contempt, the old child smashed his toys,

flung them round the igloo, and went for relief over to the
frozen seal which began to fly in chips as he cut great
chunks away with his axe. And as ridicule never contents
itself with laying a light finger on man, but always over-
whelms him once it has taken him off his guard, no sooner
had Algunerk finished his operation on the seal than the
dogs, having succeeded in shoving aside the packing case
that blocked the entrance to the igloo, rushed in, and the
igloo became a battlefield. We struck and kicked to left and
right as fast and hard as we could, but you do not know
what an Eskimo dog is when it is hungry: it will allow itself
to be hacked into pieces rather than surrender a promise of
meat. Suddenly the lamp was knocked over, and the battle
went on in total darkness. If it had not been forty below,
and if the seal had not been of vital importance to us, the
scene would have been roaringly funny. In the end, with a
final kick, we got the last dog out of the cavern . . . but there
was nothing left of the seal.

That night for the first time I ate at the same meal caribou, seal, frozen fish, and musk-ox. The caribou was excellent, especially after it had been smoked during the summer.
The fish, too, despite the fact that it was frozen so hard that
it could not be chewed. Seal meat was less to my taste, and
as for musk-ox, I never want to eat it again. Chewing its
fat is exactly like chewing tallow.

It was in the midst of this disorder that we awoke next
morning. The igloo was pitch black and Algunerk was
panting and struggling with the lamp. As soon as he heard
me stir, he let me know that his neck ached, he was ill; and
to prove it he forced himself to hawk and spit at my feet.
It was clear that he and his wife meant to linger here as long
as possible, and the reason was that, being rich in provisions,
they could not resist the impulse to consume and waste what

they had. He was very ill, Algunerk explained with his sly
eyes on my face. To-day we would rest, but to-morrow . . .
how we would run over the trail! And to be sure that we
got off, I had better set the alarm clock (which was broken)
at six. When they observed with relief that I said nothing,
was not inclined to dispute them, the whole family came
up out of its sleeping-bag and began peacefully to absorb a
huge meal.

Pretexting the cold, Algunerk asked me to warm up the
igloo with the Primus. I had come away with one tin of
coal-oil, and I refused. Instead, I lighted a seal-oil lamp
which I had brought along. Seeing this, Algunerk himself
picked up the Primus he had flung down the night before
and disdainfully poured his own coal-oil into it, letting it
burn the whole day long.

To reach Pelly Bay we had to cross an arm of the sea. The
distance straight across was a mere fifty miles, but the Eskimos never go straight across: they follow the coast, their
object being always to keep certain landmarks in sight. We
had thus described a long curve to the north and then come
slowly southeast. After five days, we were still on the sea,
although at the fall of the previous day, land had been in
sight. I tried to get them to make a forced march in order
to touch land, but they had refused. Night fell and we made
camp in the shelter of a great expanse of pack ice that rose
from the smooth surface of the sea. A sudden swell and
swirl here had raised the frozen waters, and they stood upright in fantastic shapes. Round them the drift snow was
perfect for igloo-building. For it is curious how little snow
falls in the course of an Arctic winter: at sea, often not
enough to build with; and if it were not for the drifts and
ice-cracks, it would be difficult to build a night shelter.

When we emerged from the igloo to resume the trail my heart jumped. There was still no sun, but I saw in the southern sky a chip of gold, a golden splash, the reflection of a sun that had not yet returned to our earth. In the north the horizon was a tender blue, shading into indigo and so intense that only in the desert had I seen such brilliance. But the land round us was still lifeless, anemic, colored a dead pale mauve. Nevertheless, the sign in the sky revealed that light, which for us was life, was on its way back; and my spirits were high as I ran on ahead of the dogs over the susurrant snow under my feet.

"What is the matter with that Kabloona, that he runs all day ahead of the dogs?" Algunerk asked his wife. "He is like a child, never at peace. No sooner have we started than he wants to arrive somewhere; and when we stop he is impatient to be off again."

In substance, if not in these words, this was what he thought of me, and it puzzled him no less than it irritated him. Meanwhile, he could not understand how I was able to hold out.

"Generally," he said to me, "the Kabloona hates to tramp and prefers to sit on the sled. But you . . . you never stop running."

I do not know if he spoke with admiration or with sarcasm; but I ran on, driven by a strength that was not my own. I felt no weariness, and, as so often in the Arctic, it seemed to me that I was two different men. One of these men was profoundly at peace, dreaming and reciting verses to himself while the other man ran on. One thought, the other acted; one was static, the other dynamic. And in a curious way there seemed to be no fusion of the two in me: they dwelt side by side, each ignoring the other.

For the time being, "the other" ran effortlessly on, a crea-

ture for whom fatigue was impossible since he was a mere
machine. I would think of this and smile to myself, saying
that one of me was the mechanical hare at the county fair,
running ahead of the hounds. Motivated by a mysterious
current, that other had been given a handicap, and the
hounds would not catch up with him. Human weakness
was impossible to him; the pace had been set for him; he ran
on, with the hounds in his wake, and each time that the
hounds threatened to come abreast of him, hup! a sudden
spurt left them fifty yards behind. If it had not been for
Nigak I should not have been aware that I was human.

Nigak—"South wind"— was our leader. This giant husky
had a head which seemed to me as long as my arm, and the
fur on his wide jowls made his head almost as broad as it
was long. Nature had apparently placed that fur exactly
where it was in order that, running in the wind, it blow
back at either side and protect the body from the rushing
air.

Nigak was proud of being leader; for pride and jealousy
are two recognizable traits of character in the Eskimo dogs.
But he was not only leader, he was in the true sense the boss
of the team. Each time that we stopped, he turned and
thrashed all the other dogs, one after the other. There were
seven dogs and two bitches, in addition to Nigak, but he
never touched the bitches. Once the dogs lay grovelling before him, he would sniff caressingly for a moment at each
of the bitches and then caracole up and down the line, his
curly tail wagging to left and right and his whole air speaking of pride and glory in his rank and prowess. After which
he would trot peacefully back to his place and stand in the
characteristic pose, paws widespread, powerful thigh-mus-
cles taut, claws dug in as if ready to "push" rather than pull
when the whip swished in the air. Nigak never rested, but

stood waiting to go on, and if the halt was long he would rise up on his hind legs and bark furiously as if to say, "What are we waiting for?" I have seen him break out this fourteen-foot sled, with its twelve-hundred-pound load, and drag it twenty yards all by himself.

He was rare among Eskimo dogs in his outbursts of friendship for man. Often as I ran my mind would wander, I would forget where I was. Perhaps I was in Tahiti, looking at the sun as it set behind Motu-uta; or I might be rummaging cautiously among my childhood memories. Of a sudden I would feel in the hollow of my hand something warm. It was Nigak's nose, and this was his fashion of caressing me. He would have decided suddenly that he wanted to be near me. With one great effort, he would have come up directly behind me, and there he would be, gently rubbing that truffle of his in the hollow of my hand as if to say, "Go straight on, I am with you. Eskimos say we must be beaten: believe me, a show of affection now and then does no harm." That caress would bring me back with a start, and I would say to myself that even in these barren immensities love was present though only in the nose of a dog. My heart would fill with warmth; without turning around I would close my hand gently over that nose as over the hand of a woman; then I would run on while behind me Nigak barked with power, with joy, with life.

Once again Algunerk rang up the curtain on his familiar comedy.

"You slept well? I very badly." And he forced himself to cough. I gathered that his wife was behind this.

"I'll have a look outside," he said. "If the wind is too strong, we'll stay."

"There is no wind," I said calmly, and I continued packing. Seeing that it was inevitable, they packed, too, but they hung on as long as they could.

Once we were on the trail, Algunerk said in pidgin-Eskimo, *"Nuna ta-u-tok pii-shek,"*—"I see no land."

Everybody who has lived among the Eskimos has been struck by their intuition and their ability to read the white man's thoughts. This was certainly the case with Algunerk. He knew each time what would discourage me most, and the hope of making land had been in my mind when he spoke.

He was lying, though, and it was not long before we both saw the line of the shore. And then the scoundrel insisted that he did not recognize this land, that he was lost! It was his native land, I knew. What was behind this? I tried, but could not guess, and I was not to know the answer until, a fortnight later, Father Henry explained to me that I was myself to blame. We went on a bit.

"Where now?" I asked.

He pointed successively in several directions. Was he suddenly snowblind? Was he refusing to see? Finally he recognized a promontory and soon we were down in what seemed to be a river bed. This land is so flat that you pass from sea to earth without knowing it. You have to scrape the ground with your boot in order to tell which it is.

Night fell. The heavy sled sank and stuck in the snow. The going was bad. We were in snow up to our knees and the dogs were hanging back. I knew that the parents of Algunerk's wife were in an igloo somewhere along this river, and I took it that we were bound for that igloo. But when, night beginning to fall, I said, "Are we almost there?" the answer was: "Oh, no. It is a long way off. Do you want to build an igloo?" Once again the rascal had waited for night to fall before asking that question with his innocent air—as if he had not been told again and again that the thing I detested most in the world was these haphazard igloos put up in the dark of night when shovelfuls of snow were flung on at random and failed to fill the chinks between the blocks. Six days had gone by; it was bitter cold, and where were we?

That night Algunerk let the cat out of the bag. He did not intend to take me to Pelly Bay. Instead, his father-in-law would go with me. His throat was sore.

The truth was, he had never intended to go as far as Pelly Bay; but of course if he had admitted as much at the Post, he would not have had his two foxes.

"Very well," said I. "But I traded to go to Pelly Bay. I want a sled and man to take me there, and it is your job to provide them for me and to see that I get there."

That was all he wanted to hear. Instantly he was in fine humor; he stopped coughing and I do not believe he spat oftener than ten times a minute. Next day we were on the trail again over a terrain as monotonous as the frozen sea.

Whenever Algunerk beat his dogs I would go back and sit quietly on the sled, refusing to budge until the dogs were free of his lash. But it made no difference to him. He beat his dogs out of the same impulse which made him, from time to time, beat his wife: he had worked himself up to a pitch of anger, and that was all there was to it. One after the other, he would tackle each dog in turn, growling and swearing as he swung the whip. He would pull a dog towards him by the individual trace to which it was harnessed, the beast meanwhile crawling and resisting his pulling, and howling with terror. Once he had the dog at his feet he would take the stock of the whip to it and beat it over the loins and kidneys as hard as he could. Eskimo dogs must, as a matter of evolution, have backs specially built against these beatings, for when the horrible scene was over, the dog would rise with no ribs broken and go back to its place. But Algunerk's fury was not sated by a single beating. He would run alongside and continue to slash and hit even after we had started up again, bounding among the traces with an agility astonishing in a man of his years (for he was by no means young). Now and then, to my intense pleasure, he would trip up in the traces; but he always managed to roll cleverly out of the way of the heavy sled and get to his feet swearing harder than before. On the day I best remember, he had so embroiled the traces that the dogs had to stop, and the old man beat and beat and beat them until he sank down in the snow, panting for breath. After a bit he got up, went back to the sled, and sat exhausted and motionless, his legs dangling over the side of the load. I said to him:

"You beat your dogs. It is bad for the dogs and bad for you."

He said nothing, and indeed there was nothing he could say. An Eskimo who did not beat his dogs would not consider himself an *Inuk,* "a Man, preeminently."

On the seventh day, finally, we came round a bend in the river and I saw two igloos snuggling in the hollow of a valley, nestling so deep in the snow that they looked like white molehills. One of these was Algunerk's, the other belonged to his father-in-law, whose name was later given to me as Shongili. The dogs barked, but no one came out of the igloos, and when we crawled in I saw three beings sitting as still as animals on hairy musk-ox hides. The seal-oil lamp was out. They had no blubber, therefore they could have no light; and they were sitting in near darkness in an igloo whose temperature was forty degrees below zero. This was the most wretched and degraded igloo I had yet seen.

These people were foul with grease, their long hair hung in clots, the walls of their snowhouse were black with filth. They grinned, but they said no word. It was plain that they were not used to the white man, for when I ventured a few words they fidgeted nervously and made no other sign that they had heard. Algunerk's father-in-law was not there. Where was he? All that they would say was that he was away, and they sat there before me, inert, silent, their arms huddled across their chests for warmth and their sleeves dangling empty. They were unable to lie, and it was Algunerk who lied for them. He said:

"Atata" (the old man) "has gone to visit his trap-line. He will be back this evening."

It was not true, and a little later Algunerk himself told me casually that Shongili would not be back before the next day.

There is always something a little mysterious in Eskimo life. It is heavy with silence, with things felt and not expressed, a tissue of the inexplicable that remains unexplained. I had never been so well aware of this as here.

It does not happen often, but even in our civilization we find ourselves at some time or other in a place that fills us with uneasiness. The impression is instinctive, undefinable but actual. You cannot say the fault is specifically with the walls, or the people, or the air in the house; and yet you are enveloped by something impalpable; something is radically out of kilter, and you are sure of it.

Algunerk was a mysterious character. There was a time when his name was Kakor-tig-nerk and he had two wives. His wives had died almost simultaneously, and he had changed his name to drive away the evil spirit. Meanwhile, from one day to the next he had found himself alone. A man

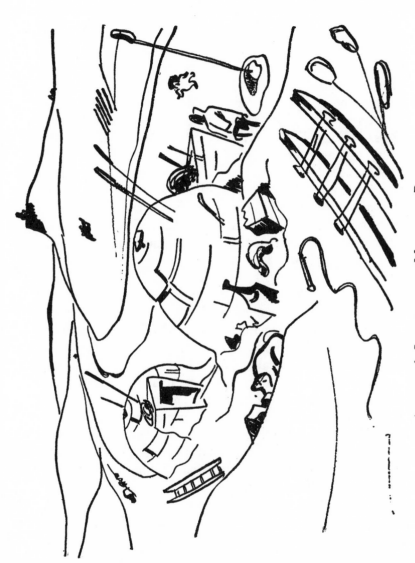

ALGUNERK'S IGLOOS ON THE MURCHISON RIVER

cannot live alone. He had gone to live with Shongili's family, had made a trade for one of the daughters, and it was that girl who was now in effect his wife and had been on the trail with us.

Now the girl—Eskimo details are always complicated—had been promised in early childhood to a man from Fort Ross. The man had never come to fetch her, and she was living in the meantime with Algunerk. He was her husband without actually being her husband (since she was betrothed to another). If that other man came down from the north, what would happen? The two Eskimos would be afraid of each other: the man from the north because Algunerk was reputed a dangerous character, and Algunerk because to kill the man from Fort Ross would bring about certain unpleasant consequences. Probably, therefore, Algunerk would give up the woman; but in that case he would be alone again, and what would become of him?

Eskimo life is filled with these unresolved problems, these items in suspense. They are in everybody's thoughts, everybody watches for them to break out; but nobody speaks openly of them. Will Algunerk come to an agreement with the man from the north? Will he kill him? Will he get some one else to kill him? A strange thing about the Arctic is that it abounds in tales and rumors, and one of the stories is that although Algunerk himself had never killed a man, yet he had prompted more than one killing, armed more than one hand that struck the blow.

Another sinister element in Algunerk's make-up was the fact that he had formerly been a shaman. Was he still a shaman? He certainly acted like one; and that half evil, half sugary glance he let flow over you out of his half shut eyes, that incessant observation of others in order to judge what effect he was producing, was a characteristic of the Eskimo

shaman. Nobody had spoken of this to me directly, though
he himself had boasted, in a moment of vainglory, "Among
the Arviligjuarmiut I am a big man." He belonged to that
clan which inhabited Pelly Bay, but he did not live among
those primitive people. Why? Why was he down here with
his father-in-law, a hundred miles from his own people, on
this solitary bend in the river? Was there a vendetta pending? Had the others driven him out?

Meanwhile, something else in this igloo was mysterious.
Algunerk's sister-in-law lived here with her father. She had
been married, but her husband had left her. (I did not learn
why.) Since he had left her, she was, according to the
Eskimo code, a free woman. In this land where women were
scarce she should have been sought after, re-married, the
more so as she had a gentle smile and was comely. But no
one came for her. No man seemed to want her. She sat apart,
by herself; and even when the seal meat went round she was
not of our circle. What taboo hung over this seemingly
inoffensive young woman?

It was in this atmosphere of the unexpressed and the
ominous that I settled down, the temperature registering
now forty-eight degrees below zero, in Algunerk's igloo.

Igloos are like men: as they grow old they grow decrepit
and are marked by humps and hollows. Our igloo was no
longer round but shapeless, and it was freezing cold. Nothing is so cold as an old igloo. The snow, that warm and
comforting element, turns to ice, and ice is a perfect con-
ductor of cold. Uninhabited for a fortnight, the walls of an
igloo become coated with a damp mould that is glacial. We
sat freezing in this mouldy ice-house while Algunerk said
to me that he had no coal-oil left for the lamp—still another
attempt to persuade me to use up my fast diminishing supply. I resisted. I boiled some rice for us, but would not fuel

the Primus stove. Once more I was in conflict with them. In their eyes, my caution was incomprehensible; but beyond that it was revolting because it represented selfishness. I knew that, but what could I do? I wanted very much to be on good terms with them, first because I had to be, and secondly in order to understand them better. On the other hand, my position was different from theirs. I had not only to get into their land, I had also to get out of it. My forethought—an element that formed no part of the life of these people who consumed whatever they got as soon as they got it—was imposed upon me. I had no choice.

So I turned a deaf ear and reconciled myself as best I could to the glacial night. The temperature was now so low that I could take no notes because the lead in my pencil had frozen. Next day, still no *kudlerk,* no seal-oil lamp. Both sides were equally stubborn. I spent the whole day in my sleeping-bag while Algunerk, bare above the waist in this temperature, squatted on the *iglerk* and muttered to himself all the day. Physically and mentally, it was the worst day I spent in all my months in the Arctic. I have said what warmth and life the seal-oil lamp creates in an igloo; I can say now that without the lamp an igloo is a grave. Out of doors the wind was sweeping up the river and raising the hair on the backs of the dogs. It bit into your skin and made you want to bite back in rage. And the day was all disquietude, all uncertainty. It went by, another went by, what would the third day be like? Lost in this dank and unfriendly abyss, I could think only that Shongili would not turn up and I should be left suspended in this clammy void, forced to hide my feelings, stifle my questions, and smile patiently . . . at fifty below. I was at the mercy of Algunerk and at the mercy of the Arctic wind: one was as unforeseeable as the other.

Going into the other igloo on the second day, I found on the ground a doll. It was a thing that might have been made not only for a child, but by a child—shapeless, covered in caribou hide, shining with fat like the Eskimos themselves, and pigeon-toed as their women invariably are. Tufts of musk-ox fur had been stuck either side the head to simulate human hair. The thing had no form, was crude, wretched, yet how expressive it was! With this bit of caribou the un-knowing artist had sewn together a limp mannikin in which the whole of Eskimo poverty and wretchedness came start-lingly alive. The fact that this doll had no face—its head was a mere ball—conferred upon it an air of universality and lent it the value of a symbol of this rude and enigmatic race; externally impassive, but brooding over its dark secrets. I took it up and looked long at it, more moved by it than I had been by any of the race it bespoke. It filled me with pity, and with admiration, too, for if it spoke of wretched poverty, it spoke no less of stoicism. When, for his obscure reasons, the Eskimo decides to die, and slumps inert on his igloo couch with arms lax and back bowed over, it is like this doll that he looks.

On the spot I gave two plugs of tobacco for the doll, and instantly I became the idiot white man. For a bit of hide that the child no longer would play with, I had given two plugs of tobacco. I had hardly left them before they began hastily to manufacture bright new dolls, dressed in new skins. Surely the Kabloona would pay five or six plugs for the new dolls! They were in Algunerk's igloo next day before I was out of my sleeping-bag, and when, in triumph, they held up the new dolls, and I wrinkled my nose (the Eskimo sign for "no"), they grumbled angrily and with-drew, convinced now that the white man was surely mad.

"Senne," said Algunerk the following morning, and I knew he was telling me that it was Sunday. This might have been one reason why our departure had been delayed. For, curious as it was, Algunerk, the ex-shaman, was on the way to becoming a Roman Catholic. With the arrival of the first missionary in these parts, he had seen very quickly that shamanism might be superseded by the new religion, and from sorcerer he had transformed himself into catechumen. Cautiously and astutely, he had been moving for months towards the re-capture of his lost influence over the natives with the aid of the new rite. He never took the trail on Sunday, because it was the day of rest; and though a given Sunday be a rare day for travelling, a day without wind such as might not come again in the week, he rested. What was more, religion had pretty well eliminated travel on Saturday: was it worth while, seeing that to-morrow we should be forced to spend twenty-four hours in an improvised shelter, in Heaven knows what weather? He practised what he had thus far been taught of the Catholic religion, and he spread its rites, if not its doctrine, wherever he went. Meanwhile, this occasion to show off before the Kabloona was not to be missed, and so I participated in an Eskimo version of Divine Service—which I was of course expected to report with due enthusiasm when I saw Father Henry.

Algunerk, his women, and his child squatted in a semicircle, holding three prayer-books printed in syllabic Eskimo, a written language invented by the missionaries. He alone could read, and as he read he turned the pages, greasy with seal fat, while the others imitated him. Each time that he began a verse he would indicate with his finger the place on their pages. Sensitive readers will wish me to spare them the details of this scene—some of them comic, others disgusting—in which Algunerk continued imperturbably his recitation, among the carcasses of dead foxes, in an igloo hung with icicles while three or four frozen seal stood round the walls with staring eyes like mediæval statues, and the puppies, their hair covered with hoar-frost, dozed at our feet. What, I wondered, could this mean to them? That the true religion might eliminate their superstitions and many of their taboos, I could believe; but how could they reconcile its teaching with their manners, with murder, wife-trading, and the rest?

After prayers, Algunerk went out. He came crawling back, pushing ahead of him a wooden box, and before the dazzled eyes of his women he unpacked what remained of the riches he had garnered at the Post, thanks to my two foxes. His greatest pride was a telescope, one of those long collapsible marine telescopes made of brass that looked as if it was the one Nelson had put to his blind eye at the battle of Copenhagen. When it was passed round for our admiration, I saw with pride (Lord forgive me!) that it was of French manufacture. Next most fascinating was a pair of tennis shoes, made in Japan. How such things happened to turn up in the Arctic, I cannot conceive. The rubber (or rubberoid) soles were frozen stiff and there was no comparing them for comfort with the sealskin native boots, even had they been of a size to fit one of these people. Algunerk drew them out of the box as cautiously as if they had been made of the finest glass, and passed them to his wife. She set them carefully down on the ground at the deep end of the igloo, whence I dare say they would never be moved.

This day was one of the longest I ever spent, partly because the extreme cold made it impossible for me to write or sketch, my lead continuing frozen hard. I remember, in the matter of cold and sketching, that one day in the Store, at Gjoa Haven, I stood trying to draw the natives while they

were trading. The temperature was so low that my breath
formed a dense fog before my face, so that I could not see
the drawing paper; and each time that I set down a few
strokes I had to hold my breath. The sketch had to be left
unfinished.

Here, on the trail to Pelly Bay, I could not even work my
cameras. They were packed in a box that was still on the
sled. If I unpacked them they would freeze solid and no
lever would work. A "dry" object should not freeze, you
say. But everything freezes in this Arctic world; and as for
metal, it becomes so magnetized that it does not merely cling
but seems to leap across space to stick to your bare hand.

Atata, the father-in-law, known to me as Shongili, finally
turned up on Monday. My first sight of him was of a man
standing waist-high in the snow, hacking with all his might
at a frozen block of fish in his cache. He was digging out
food for himself and feed for the huskies on our trail to
Pelly Bay. Round him stood the dogs, and when his axe had
chopped out a block of fish they stretched forward, bodies
taut, ready to snap. He was quicker than they were, grabbed
up a great piece and crammed it into his mouth, throwing
them the rest. Each time that one of the dogs caught a piece
in the air the others would fling themselves howling upon
the clever one, the weakest of the fighters would snap up
the fish dropped by the victim of the attack, and the whole
pack would be off down the frozen river in pursuit of the
weakling. Meanwhile the man would profit by their absence
to fill his mouth with another chunk and then, having
sucked all his fingers clean, would go back to work. Quarters of seal, frozen fish, the food of men and dogs was the
same, and while the frozen article was commoner, the rotted
was spicier and was preferred. If the Eskimos knew what

our cheeses were in truth, they would marvel even more than they do at the white man's distaste for rotten fish.

Finally we got away, Shongili and I, and all day long we dragged and pushed the sled over the ice that covered the frozen river. If I had hoped, at Gjoa Haven, to see here a land less monotonous than the tundra that lay round the Post, I was disappointed. Flat and void, there was nothing to catch the eye in this landscape except an occasional knoll, and the farther we went the flatter it became, the wider the river the more difficult it grew to find and stay in the bed. Yet there we had to stay, for the sled ran more easily over this ice than over the snow that covered the earth.

We stopped when night fell, and I had a good look at my man. The brute stood before me like an ape, mindless, round-shouldered, his arms hanging loose at his sides. The long hairs of his moustache fell over his mouth, and he giggled like a girl while he never stopped licking his fingers. All that this numbskull can do, I said to myself, is to spy upon me with his sly slanting eyes, to watch for the slightest sign of anger in me and see to it that I make him work as little as possible. Whenever I turned my back to run on ahead of the dogs, he would let himself down on the sled, and with his eyes on me would jump down again as soon as he saw that I was about to turn and look back. Algunerk had lied to me and was a dangerous character, but at least he had been energetic and quick-moving—incredibly so for a man of his years. This fellow—much younger than his son-in-law, by the way—was dull and slow of movement, and infinitely repugnant of personality. You have seen nothing at all until you have seen this Shongili, in the igloo, scrape with a knife between his toes, lick the blade, and look up at you with a great coarse laugh.

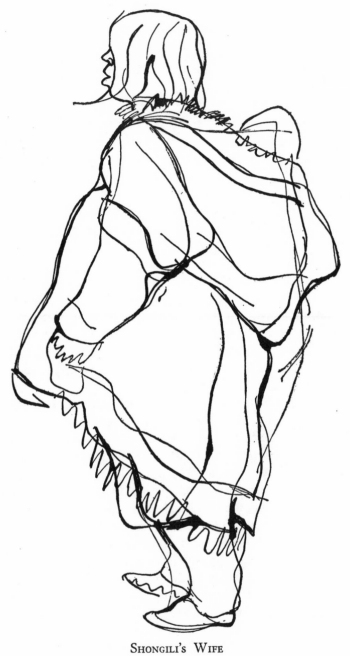

SHONGILI'S WIFE

But when he set about building an igloo he turned into another man. This rude and mindless being became suddenly an artist as he stooped with a sober, concentrated gaze over the snow. Something profound, mysterious, awoke in him, transfigured him, creating a striking contrast with the whole of his dense and brutish figure.

Choosing his snow, he moved like a man inspired, bowed over, digging in his harpoon first here, then there, moving at first swiftly, then slowly, prodding the snow with a gentleness as if afraid to hurt it. Carefully, he cut out a first row of blocks and fitted them in a circle round him. Now he stood within them, not to emerge again until his work was done. The blocks for the higher rows of the igloo would be cut out from beneath his feet, and he knew to a square foot what lay where he stood. He was an architect counting his stones, an Italian mason raising a dome. Slowly, cautiously, he built up the gradual spiral that was to be his house. The snail was here constructing its shell. Bent far over, only his rounded back showing above the first row of blocks, he dealt fine precise blows with his snow-knife. He hoisted a block, set it skilfully in place, its inner surface cut on the appropriate bias, and I could hear him puff—it was his moustache that seemed to puff—as he stared, reflected, trimmed with light strokes until the block slipped into its place.

It came to me suddenly that I was watching this man with pleasure. Ten minutes earlier I had been torn between rage and pity over this inept and exasperating creature, and I found myself now filled with admiration for his artistry. You believe, perhaps, that it is easy to build an igloo because it is done very quickly and seems to be rough and unfinished: I assure you that there are a thousand tricks in this trade, that it wants a particular skill to make use of a friable

snow, to set a wall securely in place, to reduce the dimensions of an igloo in mid-work because of a sudden the
blizzard forces you to hurry your job. And all this, Shongili
was able to do, seemingly without the least difficulty. He
knew his snow, knew all its whims, all its subtleties. To me,
for whom snow had hitherto been nothing at all, he was
suddenly revealing its quality, its true price. He respected it:
snow was to this brute a thing divine.

Yet the fact was there: the man was a brute. He would
wake me in the black darkness of our morning, stirring,
snorting under his coverings like a seal, spitting and hawking until I had opened an eye and he had my attention. I
knew what was up. He had woken: therefore I must wake:
and once awake, I must light the Primus stove and make
tea for him. Algunerk's little game had been to see that we
got off as late as possible: with this one it was a matter of
having his tea as early as he could get it. He would slip down
from the *iglerk,* bend over so low that, in true Eskimo fashion, he stood with his bottom higher than his head, and he
would scrape, scratch, dig round in his effort to waken me.
"Aiie!" he would moan, *"Aiie!"* and again *"Aiie!"*

"Una?" I would shout angrily. "What is it?"

"Kam-mak-to,"—"Daybreak," he would say.

"Not yet, confound you!"

And all this to have a mug of tea—for he had brought
no grub of his own, as I learnt only after we were well out.

There would be ten minutes of silence, then he would resume. And I, filled with loathing, would sit up in my sleeping-bag and make the tea—three great mugs for each of us,
and a couple of biscuits. He would squat, eyeing my movements, the mug lost in his enormous hands while the hairs
of his moustache swam in the liquid. And then, the tea

drunk, he would fall silent as by enchantment and sit motionless on the *iglerk* while I went back to sleep.

The Arctic is a perpetual course of lessons, and it is the weather which, with an inconceivable harshness, inflicts upon you the first of these lessons. I might be filled with grievances against Shongili: a blizzard would rise, and on the instant everything would be forgotten; it would force me to forget myself and to remember only that Shongili and I were two men fighting together in the same cause.

It started towards half past two. We were on the trail. Suddenly the wind was blowing hard. In a moment all the dogs but the nearest were in a mist,— a gust struck the sled square on and tossed it about like a straw, and through the storm came the weird howling of the invisible huskies. Strangest of all, this was not bad weather. A barometer would have stood on "Fair." This was a ground wind running at fifty miles an hour along the surface of the earth, blowing up the snow, enclosing you in a wall of snow; but the wall was not thirty feet high, and overhead the sky was blue, serene, despite the vortex in which you gasped for breath.

We stopped, built an igloo as best we could, while the dogs went to sleep under layers of snow. When we turned round, all that remained of them was occasional tufts of hair sticking up like grey patches of weed, so that we had to hunt them out, scratch about, walk upon them and boot them in order to save them from suffocation and send them elsewhere to sleep.

Here again Shongili undertook to show me what it meant to be an *Inuk,* "a man, preeminently." Placidly, he lit his pipe, prodded the ground with his harpoon, and went off in search of proper snow. While he disappeared and reappeared, I stood perfectly still. I dared not stir: if I stirred I was lost; and if I became lost . . . Finally he bent down, scratched round with his snow-knife, and cut out a block. I stood beside him, close enough to touch him, but he seemed not to know I was there. The dogs rushed for shelter into the hollow out of which the block had been cut, and he kicked them violently away. This igloo seemed to take centuries to go up. I stood beside Shongili, passing blocks to him and saying to myself, When will it be high enough to protect us from the wind? Imperturbable, he worked on. What was to me catastrophic was to him a bit of every-day existence. When the igloo was almost finished I crawled inside and huddled motionless against the wall. Shongili set in the last block and then went out into the blizzard—doubtless to dig up the dogs, feed them, bury our effects in the snow. I could hear nothing but the hollow rush of the wind, and I lit a cigarette. At last he came in—and with him the storm—straightened up, quietly beat his garments, one by one, sat down and pulled off his boots, and then, lying back, looked at me through his eyelashes, content.

Who would deny that experiences like this draw men together? And yet, though this experience drew me to Shongili, would it be true to say that he felt at all closer to me for it? Momentarily, yes; but it was he that had taught me a lesson, not I him. I admired that man. He had proved himself stronger than the storm. Like the sailor at sea, he had met it tranquilly, it had left him unmoved. It had not changed his rhythm; and perhaps nothing can alter an Eskimo's rhythm. That deliberateness which, an hour earlier, had filled me with anguish because I had been shivering with cold and fear—that slow deliberateness seemed to me now a kind of grandeur. In mid-tempest this peasant of the Arctic, by his total impassivity, had lent me a little of his serenity of soul.

Night had long since fallen. The wind beat in repeated smacks—for here where there are no obstacles to its flow it does not howl, it slaps. To keep it out as much as possible, we had stretched the tarpaulin, taken from the sled, over a part of the roof, and had set blocks of snow at the corners. It was worse than nothing at all, for the snapping of the tent in the wind was hideous. I could not get to sleep. The igloo was too short. One of my legs was in a bad way and I could not stretch it out. Outside, the dogs were whimpering; and we indoors lay like the dogs, eyes wide open listening all night to the wind.

Not all of the nights I spent alone with Shongili were, like this one, nights of horror: some were peaceful. He would have eaten, and I, too. He would be sitting on the edge of the *iglerk,* legs dangling, head forward and body supported by his elbows at either side, bottom in air, staring straight ahead. The seal-oil lamp would be giving off its gentle glow, and from time to time Shongili would crush and re-shape its wick with the back of a spoon—all our household silver—and relapse into his animal immobility. A little earlier he would have cut out, above our heads, a hole through which the smoke could escape; and after we had eaten he would have stopped it up with a ptarmigan skin. I would slip into my sleeping-bag, too weary to bear any longer the sight of that lifeless profile, that eternally recurring gesture of nose-picking and snot-swallowing. If only I might never see this man again! I would say to myself.

That, I dare say, is what we call human nature. This man whom I admired while he built the igloo, whom I loved like a brother in the storm, so that I was almost proud to feel that sentiment of fraternity in me—as soon as it was over, as soon as all was well again, this man became for me a stranger, all but an enemy, a being so odious that I could not bear the sight of him. Slowly I would sink down into my sleeping-bag, into the humid lining of the ice-covered skins. In another minute, I would say to myself, the bag will cover me completely, and I shall be alone. Down. Slowly down. Cautiously, without stirring too much, because it was so cold, I would contrive a little opening through which to breathe. A cigarette was my next thought. A cigarette to take the curse off the rigor of the trail. A beatific cigarette. I would smoke it down to the very end, burning my wind-chapped lips.

We had been out three days, and I was still limping on ahead of the dogs when the terrain changed and we were running through a narrow corridor between two chains of hills. Below the ice over which we ran, there flowed the waters of a lake, but cut out so regularly, so narrow and long, that it might have been a race-track set between grandstands. We spent a whole day on this lake, which must have been twenty miles in length, and at the end of the day we found ourselves among mountains. Mountains! I could not get over it. For months, the highest ridge I had seen ran up some fifty feet, and to find myself now surrounded by monsters a thousand feet high gave me the impression of a child lost in the landscape of a fairy-tale. They were gentle mountains, roundbacked, worn, bare and harmless, but mountains, nevertheless.

Soon we were well within them, our sled rising and dropping and rising again. The going became very hard for the dogs, and when they stopped it was always at a critical point where Shongili and I had to use all our strength to

push the load over the rise. Once on top, the fall was so
steep that we ordered the dogs to lie down (one by one,
with that long caress of the whip to which they were so
gratefully responsive) and we went off to find a way out,
Shongili to the right and I to the left. Eventually, we found
a grade that did not seem too stiff; but as it was still steeper
than we liked, we tied two sealskin straps to the hindmost
crossbar of the sled and hoped that the dogs would slide
gently down the slope while we worked our improvised
brakes at the back. But the dogs tumbled down like mad,
and Shongili and I, hanging on grimly to our straps, were
dragged along on our bottoms, braking with our feet for all
we were worth. We came out into a valley that was like an
amphitheatre, and here we paused for breath. While Shongili went off to set a trap, in which he might find a fox on
his way home, I had a look round this natural circus. The
ridges that encircled us must have been a thousand feet
high. On the slopes lay broad sheets of immaculate snow,
cut by bare brown spines. Not a wisp of vegetation grew
here, and the dead rock stood out against a perfectly serene
blue-green sky. Silence and unreality dominated the scene,
and after we had started once more I turned round again
and again to fill my eyes with the beauty of what was in
sum merely an irregular terrain, of no interest to an eye less
starved than mine.

We were still rising, and it was clear to me that we should
have to cross this range and come down the other side of
the island that we were on, in order to reach the sea and
Pelly Bay. But the up-hill work seemed never to end, and
as we moved through pass after pass I began to be worried.
Our dogs were panting: Algunerk had not let us have
Nigak for leader, and out of the nine huskies three were
young and not yet toughened by hard work on the trail.

To spare the team as far as possible, I followed the slope of
the mountains obliquely instead of driving straight ahead—
a procedure that Shongili could not understand. I began to
worry lest we be overtaken by night. Why, I do not know,
but the thought of spending the night in these mountains
sent a chill through me that I had never felt on tundra or
sea. I asked Shongili if it was far, now, to the camp of the
Arviligjuarmiut?

"*A-va-ta-ne,*" he said. (The other side.)

"The other side of what?"

He said something very quickly in a rumbling voice that
came up out of his belly. When I made him repeat it, I
understood as little as before. Then he laughed, and I flew
into a rage. (Decidedly, I was incorrigible.) I ran on ahead
of the dogs, stumbled and fell, and when I looked back I
saw him sitting on the sled. Both Shongili and the mountains seemed to be mocking me. Going back, I ordered him
off the sled and on ahead; and he, to avenge himself, began
to beat the dogs. But just as I was about to rush forward I
saw him tripped up in the harness, rolling over and over in
the snow. It gave me pleasure enough to make the next hour
endurable.

When evening came the scene was colored like a Swiss
postal card. Ahead, the sky was deep green, and behind it
was violent red, like the brief sunset of the desert. A crescent
moon hung in the heavens. I stared at all this like a man
long deprived of the beauties of nature, and it was not until
night had fallen and brought out its map of stars that I
came to myself and once again interrogated Shongili.

"Is it much farther?" I asked.

"*Una-hi-ķto,*"—"very far," he said. "Do you want to build
an igloo?"

I set my jaw. "You told me we would be there this

evening," I said, "and we are going to get there if we have
to travel all night."

"*Na-ma-kto,*"—"very good," he said calmly.

Passes, curves, and more passes. A parade of ghosts
through a ghostly land. Now I could no longer run on
ahead, because that slight sickle of a moon gave off too little
light. I stumbled forward, stared in every direction, and
once or twice I went completely off the trail and ran into a
mountain-side. We had to stop, then, swing the dogs round
with a touch of the whip, go back where we had come from,
and start again. My body tramped on through the dark
while my mind strove stubbornly to cling to some familiar
image—a peasant kitchen, a woman's face, a South Seas hut.
Shongili was now guiding the dogs; my eyes were aching
and I no longer saw where I was going. The sled scraped
over stones, for we had come down into the bed of a creek.
It must have been midnight, and Shongili had ultimately
admitted that the camp was not far off. Finally we saw,
straight ahead, the sheer wall of a high rock at the foot of
which igloos glimmered white in the moonlight. This was
the camp; but as in all tales of buried treasure, it was empty.

I had been thirteen days on the trail and my story was
beginning to be the story of the man who never got there.
There was nothing to do except to go to sleep. And as we
had travelled part of the night, had had to build an igloo
by moonlight, and men and dogs were exhausted, we could
not decently be off again before break of day.

We slept, and next day we were delayed. For one thing,
the runners had lost part of their veneer of mud and ice,
and without re-mudding and icing we could not go on. For
another my sealskin boots had burst at the soles, and had to
be re-sewn. While Shongili patched up, I had a look at the

empty igloos. These were veritable troglodyte caverns; and as the snow here was thick, their floors were about three feet below the porch. That is, all the snow-blocks needed for the building of the igloo were taken from the surface of what was now the floor. Within, I seemed to be in the Roman catacombs: there was a central lobby, there were lateral igloos, and everywhere I saw niches for dogs and for the storage of food and household utensils. This was true snow architecture, with passages and perspectives in every direction.

But these igloos were chilled and mouldy, strewn with the usual repellent débris of abandoned snowhouses. For all the care that had been taken with them, they would never be lived in again.

Somewhere I have a sketch of Shongili on the floor of our igloo looking for his lost pipe. He was on all fours in the characteristic attitude of the Eskimo, bottom in air and nose to the ground, snorting and sniffing like a hunting dog in the field. His hands were wonderful to watch: the fingers were never spread; there was no feeling and fumbling behind box or sack, but a repeated clawing and scratching that was positively not related to anything human. From where I sat I had a three-quarters view of his face: an enormously long ear covered with hair, a lean and prominent jaw-bone, and the stiff and untrimmed moustache that seemed to come out of his nose and turn into a fuzzy spider that ran over the ground on its own hunt as the face went round and round. He was muttering as he crawled, and the sound *pa-i-pak* returned often enough in his speech to tell me that it was his pipe that he was looking for. He had made it himself, the bowl out of soapstone, the stem out of two bits of driftwood bound together with caribou nerve, leaving the smoke to be drawn into the mouth between the two pieces of wood—for the Eskimos have no tool with which to bore a long hole. I thought of that driftwood floating eastward from the Mackenzie River through the Glacial Ocean and then down McClintock Channel to be cast up here in Shongili's mouth. What a strange end for that bit of wood!

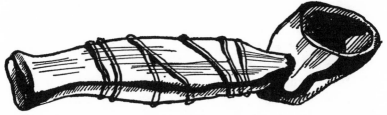

"Pa-i-pak," he continued to moan, but the moment I started the Primus he straightened up and squatted on his knees, head slightly forward and arms folded across under his chin in the habitual pose of the Eskimo waiting for his tea.

That day I was tempted and fell. With his usual thoughtfulness, Paddy Gibson had shoved into my sack a Stilton cheese to cheer me on the trail. "What a treat!" I had said to myself, but after I was out it occurred to me that the cheese would be a much greater treat for Father Henry, if I found him at Pelly Bay. Father Henry had been living for six years among the Arviligjuarmiut, a solitary missionary sharing their life, and, so far as I knew, never coming away from his remote "parish." I put the cheese away for him, and though I had looked at it hungrily from time to time, I had hitherto not touched it. But the day we got finally over the mountain range it was too much for me. Morally and physically, I need the reinforcement of this cheese, and I gobbled up a good quarter of it before shame stopped me.

Next morning, after the usual music-hall turn by Shongili, we struck camp, rounded a point, and found ourselves in the heavy ice of the open sea. A strong wind was blowing and plumes of snow ran before us over the ice. Shongili took fright—at least he said he was afraid: there were many things I should never know about these Eskimos. Soon he spoke to me about turning back. This weather, he said, was bad, bad.

"You don't like it?" I said.

"*Oo-van-ga na-mang-ni-kto,*"—from which I made out that he did not like it.

"It suits me," I replied curtly, and I ran on. But it was no pleasure, for Shongili seemed not to know where he was. He wove to right and left looking for traces of sled-tracks, and the dogs and I would stop until he returned and gave the signal to go on. Eventually we went off at an angle, still over the sea, and after a good hour in a straight line the wind dropped and visibility was about half a mile.

Suddenly I saw a black dot against the white background.

"*Inuk!*" (A man!) I called out.

"*Na-oo?*" Shongili had not seen it.

I pointed, we moved towards it, and there was no doubt about it: that black dot was a man. In this land of one million square miles inhabited by six thousand men, the sight of a human being is overwhelming; it creates an emotion that is like a seizure, difficult to describe. A man, yes! You stare and stare at the black dot. You hesitate to believe that you are not alone here in this immensity through which you have for days been wandering. You are tempted to reject the evidence that another human being may be squatting in full view over his hole in the ice, or moving to join you.

We trotted forward, and the black figure floated before

our eyes from left to right, revealed and then concealed in
the puffs of snow raised by the wind. Actually, the man was
still enough. He had not seen us, folded in two over his
seal hole as he was. But as we came nearer he turned and
straightened up, roused by the shout with which we urged
on our dogs. ("*I-no-ralu!*"—"A man indeed!" you shout to
them, and they, knowing what you mean, trot faster.)

Some yards from the seal hole lay a small sled and two
dogs. We stopped our team near by with a gentle "Hoo!"
slipped the whip under the lashings of the sled, and went
forward. But we moved Eskimo fashion, cautiously; and he
stood Eskimo fashion, firmly without stirring. So two
animals meet. Within a few feet of him we stopped. It was
his turn to come forward. A smile—very formal; a hand-
shake—high up and very Asiatic. Contact!

The man called to his dogs, and, leaving his sled, hitched
his team to ours, and over the ice we ran. Two hundred
yards farther on, another shadow emerged through the grey
air, this one like the first folded over a seal hole in the con-
ventional posture. We stopped, went through the formali-
ties of the greeting, added his dogs to ours, and were off
again. One by one, in this fashion we picked up six Eskimos,
and now they stood round me on the ice, harpoon in hand
and no word spoken. Shongili broke the silence:

"Kabloona," he said simply.

"*Kabloona-ralu!*" "A white man! A white man!" the six
men rumbled. They were startled.

One of them approached near enough to touch me, and
I could see his eyes shining in the middle of his hood.

"*Kina-oo-vi?*"—"Who are you?" he asked.

"Mike," said I, giving the nickname.

"Ma-i-ke," they repeated; and with this they became
loquacious.

When we had chatted together for some minutes I asked if it was far to where Ka-i-o lived? (Ka-i-o, "the Red," was their name for Father Henry.)

"It is far," they answered, "but the igloos are near."

"The igloos are near," Shongili repeated hastily. He wanted no more travelling that day.

These were the true, the pure Eskimos, the Eskimos who knew not how to lie. Of course it was not far to the house of Ka-i-o; but to say that it was, was not to lie to me. It was an expression of their amazement at the appearance of a white man among them, a phenomenon so extraordinary that they must hold fast to it. Gently, but decidedly, they were determined to detain me.

One of them made place for me on the tiny sled behind him—a sled so small that I could scarcely keep my seat on it, especially as there was no room for my legs. Is it a species of sled-driver's evolution, I wondered, that has made their own legs so short? For mine are not long, yet they were scraping and jerking over the ground. The man drove furiously and we bounded from one hummock of frozen ice to the next, skirting ice-cakes, curvetting and bouncing in the flying wind, until I thought I should be sent sprawling at any moment. But my host was a wonderful driver, and as he drove he clicked and clacked with his tongue and sent forth bird-like cries that seemed to madden the dogs while it guided them so skilfully among the obstacles with which this grainy pack was thickly strewn. To left and right of us other sleds were racing in the same direction, but we outran them all. Finally, when they were well behind, and the self-esteem of my driver (together with his pride at driving the Kabloona) had been well merited, he turned round, and for the first time I saw his face. He had only one eye, but

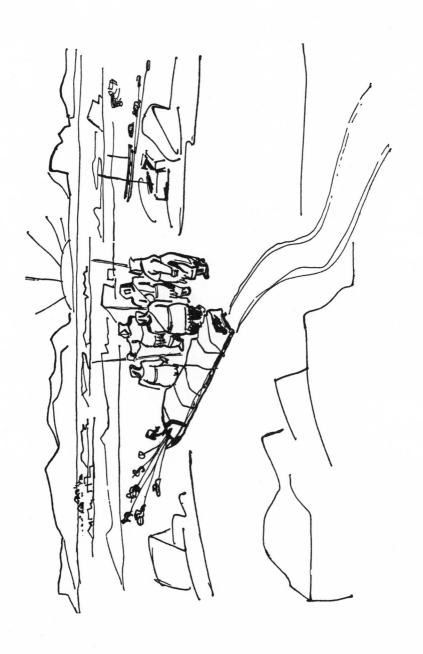

he looked a pleasant fellow, laughed cordially, and I felt that already we were old friends.

One after the other, the little sleds flew into camp as if covering the last lap of a race, drew up short, and stopped dead. From every side, men and women poured out, and I shook hands as nearly in the Eskimo fashion as possible so that they might not think me a barbarian. This done, everybody slipped back into his igloo and left me alone with my host.

What a difference there was between our hasty habitations of a night and this admirably built and chinked snowhouse, banked all round for warmth, glowing inside with the gentle pulsing of the seal-oil lamp, its stillness the product of leisure and contentment, not of morbidity and fatigue.

Next morning I was out of my sleeping-bag before my hosts, and had begun to pack my things. They lay staring at my agitation. Once more the barbarian, the Kabloona that I was, showed itself unfortunately. With the white man's impatience, with the white man's stupid distortion of true values, I blurted out crudely that I must be off to see Ka-i-o. I would be back, I said, but I could not linger. Also—see to what depths of gracelessness the white man can descend! —to make matters worse I added that later I should want a man and sled to take me back to King William Land and was ready to pay two foxes for the service.

I had said exactly the wrong thing. My words were met with silence. They stared at me from their sleeping-bags in a silence so long that it almost unnerved me. I felt as if I were in their eyes an insect disrupting with its aimless and angry buzzing the tranquil peace of their igloo. Finally an old man said with a mocking and yet gentle smile:

"Sleep. There is time enough."

But I was too deeply in the wrong to retreat; and besides, I was determined that I should reach Father Henry that same day, come what may. So, saying what I could to repair my disgrace and soften their judgment of me, I finished my packing. At that moment Shongili crawled in.

"You have forgotten to visit," he said. "I go to make the round of the igloos."

It was true. I had neglected the first article of Eskimo behavior. Two lessons in Eskimo manners had been administered to me within the hour, and half the morning was to be lost in visits. But we got away, and were guided by one of these Eskimos—so great was their courtesy—on his swift small sled.

Pelly Bay, which we were now crossing, is a great pocket of the sea over a hundred miles long and twenty miles wide, filled with endless chaplets of small islands. As we moved among these islands I thought again how different this was from King William Land. Gone was the void without contour, the monotony in which nothing was present to comfort the spirit. Here was a world of shapes and surfaces to which the eye could cling. Here were bluffs that rose abruptly five hundred feet above the sea, and for a man so lately come from the tundra, a man who had spent last night in a five-foot igloo crouching at the base of one of these bluffs, they towered like topless mountains, rose like cathedrals seen from their own porches, higher than Manhattan when it suddenly emerges to greet the traveller from overseas. King William Land had been oblivion: this was grandeur.

We drove for three hours among the islands, most of them inaccessible and serving in the spring as natural sanctuaries for half the birds of North America. I could imagine them hovering and fluttering in clouds round these towers like pigeons round the steeples of our churches.

The sled ran on, winding in and out, coming to an ice-crack and making a wide detour to avoid it, while I thought of the man I was to see. As we neared the promontory that was our destination, our guide whipped up his swift dogs and was out of sight in a moment, hurrying ahead to bear the stupendous news of the arrival of the Kabloona. Here was a land that only three white men had seen in a century, and here, I said to myself, lived a priest who was my own countryman. During the seventeen days on the trail, time had ceased to exist for me. Now time had returned, and it was not a matter of days but of seconds before I should see that man. We rounded a bend, and ahead of me I saw a hill on the slope of which three forms were running. When, a moment later, we drew up at the foot of that hill, I sprang down from the sled and started up the slope. At that moment I saw Father Henry.

Coming down to meet me was a tall, slim, bony figure—more than thin, translucent. Like all ascetics, he induced in one an impression of transparency which no quantity of Eskimo coverings could conceal. He was not much taller than I, yet as he came down the slope he seemed infinitely tall. On his head was a fur bonnet with earmuffs such as I had never seen in these parts but is common below the Barren Lands. Beneath that bonnet shone two very bright blue eyes, half spiritual and half childlike. A reddish blond beard of patriarchal length flowed over his woolen parka, and his legs were encased in boots trimmed with polar bear fur.

He was coming down hill very fast, as if the arrival of a white man at Pelly Bay were indeed an event. One look at those blue eyes, and I forgot all my little schemes. I had planned to address him first in English, in order to tease him; and then, when I had fooled him completely, I should say to him in French with a laugh, "Well, Father, and how are things going?" to see the look of amazement that would come into his face.

But all this went straight out of my mind. His eyes were too candid; and when he came up to me I put out my hand and said in French:

"Father, here is a Frenchman come to visit you."

"Dear, dear!" he said. "And—and your name, if you please?"

Together, we walked up the slope.

Chapter II

I AM going to say to you that a human being can live without complaint in an ice-house built for seals at a temperature of fifty-five degrees below zero, and you are going to doubt my word. Yet what I say is true, for this was how Father Henry lived; and when I say "ice-house for seals" I am not using metaphorical language. Father Henry lived in a hole dug out by the Eskimos in the side of a hill as a place in which to store seal-meat in summer. The earth of this hill is frozen a hundred feet down, and it is so cold that you can hardly hold your bare hand to its surface.

An Eskimo would not have lived in this hole. An igloo is a thousand times warmer, especially one built out on the sea over the water warm beneath the coat of ice. I asked Father Henry why he lived thus. He said merely that it was more convenient, and pushed me ahead of him into his cavern.

If I were to describe the interior, draw it for you inch by inch, I should still be unable to convey the reality to you. There was a wooden door framed in the side of the slope. You stooped to enter the doorway and found yourself in a passage. On the right, standing as usual on end, were a half dozen frozen seal powdered with snow. On the left

lay a bitch, suckled by a puppy. Ahead was a second door
and behind it a second passage about ten feet deep and so
narrow that you went through it sidewise, so low that your
hood scraped the snow that had drifted in and sent it down
into your neck. At the end of this passage was the hermit's
cave.

Two seal-oil lamps were burning as I went in. These
lamps light up an igloo, because an igloo is circular and
more or less white: here they gave off only a faint gleam
and the corners of the cave were hidden in darkness. The
lamps stood on an empty barrel at the left of the door.
Above them hung the drying rack, a sort of net suspended

FATHER HENRY'S ICE-HOLE FOR SEALS AT PELLY BAY. THE BOARD
RUNNING ALONG THE LEFT WALL WAS USED AS AN ALTAR FOR
MASS. A SMALL CRUCIFIX LEANS ON THE SHELF IN THE UPPER
RIGHT CORNER. ALL THE EQUIPMENT NECESSARY FOR LIVING
IS CROWDED INTO THIS SMALL SPACE

from three nails in which, if you looked hard enough, you could see a glove, a boot, but surely not a pair. At the right a shelf had been nailed up, and on it stood a queerly shaped kerosene lamp, the lid of a pot, a circular Eskimo knife, a rag, an empty tobacco tin, and a box of salt. Straight ahead, facing the door, was a couch.

Compared with this hole, an igloo was a palace. From the door to the couch opposite measured four and one half feet. Two people could not stand comfortably here, and when Father Henry said Mass I used to kneel on the couch. "If you didn't, you would be in my way," was how he put it. It was so small that when I came in from outdoors I never contrived to shake the snow off my coat without shaking it all over the couch.

The couch was a rickety wooden surface supported in the middle by a strut, over which two caribou hides had been spread. On these three planks forming a slightly tilted surface, Father Henry slept. To the right was a hole in the ground, which we blocked in part by the packing case containing my effects.

"The box will be your couch," said Father Henry; "and if you remember to keep out of that hole, you'll be perfectly comfortable."

Father Henry has no table knife, and I doubt that he has ever had a fork. His spoon disappeared a few days before my arrival, and he thought it might have fallen into the hole. I pushed the box aside and began to hunt for the spoon. After I had pulled up a dozen frozen fish-heads, an old parka, a sack with a bit of flour still in it, and five Arctic-hare hides, I found the spoon.

No white man has anything to boast of in the Arctic, but Father Henry no longer had the little with which he had started. Whatever he had possessed on first coming out here was to him part of a forgotten past, and he referred to it as "all those things." It had helped in the beginning, but now "all that" was superfluous. What, for example, did he want with a plate when his only meal of the day was a lump of frozen fish, eaten on waking in the morning? What good was that lamp to him, since he had no kerosene? How could he have used a pen here where ink froze? A napkin, which would have stiffened like a board in this cold? The only thing to do was to lick one's fingers, and indeed the gesture had become automatic with him. But since he knew that I was what Frenchy Chartrand at Coppermine had called a "cream puff," he gave me a ptarmigan skin to wipe my fingers on. This is the classic towel of the Arctic. It lasts the whole winter through without washing, and if you really mean to honor your guest, it is with this ptarmigan skin that you wipe his plate.

Father Henry lacked every object known to the civilization of the white man. "Those things make no sense here," —and with that phrase he disposed of the subject. When I unpacked my gifts for him, rejoicing in advance over the delight they would give him, he stood by shaking his head. No, he can longer eat white man's food: not even rice. He cannot digest the stuff. "That sort of food doesn't keep a man warm. Frozen fish, now . . ." He loves frozen fish. There is nothing like it, he says, to warm you inside. Doctors tell you that you ought to vary your diet. Well . . . For six years he had been living on nothing but frozen fish, and he was none the worse off for it. When he awoke he groped on the ground, picked up a great chunk of fish frozen so hard that he had to thaw it out a little with his lips and breath before he could bite into it, and with this he regaled himself. It was succulent, it warmed you up, it

sated your hunger, and you felt fine. As for eating in the
evening, no: it would have kept him awake all night.

Despite this discouragement I continued to unpack. The
cheese: I should finish it myself. The cigars (Gibson's gift):
there was a Belgian priest at Repulse Bay who loved cigars,
and they were put aside for him. The pipe: poor Father
Henry! He had had a pipe. Smoking it from time to time
had been his only luxury. But my Lord Bishop had asked
all his missionaries to make one supplementary sacrifice,
and Father Henry had sacrificed his pipe. I protested; but I
do not believe I quite got him to promise to smoke again.
As for the rest of the gifts, he took them and put them to
one side, saying absentmindedly, "Very kind, very kind."
His thanks were an acknowledgment of the intention: the
gifts themselves had no meaning for him, no value.

His possessions were limited to lamps, dogs, sealing nets,
and clothes. He spent a great deal of time looking to his
lamps, and the Eskimos teased him about it. "You do it
better than we do," they would say with their smile; and
it is a fact that nothing wants so much attention as a seal-oil
lamp. You can spend hours trimming the improvised wick,
shortening or lengthening it, adding more seal-oil—or rather
blubber which, melting, becomes oil—when you hear it
splutter. It used to make me smile to see Father Henry, in
the midst of his Mass, between the syllables of an *Introibo
ad altare,* turn from the plank on the right that was his altar
and trim the wick while he continued his service.

It was six o'clock next morning when I awoke. I had
slept badly on my box, unable to stretch my legs and half
fallen into the hole. Father Henry had long been up and
tended to his lamps, and now he was sitting on the couch.
He had slept in his clothes: one could not do otherwise in

this terrible cold that rose from the earth, and he was sitting
motionless, fearing to wake me, murmuring his prayers to
himself. Now that I was awake he prepared his altar by
shoving to one side the kerosene lamp and empty tobacco
tin, and the Mass began. I "served," squatting on the couch.

"*Dominus,*" said Father Henry; and then ducking beneath a beam overhead he appeared round the other side:
"*Vobiscum.*"

And I, from the couch: "*Et cum spiritu tuo.*" . . .

When he heard confession from one of the natives, his
box was the outer passage and the scene took place under
the vitreous eyes of the frozen seal. In this virtual darkness,
at fifty degrees below, the two men would kneel and murmur together.

All day long I was weary, unable to get warm. I lay in
my sleeping-bag and drank tea, and as Father Henry drank
with me we chatted. I tore the paper off a packet of biscuits and said as I threw the wrapper away:

"An Eskimo would pick up a bit of paper like that as
soon as you threw it down."

"So would I," Father Henry said calmly, and he picked
up what I had thrown away and put it on a shelf. He told
me how he had been informed of my coming. Nothing
could better display the mentality of these natives.

An Eskimo had come running into the cavern and had
stood breathless before him. He was the bearer of astound-
ing news and proud to be bringing it. But he did not speak.
It is ill-bred to be in haste, and it is ill-bred also to attack
any subject directly. So, shaking the snow from his clothes,
he had taken a mug of tea from the unsuspecting priest
and had drunk it in silence. Then, having cut himself a
slice of fish, he had eaten, and smoked a cigarette. Time
passed, and Father Henry went about his household tasks.

Eventually Father Henry asked him a question.

"Kis-si-wi?" (Are you alone?)

"Nak-ka." (No.)

"Kina-lo?" (Who is it?)

"Oo-shu-tik-sak," said the Eskimo, giving Shongili's true name and refraining from mentioning me.

"Sug-mat?" (How does that happen?)

The Eskimo looked at Father Henry and smiled. Now he was heavy with his news, electrically charged, bursting to speak, proud of his mission of annunciation. And yet he was silent again for a time. Finally he exploded:

"Kabloona-ralu!"

Father Henry stopped short and turned round with a start.

"What is his name?"

"Ma-i-ke."

All this meant nothing to Father Henry, for he knew nothing about me, not even this nickname by which I was known among the Eskimos. (Of themselves, the Eskimos might have called me "He of the Long Ears" or something equally flattering.) He hunted round in his mind. Who could it be?

"What does he do?"

"Nu-nang-juar-le-rie." (He draws the image of the earth.) The Eskimos had seen me sketching.

"Is it Learmonth?"

"That is not his name."

"Is it a policeman?"

"I believe not. He went into the igloos. He saw the Cross. He 'follows' as we do."

"Does he speak Eskimo?"

At this point Father Henry said to me: "Observe the delicacy of these men. He might have said, 'Badly.' Instead, in order not to hurt any one, he said, 'All that he has said to us, we have clearly understood.'

"Then," Father Henry went on, "they brought you gradually into Pelly Bay. I was at work shovelling the snow away from my door while one of them on the watch called out to me: 'He is in sight. He is turning the point. He will be here in a moment.' And I, hunting feverishly for my gloves! 'He is very near.' And then, just as I started out of the door: '*A-ood-lar-mat,'*—He has arrived!"

We talked of many things and among others of dogs, for Father Henry had a superb team of which in his selfless way he was proud.

"The more I see of the dogs," he said, "the better I understand the men. The same defects; the same qualities. And how different they are from our dogs at home! What hypocrisy there is in them at times, and with what pleasure they play tricks on you, turning round each time to give you the same jeering look. On the other hand I have known them to go a week without food, trotting along at a steady pace with no single whimper of complaint. To go three or four days hungry is their frequent lot, and when night falls and the sled is stopped, they will lie down and go to sleep unfed, as if they expected nothing better."

I expressed my regret that I should never know the Eskimo language well enough to grasp its inner essence, and should therefore never know the men who spoke it, seeing that language is the faithful mirror of a people's spirit.

"If you knew what condensation there is in their language!" Father Henry exclaimed. "Their phrases are as sober as their faces. A gleam in an Eskimo's eye tells you more than a half dozen of our sentences concerning desire, repugnance, or another emotion. Each Eskimo word is like that gleam: it suggests at once what has happened and what is to come, and it contains that touch of the unexpressed which makes this people so mysterious and attractive.

"Their shades of expression are infinite," he went on. "They are Asiatic, and perhaps for that reason imperceptible to us. We are so habituated to our simple yes and no that we ignore the existence of a scale of gradations between affirmation and negation. It took me a long time to understand what was going on in their minds, and many things had to be revealed to me before I knew where I stood with these men. They would explain: 'He did not refuse to do as you asked; he merely told you that there were obstacles in the way.' Or: 'He did not deceive you, he did not lie to you; he merely omitted to affirm the thing to you.' It was hard for me to grasp the care they took not to commit themselves. Each time that they speak they leave themselves a back door through which to retreat. For example:

"An Eskimo comes in from trapping. There are several visitors in his igloo. He picks up the snow-beater, and when his clothes are free of snow he takes them off. All this without a word. Then, as he knows that the others are waiting for him to speak, he says: 'Those foxes! There is no way to get them.' Silence. 'And besides, I'm not good for much any more. An old man.' Again silence. Finally, still as if he were speaking to himself: 'But I got three to-day.'"

I told Father Henry of my trouble getting to Pelly Bay. He was astonished.

"How could it possibly have taken so long?"

"I can't say. And yet, Heaven knows I told those men often enough that I was in a hurry to get here."

Father Henry laughed. "That's it then," he said. "That explains it. You are lucky to have got here at all. You deserved to be led round and round in a circle to teach you a lesson."

And he told me how he went about getting a sled up to Repulse Bay in double time.

He would send for an Eskimo and say to him: "I want you to go to Repulse Bay. It will take you a good bit of time. You are young; probably you do not know the way very well; your dogs are not worth much. Still, nobody else is available, so go along."

Time passes, and the Eskimo is back from the trip.

"Well?" says Father Henry to him.

The man looks crestfallen. Things went badly. The weather was worse than he had expected. Then one of the dogs fell sick. And there were other difficulties, each of which he lists with scrupulous care. But he had gone and come in twelve days, just the same, and he knew that Father Henry knew that was fast travelling.

When we spoke of Eskimo murder, Father Henry told me about a man now at Committee Bay who had come to him one day, and, after the usual tea and silence, had said to him suddenly:

"I took the old woman out on the ice to-day."

It was his own mother that he had driven out and set down at sea to freeze to death. He was fond of her, he explained. He had always been kind to her. But she was too old, she was no longer good for anything; so blind, she couldn't even find the porch to crawl into the igloo. So, on a day of blizzard, the whole family agreeing, he had taken her out, and they had struck camp and gone off, leaving her to die.

"With God's help I hope in time to change these things, to soften some of their ways," said Father Henry; "but it is difficult. They live a hard life, and it is in all respects a material life. They would say, if they knew our words, that they had to 'face facts.' That man had indeed been a good son. You must have seen yourself how they look after the aged on the trail, running back so often to the sled to see if the old people are warm enough, if they are comfortable, if they are not perhaps hungry and want a bit of fish. And the old people are a burden on the trail, a cause of delay and of complication. But the day comes when, after years with no word of complaint, the young people deem the thing no longer possible, and they leave the old man or the old woman on the ice. The old people are told in advance what their end is to be, and they submit peacefully without a word of recrimination. Sometimes, indeed, they are the first to suggest this end for themselves."

There are violent murders, however, that are harder to explain. The murder, for example, that results purely from the instinct of the hunter. One of Father Henry's stories I had already been told at King.

Three men were on the trail together. Evening came and they built an igloo. They sat talking and smoking. The igloo had been hastily put up and a wide hole appeared overhead which one of the men went out to patch up. As the two others continued to sit and smoke, one of them chanced to raise his eyes. Overhead the third was patching the hole. His loose clothing had parted, and his great brown belly was bare and visible as he worked.

"A fine belly," said the first Eskimo.

The other raised his head. *"Eh-eh-eh!"* he affirmed with appreciation, "a very fine belly."

They continued to stare at it. The first man spoke again: "I could stick my knife into a belly like that."

The second man said nothing. He stood up and planted

his snow-knife into that belly. It was irresistible: the belly was too fine.

Father Henry having asked why I had come into these regions, the simplest thing for me to tell him was that I was studying Eskimo manners and trading for primitive utensils. The fact that Eskimo life and objects might be of interest to me must have seemed to this priest pure futility.

"You bother with those things, do you?" he said. It was clear that they had no value in his eyes. Nevertheless, to give me pleasure, he sent for a native called Nibtayok, who arrived with a few articles in a sack. One of these pieces fascinated me and was highly valued by Nibtayok, too, for it was the product of a great deal of labor. It was a *kayok-tak,* a bowl made of the hollowed out skull of the musk-ox. Out of it the natives drank seal blood. These bowls were now so scarce that I had never before seen one either on King William Land or at Perry River. I was about to offer a tin of tobacco for it, and for the rest a packet of cigarette paper; but, uncertain that this would be enough, I asked Father Henry to find out for me. Nibtayok's face brightened the moment the question was put to him.

"A-lie-na-i!" he answered. (I should think so.)

Nibtayok was the only man left in camp, the others having gone off sealing, and I took advantage of his presence to ask him about Eskimo superstitions and legends. This astonished Father Henry.

"I should never have thought of asking about such things," he said; and I teased him a little.

"How," I said, "can you expect to uproot their superstitions if you do not know what they are? You told me yourself that the surest way to be rid of these things is to show bit by bit how ineffectual and absurd they are."

"True, true!" he said, but his mind was on other things and I sensed that for him all this was nonsense.

When I had questioned Nibtayok for about twenty minutes he became exhausted and his eyes began to blink.

"I am sleepy," he said.

Twenty minutes was as long as an Eskimo could go on thinking. And besides, the white man's way of putting his questions made the operation difficult. I would ask a question directly, to begin with. Then I would have to attenuate it, explain in roundabout fashion what I was getting at; and the explanation itself took so much time, that listening to it wearied my man. He had to be reassured about each subject of inquiry, convinced that he need not be afraid to answer, so great is the fear among them of committing themselves.

Nibtayok took me with him on a tour of the camps. This was the season when the whole clan were scattered over the ice throughout the length of Pelly Bay, and to see them one had to go visiting.

As we were about to leave, Father Henry gave me a bit of advice. "Be sure not to run alongside the sled," he admonished me. "Nibtayok would be horribly vexed, for my Eskimos do not do this. Besides, his dogs are very fast, and you might soon find yourself left behind."

I had scarcely time to fling myself on the sled before we were off at a gallop, and for three hours we went on without slackening speed. How different from King William Land! Nibtayok had only to call out to the dogs, and they responded magnificently. Snow on King was often a hindrance; here it was a kind of airy carpet on which we seemed literally to be flying, not dragging ourselves along on a sled that creaked like an old farm cart.

Our first visit was to Nibtayok's father, and here a little incident took place which revealed to me in a flash another trait of this race—the lengths to which Eskimo shyness can go.

Nibtayok's father was a very interesting old man, one of the few, even up here, who clung to the old ways. For example, he still hunted the caribou with bow and arrow. His name had once been Orpingalik; now he called himself Alakannoak and lived with two or three others not far from Father Henry's ice-house.

We found him and his friends at their seal-holes on the ice, each with two dogs on a lead to sniff out the *aglu,* or air-hole of the seal. As soon as they saw us, they gathered up their implements and mounted their sleds. They did not greet us, and it was as he went forward to his sled that I saw that Nibtayok's father was a rosy-cheeked, bright-eyed ancient, as round as a ball in his white *kuliktak,* or outer coat. He was the only Eskimo I ever saw who had a full square-cut beard, the beard of one of our peasants at home and not merely the nine scraggly hairs on the chin that constitute generally the whiskers of the Eskimo. We drove off to their igloos, Nibtayok's father seated on a sled so small that it was hidden beneath him. With his legs widespread, his short arms stiff at his sides, he seemed to be pulled by the dogs on his bottom over the ice. The two dogs, one black and the other white, ran with a steady flowing gait that was beautiful to watch, and when they were thirsty they merely put their heads down to the ice, opened their mouths, and filled them with the snow that blew in as they ran on at an unvarying pace. The old man never stirred but seemed stuck to his sled, rising and falling as it rose and fell over the bumpy surface of the ice.

We arrived, stood up from the sleds, and made ready to

greet one another. It was at that moment that the thing happened. Alakannoak came across to me and raised my hand with the greatest grace. Then he went over to his son. But to my astonishment, Nibtayok turned away and pretended to be watching something on the horizon. Later, I asked if they had quarrelled, this father and son. Not at all. It was a long time since they had seen each other, and the son had been too shy to look his father in the face.

As we moved from camp to camp I was surprised everywhere by the spaciousness, I might almost have said the magnificence, of these igloos. Their porches were invariably built to contain two good-sized niches, one for the dogs, the other for harness and equipment. In some camps I found again the communal architecture of which I had seen a deserted specimen on the trail—three igloos so built as to open into a central lobby. Each igloo housed two families, one at either side the porch, and was lighted by two seal-oil lamps. I measured them and found they were twelve feet in diameter,—so wide at the axis that the *iglerk*, which in the King William Land igloo fills three quarters of the interior, took up less than half the floor space. The seal-oil lamps, or more properly, vessels, were nearly three feet long. All this luxury was explained by the presence of seal in quantity, whereas round King, seal is, to say the least, not plentiful.

Back of each lamp, on a sort of platform of snow, lay the usual larder of the Eskimo rich in provisions, into which every visitor was free to put his knife and draw forth the chunk of seal or caribou or musk-ox that he preferred.

What was admirable about the architecture of these igloos was that it permitted at one and the same time a private life and a communal life. Each woman was free to trim her lamp and sit quietly over her sewing or scraping of hides, attending in silence to her own concerns; but it was also possible for her to converse with the others across the lobby while she worked, to drop her work and, with the child in its hood at her back, come across to sit with her neighbor; or all of them might, if they wished, collect for a chat in the central lobby.

Thanks to the abundance of seal, these people exhibited to me a powerful and dignified community, a life that might have gone on in an ancient civilization with its matrons, its patriarchs, its forum in which the will of a people expressed itself in common discussion and decision. Each detail of life was here an episode: the waking in the morning and first trimming of the lamps; the feeding of children and men and dogs; the hubbub of departure for the sealing; the chatter of the matrons, and their housekeeping; the return when evening fell amid the barking of the dogs, the swearing of the men, the hauling in of the seals; and finally tea, the women sewing or serving while the men stood waiting for their steaming mugs to cool, snorting, joking, cutting off large chunks of meat, and feeling themselves indeed that which their name implied, *Inuit,* "Men, preeminently." What I was seeing here, few men had seen, and it was now to be seen almost nowhere else—a social existence as in olden days, a degree of prosperity and well-being contrasting markedly with the pseudo-civilized life of the western Eskimo and the pitiful, stunted, whining life of the King William clan with its wretched poverty, its tents made of coal-sacks, its snuffling, lacklustre, and characterless men clad in rags; that life like a dulled and smutted painting with only here and there a gleam to speak of what it had once been.

The generosity and courtesy of their hospitality struck me as forcibly as the grace of their life. Hardly had I come into the igloo before my clothes were taken from me, my boots and socks drawn off my feet and hung to dry on the rack. It was as if my presence honored the igloo, and when my clothes were later handed back to me by a little girl in a gesture whose shyness was charming, I saw that they had not been dried only, but scraped clean and soft as well.

I had not been five minutes on the *iglerk* before I heard gay giggles in the next igloo. Bending forward, I looked in and saw—my own image. They were mimicking me, and it was the wife of Ikshivalitak who, seated on her *iglerk,* was taking me off. There was "Ma-i-ke" himself, me to the life, jerky and nervous in gesture, peremptory in speech, practically giving orders: "I want to trade utensils." "I want," not—as it should have been—"I should like"; and my confusion between the two modes of expression sent them into gales of laughter. The notion that I, a white man, alone in this immense country, their country, should take it upon myself to give them orders ("I want . . .") was to them highly comic. And then, the woman continued in my own pidgin-Eskimo, *"Na-mang-nik-to tap-ko-a"* (This thing is worthless): and off into laughter they went again. The idea that objects which they knew to be precious might be said by me to have no value, was very funny to them.

And the mimicry was done with so much art, with such perfection in reproduction of the intonation of my voice, that I was stupefied. These people had never seen me in their lives until ten minutes before, and then in the hubbub of our arrival; yet they had picked up instantly the characteristic traits—the nervousness, the impatience, the stupid arrogance of the white man who thinks himself master wherever he goes. I had never been parodied like this, with an insight at once so penetrating and so little aggressive. Small wonder that I burst out laughing myself.

I made a humiliating discovery among these people, which was that I did not know their language. On King William Land I thought I knew it, but that was because those Eskimos, in their contact with the white man, spoke pidgin-Eskimo in order that he might understand them. Here pure Eskimo was spoken, and I understood scarcely a word. It was embarrassing. I found myself in an igloo with an old man named Krepingayuk and his wife. He was a gentle old fellow, bearded, and speaking in the high-pitched voice usually affected only by a shaman. This respectable old man, with his pious old face, was said to be twice a murderer—his second killing having been done in order to keep to himself the wife of the man he killed, who had been a shaman. He had simply tipped the late husband into open water and had come back saying that his companion had drowned. Everybody was quite sure what had happened, but as so often in Eskimo occurrences, it had been impossible to get at the truth. His wife—probably as the result of having lived with a shaman—spent hours bowed over the lamp, murmuring to herself in true shaman fashion. They would speak to me, would see that I did not understand, and then a long colloquy would be held between them. Was it possible that a man might not know their language? The old chap would try again, repeating carefully several times his words, and when, again, I let him know that I did not understand, he would smile incredulously.

The igloo was constantly filled with visitors come to see the Kabloona. They would come in one after the other, stay only long enough to examine me closely, and then slip out through the porch in order to take home their impression of me. When the parents hadn't time to spare for this scrutiny, they would send a child, and the child would report my appearance and gestures, from which they would draw their conclusions. I, meanwhile, sat not daring to speak or move, conscious that all the words and gestures of the white man were in their eyes violent, direct, and ludicrous. If only Father Henry had been there!

In the way of nourishment, I had brought with me only tea and biscuits, and these I distributed with the feeling that they hardly constituted the acknowledgment of an honored guest. But my hosts appeared to be delighted, as if the intention were the important thing, not the gift. Constantly, I was asked my name—the question was phrased thus: "Who are you?"—and the name, "Ma-i-ke," was repeated again and again. Women would shake their children half out of the hood and say to them:

"Look! Who is this?"

"Ma-i-ke!" the children would answer promptly; and as they gazed at me with sober faces and unblinking eyes everybody present would laugh with pleasure.

Except for Father Henry, these women and children, and even some of the men, had never seen a Kabloona, and they dealt with me as with a friend. True primitive hospitality consists not merely in welcoming the stranger but in seeking to incorporate him into the community. Their intent is to keep him among them as long as possible, and his slightest indication of appreciation increases their hope that he will stay on with them. They discuss at length precisely where and how he is to be lodged, and what can be done to make his visit pleasant. Once he has distributed his little gifts and brewed them a mug of tea, he has done his part. It now becomes their part to look after him solicitously, to see that he is well fed and comfortably bestowed. And if the stranger speaks of leaving them, he will find that he has offended them.

My first call that day was upon Krarsuvik, an ancient

dame who suffered from a malady common among the
Eskimos—the cataract—but who could nevertheless see me
well enough with her almost disturbingly direct glance. She
sat very stiffly on her *iglerk,* and in the face beneath her
carefully braided grey hair, as in the carriage of her head,
there was an impressive dignity combined with a great
vivacity of spirit. She was obviously a dowager of quality
and character, and I confess that with her brief and em-
phatic manner of speech, and her steady gaze, she intimi-
dated me. Each time she spoke it was apparent that she
spoke both amusingly and to the point, and nods, murmurs,
and laughter greeted every one of her sallies. It was clear
that whether her eyes permitted her to see me well or ill,
she had taken my measure.

I had brought her a pound of tea and had set it down
beside the lamp at her elbow. Her hand went out, picked
up the tea, and she put it away behind her without a word.
You may consider that this was not very courteous of her,
but that is because you do not know their ways. The tea
was held in reserve until her husband returned from his
sealing. Then, when the igloo was filled with guests, she
unwrapped it, and as she put it in the pot she said:

"This must be much better tea than our own, for it is
a gift from the Kabloona."

They go two hundred and fifty miles for their tea—the
length of the road to Gjoa Haven, though not in a straight
line—and in this igloo alone they drink sixty pounds of it
in the course of a winter. Into a pot of cold water they drop
handfuls of tea, which is then heated slowly, never coming
to the boil, over a seal-oil lamp. After two hours the tea is
ready, and the mistress of the igloo fills all the mugs that
stand in rows before her. When the tea has cooled off—for
the Eskimos cannot take any drink hot—each man and

woman picks up a mug of the ink-black liquid and sips it
noisily. The mug empty, they wipe the leaves up with their
fingers and eat them. The teapot is never emptied of its
leaves, but each time a fresh handful of tea is added.

I asked Krarsuvik if she had not old things—*o-to-kak*—
to trade. She had nothing to trade. What this meant was
that my proposal wanted thinking about, for when her husband came in at the end of the day they held a murmured
colloquy with a great air of casualness, after which she
turned back to me, opened a chest, and produced a number
of objects from which, evidently, he had consented to part.

It wants very little time to return to the primitive. Already I had ceased to feel the need of the appurtenances of
our civilization; and yet I had been reared in a fair degree
of comfort, I was rather more than less sensitive than the
average, and I was even, in a manner of speaking, an "intellectual." After a brief few weeks, all this had dropped
away from me. I do not mean that I had stopped yearning
for telephones and motor cars, things I should always be
able to live without. I mean that the thought of a daily
change of linen was gone from my mind; that a joint of
beef would not have made my mouth water, and I loved the
taste of frozen fish, particularly if it had frozen instantane-
ously and retained its pristine savour all through the winter.
As a matter of fact, I do not remember being served anything in France as much to my taste.

Besides, Father Henry was perfectly right: the white
man's diet would never have lent me the power of resistance
needed for this life. Boiled rice warmed you while you ate
it, but its warmth died out of you almost as soon as it was
eaten. Frozen fish worked the other way: you did not feel
its radiation immediately; but twenty minutes later it began

to warm you and it kept you warm for hours. As for raw
meat, with its higher vitamin content, the advantage of
eating it frozen was that you could absorb enormous quantities of it; and after a hard day on the trail there was no end
to what you ate. Even the taste for rotted food came in time,
though I never reached the point of considering it a delicacy.
"In the beginning," Father Henry admitted, "I was like
you; I always chose the freshest piece. But one day I happened upon a bit of *ti-pi,* the high meat, and I said to myself,
'Mm! not bad!' Since then fresh meat has seemed to me
almost tasteless."

Father Henry and I took to each other from the beginning. A seal ice-house brings people together more quickly
than a hotel room, and a good deal more intimately. Conversation in such a place is frank and honest, untrammelled
by the reticences of society.

I said to him one day: "Don't you find this life too hard
for you, living alone like this?"

"Oh, no," he said; "I am really very happy here. My life
is simple, I have no worries, I have everything I need." (He
had nothing at all!) "Only one thing preys on my mind now
and then: it is—what will become of me when I am old?"

He said this with such an air of confessing a secret weakness that my heart swelled with sudden emotion, and I tried
clumsily to comfort him.

"When you are old," I said, "you will go back among
the white men. You will be given a mission at Chesterfield,
or at Churchill."

"No, no, no!" he protested, "not that."

What could I say? I had no right to press the point. But
at that moment I wished with all my heart that every man

who had a warm house and assurance of a comfortable old age might see this lone priest in the Arctic.

Another time I expostulated with him. "You cannot live like this," I said, "devoid of everything. You are not responsible to yourself alone. You have a mission to fulfill, and you must equip yourself for it, must have those things that will ensure your health and well-being so that you may fulfill it properly. Let me take back those foxes of yours"— offerings brought by the natives—"and trade them for you at the Post. I'll send you back the things you need."

He refused categorically. "No, no. I have not the right to dispose of the foxes. They belong to my bishop."

"Never mind your bishop!" I said. "Let me have those five foxes."

But he was unshakable. "No," he said, wagging his head; "impossible!"

"Very well," said I crossly. "You need harness, nets, rope —not for yourself, but for your mission, and I am going to send them to you. You will force me to pay for them out of my own pocket."

Ah, the poor man! I had faced him with a case of conscience, and he was upset. "All right, all right," he agreed. "But it is very bad of you to put me in this position. I'll let you have the foxes."

He didn't, though. When time came for me to leave, his scruples had returned. "I've thought it over," he said, "and I find you are wrong. There is nothing I need."

I had been with him several days when I began to see that something was gnawing at him. Something was on his mind, and he was going round and round in a circle.

"Come," I said, "What is it? You have something on your mind."

It must really have been preying on him for he made no
attempt to evade me.

"Ah, well," he said. "You see for yourself how it is. Here
you are, a layman, enduring these privations, travelling
'tough' "—another locution of the North—"depriving yourself of your only cheese for me. Well, if you do these things,
what should I, a religious, be doing?"

I stared at him. His eyes were hollow, brilliant, strangely
brilliant. A religious, indeed! What a distance that one word
suddenly placed between him and me! This man was animated and kept alive by something other than the power of
nature. Life had in a sense withdrawn from him, and a
thing more subtle, more mysterious, had taken its place. He
was doubly superior to me, by his humility and by his mystical essence as priest. "I am of the most humble extraction,"
he had said to me. He was a Norman peasant, and it came
to me suddenly that if he had chosen to live in this seal-hole
instead of an igloo, his choice had been motivated in part
by the peasant instinct to build his own sort of farmstead,
even here in the Arctic. He took no particular pride from
his origin, nor is it because he referred to it that I speak of
his humility, which was Christian, not worldly. He was a
direct, simple, naked soul dressed only in the seamless garment of his Christianity.

By grace of that garment, his flesh was as if it were not.
When I said, for example, "It is not warm this morning,"
he would answer mechanically, "No, it is not warm"; but
he did not feel the cold. "Cold" was to him merely a word;
and if he stopped up the door, or livened up the lamp, it
was for my sake he did it. He had nothing to do with
"those things," and this struggle was not his struggle: he
was somewhere else, living another life, fighting with other
weapons. He was right and I was wrong in those moments

when I rebelled against his existence and insisted rashly that he "could not live like this." I was stupid not to see, then, that he truly had no need of anything. He lived, he sustained himself, by prayer. Had he been dependent only upon human strength he would have lived in despair, been driven mad. But he called upon other forces, and they preserved him. Incredible as it will seem to the incredulous, when the blizzard was too intense to be borne, he prayed, and the wind dropped. When, one day, he was about to die of hunger—he and the single Eskimo who accompanied him—he prayed; and that night there were two seal in their net. It was childish of me to attempt to win him back to reality: he could not live with reality.

I, the "scientist," was non-existent beside this peasant mystic. He towered over me. My resources were as nothing compared to his, which were inexhaustible. His mystical vestment was shelter enough against hunger, against cold, against every assault of the physical world from which he lived apart. Once again I had been taught that the spirit was immune and irresistible, and matter corruptible and weak. There is something more than cannon in war, and something more than grub and shelter in the existence of this conqueror of the Arctic. If, seeing what I have seen, a man still refused to believe this, he would do better to stay at home, for he had proved himself no traveller.

For three days, sleds had been running between the different camps of the Arviligjuarmiut to arrange in advance for some one to drive me back to King William Land. I had said to Father Henry that I should wait until he found an Eskimo who had an errand at the Post, and that I hoped the man would not be a worthless fellow like Shongili. Father Henry had taken a mental census of the clan, very conscientiously, and then declared that the best man for the job was Ittimangnerk.

This was the start of a series of complicated manœuvres. First, someone had to be sent to Ittimangnerk to let him know that Father Henry wanted to see him. Off went a sled to the camp where he was thought to be.

The sled came back with Ittimangnerk's brother, Manilak. It appeared that Ittimangnerk was far to the north, hunting the seal in the open waters.

With a note from the priest, Manilak started for the north. Either he would bring back his brother, or he would bring an answer from his brother. We should have to wait several days, meanwhile, for Ittimangnerk was sixty miles off. By the time we had his answer there would have been done one hundred and sixty miles of travelling on my account.

Five days later, Manilak came back, bringing with him, written in syllabic Eskimo, a letter from Ittimangnerk so beautiful that I must transcribe it:

"Since the white man has no companion for his journey, I shall go with him. I greet the white man. I go now to hunt seal for the journey. What shall I do? I will be so shy with the white man. Write to me. Encourage me. Ittimangnerk greets the Priest."

We decided as follows. When time came for me to leave, Manilak would fetch me and would drive me as far as a camp situated half way between Pelly Bay and the open water. There I should be met by his brother, and we would proceed together to King William Land. Manilak should have done two hundred miles of trail for me out of pure goodness of heart.

This was the coldest season of the year, when the thermometer was never higher than fifty degrees below zero.

The trail back was bound to be hard, and though I hoped for much from these true Eskimos, I could not look forward to the journey with entire ease of mind.

Father Henry gave me a walrus tusk, and I left him divers little gifts,—among them a half sack of flour, five candles, a knife, a half bottle of rum (from Gibson). Probably he would never make use of any of these things.

As I was about to be driven off he took both my hands. "Your visit has done me a great deal of good," he said. "I believe that I shall be a better man for your having been here." I have wandered pretty much everywhere; nowhere have I heard words more beautiful.

Chapter III

IN FATHER Henry's ice-house I had been a man. Here on the trail I was once again to be an insect, creeping over the face of the northern wastes. Had I been an Eskimo I should have pulled out without a wave of the hand: a white man, though I had choked up at the priest's farewell, and words would not come, I lingered long enough to take both his hands in mine and bob my head by way of leave-taking.

Our sled pulled swiftly out. Looking back, I saw that Father Henry had disappeared without waiting for us to round the point. He vanished; his hill stood bare of life; and in a few minutes the hill itself was as a grain of dust.

This was a different trail from all I had known before. My road to Pelly Bay had been a journey through a mist— the air grey, my being distressed, my mind conscious of reasons for despair. Now everything conspired to procure my happiness. To the affection I felt for Father Henry, the veneration that warmed my heart, there was added the comforting presence of these uncontaminated Eskimos whom I felt to be my friends. I had the impression that all Pelly Bay was thinking of me, wishing me well; and the feeling that a whole people might be concerned for my well-being was exhilarating.

With this went the fact that during my weeks in the ice-
house the sun, without my perceiving it, had returned to
fill the world with light. On the trail out we had had daylight (to call it that) from half past eleven until half past
one in the afternoon. Beginning at half past one, darkness
had flowed over us, and thereafter, for several hours, depend-
ing upon the changing moment of the rising of the moon,
all had been black. Fainter in the first days, brighter as the
moon filled, her rays had lighted our way. Day as well as
night—to speak by the clock and without reference to degrees of visibility—she had always been somewhat visible,
but the help and comfort I had been able to derive from her
had varied with the days, with the state of the weather, and
with the schedule she observed independently of my wishes.

In this season of the year a week made all the difference.
Here was the sun returned and glittering on the sea, transforming it into a wide expanse of smooth pink upon which
the ice-cakes rose, pale green and translucent as we fled between them. With the wheeling of the seasons, the earth
died and was born again. Mercy and Redemption followed
the season of Sin, and the Eskimos were as conscious of the
fresh tenderness as I. We chatted and laughed, ran alongside the sled, filled our pipes from one another's tins, spoke
to the dogs, and felt ourselves regenerated.

We stopped briefly at one camp on the trail, and there I
traded for a few objects, but my store was so low that I
could give nothing in exchange.

"No matter," said these gentle people. "Send us what you
like from King. Ittimangnerk will bring it back with him."

Manilak had brought his wife along and we were three
on this first leg of my journey. We might have stayed in
our places on the sled, the dogs were tough enough; but

to ease their load he and I took turns running alongside. He would run while I sat and smoked, and when he came back it would be my turn to be on my feet.

The temperature was still fifty below, and though we did not feel it in the sun, as evening drew on the cold became piercing. I discovered that if I ran too long at a time, I was seized with violent fits of coughing. Manilak and his wife both began to suffer from nosebleed, a thing common among the Eskimos and likely to be serious. I have known it to go on for several days, and men have died among them as the result of the loss of blood. These two bled for hours and left a stain on the snow behind the gliding sled.

We went on long after dark—without a word from me! —and finally, after we had several times bumped into ice-cakes and been obliged each time to disengage the sled, the wife turned towards me and pronounced the magic word, "Igloo!" Ahead of us was a camp, and we could see through the snow-houses as through frosted glass the glow of the seal-oil lamps; distant and faint as always, but, as always, a sign of friendliness and of life. Almost without transition we slipped into the hospitality of the igloo and were embraced by its sudden warmth, its radiation of the sense of family life, and were sitting shortly amid the laughter and the snortings in a circle round which great pieces of hot seal-meat went clockwise from mouth to mouth.

We stayed here two nights and a day. On the morning following our arrival I watched the men as they prepared to go out sealing after a leisurely meal on waking. The change in tempo from the leisure of their "breakfast" to the speed and agitation of their preparation for the hunt was startling. Just as, in our cities, a downpour of rain suddenly alters the rhythm of civilized man, so here men are precipitated by the cold. They pass abruptly from the inertia of the igloo to the agitation of the hunt, scurrying as if they had not a moment to lose; and while the men are swiftly at work, the women are coming out of the igloos with those things which are always remembered only at the last second. The hunters bend over to lash their sleds, straighten up, look at the wind, scold their dogs, bend down to their work again. Like all nomads, the Eskimos have that particular faculty of being able to collect their belongings in a flash and strike camp at the least sign of danger. This whole community could have been away in an hour, leaving the igloos clean, had the occasion for moving arisen. It is not only that they were habituated to this; everything contributed to it: men, dogs, tackle, utensils—all these formed a single whole that seemed, when the moment came, to collect itself automatically out of a single impulse.

It was here that I met Ittimangnerk. The others played a game with me, hiding him in their midst and asking me to pick him out. And as I pointed successively at several before identifying him, the game was a great success and they roared with delight. What a bad eye the Kabloona had! But they were so friendly in their laughter, so affectionate, I might almost say; their need to play a game was so clearly instinctive that one could not but laugh, too, and play it with them.

That day was perhaps the warmest in human companionship that I have ever spent. When they came home in the evening they surrounded me with a degree of solicitude rare among men.

"Are you not hungry?" one would ask when I stopped eating to draw breath. And another:

"Give him more tea."

"He says the caribou is wonderful," a third would let

the igloo know; and still another would take my pipe from
my mouth and send it round the circle, each man drawing
once on it and expressing in his face the delight with which
he savored so wonderful a smoke as the Kabloona had
furnished him. Could there have been a simpler and more
heart-warming fashion of saying, "You are one of us?"

Next day I was away with Ittimangnerk, his wife, and
six frozen seal laid in a row on the sled. Before leaving,
Ittimangnerk made himself a vessel to hold seal-oil. He cut
out a block of ice, trimmed and shaped it to the desired
form, and stretched a sealskin over it. In ten minutes he had
a receptacle so rigid and resistant that he was able to bore
holes at opposite sides and fix handles to it.

When we made camp that night I saw again the difference
between these Eskimos and those of King William Land.
Once the igloo had been built they sat motionless, side by
side, their hands folded under their chins in the characteristic attitude. Their shyness was so great that they dared
touch nothing. There was no pillage here. They would not
have permitted themselves to open anything that was mine.
Husband and wife sat still. From time to time each sent
the other a glance, and a gust of stifled laughter would
come out of them, as from well-behaved children about to
be served their favorite delicacy. The Kabloona was going
to give them things, but they would receive them as gifts,
not as things due them and to be demanded if the giving
were delayed. And such was their modesty that they never
made the first gesture but waited for me to give the signal.
Almost they embarrassed me; and their concern lest they
disturb me was so great that I seemed to myself a chaperon
taking a pair of lovers on their honeymoon.

Through the smoke in the igloo I watched Ittimangnerk's

wife one day as she did her hair. Like women everywhere
in such a moment, this concern absorbed her totally; she
was alone with her femininity in a world of her own, and
I might have been looking at her through glass, so little was
she concerned over my presence. She was very pretty, and
unlike most Eskimo women was refined of feature and
graceful and vivacious in gesture and expression. Her words
were few, but her secret and mischievous eyes were eloquent,
and each time that she glanced at her husband a particularly
soft and vivid gleam came into them.

I sat beside her and took pleasure from her pose and movement. She would tilt her head slightly downward and turn it
to the side, and her bright eyes would follow the comb as it
moved slowly and lovingly through the hair which, longer
than that of most Eskimo women, hung nearly down to her
waist. Looking at her, I became aware that I had lost the
white man's canon of female beauty, and that unknown to
myself these women had become attractive in my eyes. They
are not pretty in our sense of the word, but they have a charm
peculiar to themselves. Sitting with bent heads over their
work before the seal-oil lamp, outlined against its glow, they
seem to be meditating secret plans. There is something impalpable in the women of primitive societies, some spring
or power which they never reveal, a rumination upon the
life of their family or clan which determines to what use
they will put their power; and it is always they who prompt
the decisions of their men and enjoy their triumphs in secret.
I am not sure that I do not prefer this to the shrill intervention of women in affairs in our civilized communities.

More and more as I lived with these people I found that
I was changing, was adapting myself to their way of life.
I had ceased to be critical of it, had accepted it. From talk-
ative, for example, I had become laconic; and if you think

of it, how many unnecessary words we pronounce in our
society! Language, I began to believe, was made for the idle;
and we on the trail were never idle. Three people journeying
over the ice form a tacit community. Each plays his part,
does his job, as well as he can, and does it in silence. So it
was with us, and the understanding between us was perfect.
As soon as we saw a hill ahead, without a word all three
sprang down and pushed the sled. Whether it was to ice the
runners, to disentangle the harness, or to make tea, our
movements were coordinated; the result was an unforget-
table impression of harmony and serenity. And once the
work was done we would roll cigarettes out of our common
tin while a smile as of connivance flashed between us.

Each night the igloo went up in no time at all. Working
outside with her native shovel, the wife would tamp the
snow into a fine powder and cover the whole house with
it, so that the chinks were solidly filled. The husband would
chain the dogs in place after he had built our shelter. Indoors, as busy as an old housewife, I would bestir myself.
Comfort in the igloo is a matter of organization. Everything must be within reach, once you have seated yourself
on the *iglerk,* and each object must be present in its appointed place. The matches are here, the "drinking snow"
there, and without stirring, merely by putting out your arm,
you should be able to boil water, reach the tobacco tin,
change the position of garments hanging on the drying rack
above the lamp. I had by now become so oldmaidenly that
nothing in the world could have persuaded me (O, Gibson!) to alter the disposition of these objects. I had become
the bourgeois of the igloo—and it is a fact that one may be
a bourgeois here as easily as in Angers. I had grown as
maniacal as a Paris concierge, except that here the snow-
knife took the place of the broom and our floor was the

frozen sea. Once everything was in shape, I took my seat in the middle of the *iglerk* with the identical smug satisfaction of a concierge in her lodge, her latch-string on her right, stove on her left, and cat on her knees. And, like her, I listened to the droning of the water in the kettle while my candle stood alight on the sugar-box.

This was comfort! On the other hand, once you were asleep everything changed. In the course of preparation, what with the lighted lamp and the heat generated by activity and your native supper, the igloo had warmed up considerably and it was no hardship to strip off a few clothes and slip into your sleeping-bag. But when the lamp was out, the temperature dropped. Gone was all the cosiness of the concierge's lodge. We would lie in our bags like corpses while the Arctic spread over us its mantle of ice and in our sleep we moaned like children. I was not yet an Eskimo, and sleep continued to elude me. My bag would crack as I stirred, for it was a block of ice. Ice filled my hair, and it covered my face for the reason that my breath froze the instant it left my lips. And when, in despair, I let myself all the way down into the sleeping-bag, I stifled and had to come up again for air.

It was like this night after night, and when you awoke in the morning the igloo was filled with a grey mist through which it was hard to see. You were a long time making up your mind to stir. The evening before, everything had been so disposed as to demand the least effort from you; in the morning, even to bring up your arm out of the bag and get the Primus stove going was torture.

And you could not shave. It is extraordinary how much worse this made everything. "There are days," Father Henry had said to me, "when I am so covered in ice that I cannot speak." It was the same with me, though I could show no

luxuriance of beard. But as the hair grew out on cheeks and
chin and lip, the ice would accumulate on it, and this ac-
cumulation was burdensome, was actually heavy. It had to
be removed. Had I been able to take off my mitts, I might
have melted it away in my hands; but that was impossible.
So I would tug at it; my face would bleed; the blood would
freeze; and between frozen blood and dark patches of frost-
bite on nose and cheeks, I was no beauty. Sometimes I
would think, as I ran beside the sled, that I must look like
a chandelier in movement. I would laugh; the act of laughing would tear at the ice and send sharp pains over my face;
and I would stop.

I was cold, freezing cold, but I never shivered. Cold in
the Arctic is not like cold at home. It is not in you, but
round you. There is no humidity in this country, which is
the driest in the world, with no more than fifteen inches
of precipitation, ordinarily, in a year. You wander through
this cold dry as a bone.

We crossed the mountain range and came out into the
long lake, forcing our dogs, building our igloos as late as we
could and starting out as early as possible in our haste—
in my haste, of course—to make King. One by one I saw
again the igloos which Shongili had built for me on the
journey out, and to see them again filled me with a curious
sensation. Each of these little heaps of snow had contained
a part of my life, I would think with a jolt of recognition;
and instantly indifference would follow this thought as we
ran on.

On the fifth night of travel we spied the beacon that
marked Algunerk's camp at the bend in the river. I saw it
first, and pointed it out to my companions. Already the dogs
had seen us and signalled our coming, and the family were

out of doors. They greeted us warmly when we drove up, unharnessed the dogs for us, and in a moment we were through the porch.

That night I ate the biggest meal I have ever eaten. I was hungry, I was exhausted, the cold was as severe as ever, and I had taken almost no food since leaving the Arviligjuarmiut camp. Algunerk was already hacking away at a seal when we straightened up in the igloo. The seal had been dragged into the middle of the igloo by a rope run through its nose. Then Algunerk's axe had been thawed out, for otherwise it would not have cut. Now he was going at the seal like a woodman chopping down a tree. We were too hungry to wait until he had finished, and we grabbed at the chips as they flew through the air and swallowed them where we stood.

We ate for twenty hours. What a farce the white man's table is! Whole quarters of seal were swallowed, snow and all; and the snow grated between our teeth as we bit into the meat. This cold dish finished, we began on the next course. I had contributed half a sack of rice, which was boiled with ten or twelve pounds of caribou meat; and while we chewed seal blubber from one hand, we dipped the other into the steaming vessel of caribou and rice.

Next morning we had hardly awoken before the feast continued. Frozen fish was our first delicacy, even before the tea was brewed; and the fish was followed by seal. This time it was one of Ittimangnerk's seals that went; and we were still in our sleeping-bags as we chewed it. The turn of the dogs would come later, and what we had eaten, they would eat. Ittimangnerk, who was well bred, had begun by cutting away the choicest morsels of seal and passing them to his host, and Algunerk had put them aside without a word.

Between meals, as it were, we ate *peep-se,* dried fish. It tasted as if smoked and made an excellent appetizer. Innumerable mugs of black tea were drunk, and then, our appetite returning, we stripped off long slices of lake fish and passed them round, each taking his bite, cutting the rest off with his knife close to the lips, and handing on what remained. A fish would go round so swiftly that I could scarcely swallow fast enough. I had to pass my turn twice, which made them laugh. There was a little boy of six years, and he was brought into the circle: it would teach him to be a man.

How I understood Ka-i-o! How clear it was that if I had tried, in this land, to subsist upon white man's grub, I should long ago have frozen to death!

We smoked. The pipe went round from mouth to mouth, and nothing seemed more natural than this denial of the notion of "mine and thine." I was sure that *meum et tuum* must have been a theory invented after the fact by the first man who conceived that he no longer had any need of his neighbor. We Eskimos—so to say—were a community. It was not precisely that everything here was owned in common, for it was not; it was better than that. It was, if I may say so, Christian. Each member of the community was concerned to see that all the others were provided for; and if there was a feast, and one member was not present, he was sent for, or his share was put aside for him in that corner of the igloo called—in the English of the North—"the Big Feed." I had learnt by now that it was best never to consider my grub exclusively my own. If the white man wanted to contribute to the community, there was but one way to do so, and that was to turn over all that he had brought, the first day. Thereafter he would be fed without a word as long as he remained among the Eskimos. Thus went the hospitality of the *Inuit*.

Algunerk had insisted upon doing things properly. He had offered us all the meat in his igloo, and he had used up all the coal-oil he possessed. And when the tin was empty, with what a grin of joy he flung it with all his strength across the igloo!

Now it was the dogs' turn. Ittimangnerk chopped up a seal for them. Unblocking the porch, he let them in by twos, and they flung themselves like wild beasts, like a bull springing forth into the arena, upon this meat. These were not animals, this was hunger itself that made its violent irruption among us. Their hunger was so great that they could hardly eat, and we tried in vain to calm the brutes. Scarcely had they snapped up one piece than another seemed to them better, and they circled furiously among the chunks of seal on the ground. The dogs did not chew; they gulped. These were to our dogs what the Eskimo is to us who live Outside.

Evening came. Three of Ittimangnerk's seals were still whole, standing against the wall like gods about to be overthrown, but gods still, blood-covered and fantastic. The ice glittered in the light of the lamp, and heat and cold dwelt here together in their familiar contrast. I shall never cease to chant the beauty of the seal-oil lamp; and here again I asked myself, How can a length of cotton wick, fashioned into a saw-toothed strip and floating on melted blubber, spread such an astonishing measure of friendliness and companionship? From this glow there emanates the warmth and the security that constitute the true and inner meaning of the word home. Here among these shadows, in these mysterious recesses, the almost incomprehensible Eskimos eat and laugh, live a material existence of inconceivable brutality and at the same time a spiritual life of infinite subtlety, full of shades and gradations, of things sensed and unexpressed.

I had stopped counting the passing days. Gipsies of the North, we were wanderers moving from place to place, all our wealth upon our backs and our sleds, savoring the strange taste of "this continual passing and this continual perishing." The time had come to go on, and at eight in the morning I was shoving my packing case through the porch when I saw Algunerk preparing his. I had asked him the day before if he meant to go with us, and he had answered no. Now both he and his father-in-law were making ready. One should never ask questions, and never, as Roman Horace was not the first to remark, be astonished at anything.

We crossed the sea, this time in a straight line instead of following the curving coast. It amused me to see how much faster Algunerk and Shongili travelled to reach the Post than when coming away from it. Just at sunset, one evening, I spied land and sang out, *"Nu-ana!"* On the instant everything stopped: the dogs themselves pricked up their ears, and we stood on our sleds and stared long at the welcome sight. But the land was still too far away for us to make it that night, and we sought a place to camp. Finally we found an ice-crack on the edge of which there was snow enough for our purpose, and we raised the igloo. *Nu-ana!* The word is rich and fertile in sound, like the earth itself.

It made my heart swell. I had need of it, and after the hardship of the trail I was filled with warmth and tenderness. *Nu-ana!* What dreams I could have dreamt had I not been so cold!

Next morning the weather had changed and the shore was invisible. We tramped for four hours, the dogs pulling on the harness against a head-wind as if they knew what was in our minds. From moment to moment we expected land to re-appear, but there was no sight of it. Was this another of the Arctic's practical jokes? Or had we wandered too far to the north and missed the coast altogether? Algunerk was leading us, and I had said twice to Ittimangnerk that *Ot-cho-ķto,* the Post, was on our left; but he assured me that Algunerk was right. No Eskimo would say that another Eskimo was mistaken.

The sun began to sink, evening fell, and of a sudden the wind dropped, the air cleared, and land was again in sight. We stopped.

"*Ot-cho-ķto?*" I asked Algunerk.

"*Ot-cho-ķto,*" he replied laconically. What we saw, he went on to explain, was an island that lay just off Gjoa Haven.

We pushed on with the emotion of sailors home from the sea. Now the land was plainly visible, and we looked at it again. Alas, it was Point Mathiesen. We were fifteen miles to the north of our route!

The heart went out of me. I was not an Eskimo, I was a Kabloona. My mind might tell me that I preferred their life to the grubbing rapacity of the tradesmen at home, to the spate of idle words that flowed over a cocktail party among my kind. My nature might go out instinctively to their simplicity, their communal existence, the friendly glow of the lamp and the fraternal calm of the igloo. I was none the less a white man in my physical being, in my lack of training and insufficiency of endurance for this life. Another night in an igloo was something I could not contemplate.

My distress must have showed itself in my face, for they stared at me a moment and then asked if I would mind reaching the Post in the middle of the night.

"We can make it to-night," they assured me. And I said: "No matter at what hour! Let's be off!"

A long line of land was still visible far on the left, but it was very far, the sun was sinking fast, and there was not a minute to lose. I took it for granted that we should start on the instant; but they were Eskimos. Algunerk went calmly about the business of disengaging the dogs' traces. Then the three men lighted their pipes and began a detailed discussion of the respective qualities of their dogs, of a bitch that had particular reason to be restless; and from this they went on to a great deal of joking. I, meanwhile, tramped to and fro, which seeing, Algunerk came over to me after a time and said with a smile:

"Do you think we might go on now?"

We whipped up the dogs just as night fell.

I had been dragging one leg all the way back from Pelly Bay, and that leg had suddenly failed me—probably because my morale was low. In any case, I sat on the sled that night, once again a white man, once again viewing the Arctic as my personal enemy. The wind blew, and there was no shielding my nose from it, however I turned and twisted on the sled. As for the shore line, I wanted no longer to look at it, for each time I looked it seemed farther away.

The sun went down and the world became again that grey cotton-wool in which you float without being able to see your own feet. The grating of the runners on the ice was the only indication that we were on the march.

After the half-light, total darkness, accompanied by the usual despair of ever arriving. But I did see, suddenly, land on my left and knew it was Fram Point, which is to say Gjoa Haven. At that moment Ittimangnerk pronounced the word, "Igloo," and I saw the lights of the Post. Where, suddenly, was my fatigue? What a weakling I had been to collapse like that!

We entered the mouth of the bay, stopped at the foot of the ridge, and found ourselves lighted by an electric torch. Was this Gibson? No, it was Utak's brother. All together, we pushed the sled up the rise and it fell as if dead tired into a hole in the snow near the Store. I ran to the Post and was welcomed home by the comfortable and impassive Gibson.

"Hello! Here you are again," was his greeting.

If only he had known what it meant to be here again! I let myself sink into a chair and rejoiced in the warmth of the room. Like an Eskimo, I muttered again and again, "*Unak-to-alu,*"—"It is warm, it is warm. I shall eat to-night," I said to myself. "And I shall take off all my clothes." It was thirty-five days since I had last washed my face and taken off all my clothes.

Next morning I was still tottering. I got up and lit the stove. My head was heavy, I was incapable of forming sentences, and I sat staring round the room. No *Inuk,* no "man preeminently" I! Cups. An alarm clock. A wash-basin. Impossible. I was emerging from a dream. And what did I look like amid all these familiar objects? I went over to a looking-glass. I was horrible: greasy hair stuck to my forehead; a month's growth of hair on the face; wrinkles that were corrugations. The eyes wild and haggard, the cheeks spotted with brown patches of frost-bite. My nose was shapeless

and peeling. I sank back into the armchair, murmuring to
myself that this was all in the past, I should come to life
again after a few days. Meanwhile it was wonderful to sit in
a chair and do nothing, think nothing at all.

It was hard for me to sleep. The thermometer indoors
stood at freezing, at thirty-two above, and I was stifled by
the heat. I who had never coughed on the trail began now
to cough like an old man. I was ravenous, and when I went
to bed I took food with me. But I was too weary to eat. My
stomach was as if dammed across, and after the second
mouthful I could not go on. Yet a moment later I was
hungry again. Dead with fatigue I was, and so I was to
remain for several days.

Part Four
The Trail Back

Chapter I

To LIVE dependent upon the Eskimos was to live from day to day, suspended in uncertainty. I had arranged with Kernek—he who had failed to carry out my mail—to be taken south from King William Land and then westward along the shore of the Glacial Ocean to the Hudson's Bay post at Perry River. It was early March, and we were still in a season when travelling was governed by the moon. Thus it had been possible to fix a date for my departure; and to make doubly certain I had drawn for Kernek and given him a calendar of the successive phases of the moon from which he might know exactly when to return to Gjoa Haven to fetch me. He had not returned—there are so many things that can intervene to change an Eskimo's plans!—and after waiting three weeks I sent for Utak who, with a Perry River native called Peruanna, agreed to take me out.

We left on a day of radiant sunshine, the frozen waters luminous as far as the eye could see and the atmosphere so still and serene that it seemed to be happiness itself I was leaving behind. The Post at Gjoa Haven that once had closed round me like a prison was now in my eyes an asylum of peace; and Paddy Gibson, that innocent object of my unhealthy wrath, standing now on a knoll with his arm raised in a sign of farewell, lives on in my mind as the symbol and substance of true hospitality.

The dogs were on their feet, we were pulling out, when I saw of a sudden Utak's mother, Niakognaluk, coming down the slope from her igloo. I have said already that the Eskimo parts from friend and family without a word of adieu, without a wave of the hand. The old woman, whom I had first seen so many months before as she sat with her dog scraping skins in the light of her lamp, came up to me, put out her hand in a brusque movement, and turned instantly away to be off with bowed back to her igloo. Peace to thy ashes, Niakognaluk!

The first day out we ran into a blizzard, and I was lucky in the company of Peruanna. Swifter than Shongili, he was no less thorough in his building of an igloo, and he knew well enough that the snowhouse might have to shelter us for some days against this storm. Once the igloo was up, he ran round and round outside, patting down the snow into the chinks with his hand so that it would freeze hard and keep out the wind. Then we stretched our sled-cover over the igloo and placed great blocks of snow at its corners to hold it down. But the wind howled all night, the sled-cover was blown loose, and it flapped and snapped without ceasing in the night-long gale. Next morning we moved aside the snow block that filled the entry and saw the storm pass before the porch where the dogs slept buried in the snow. The wind drove us back into our lair and we sealed ourselves up again as quickly as we could. During this minute or two of investigation, the igloo had filled with a fine powder.

We spent the day in our clothes, hoping from moment to moment that the wind might die. My Eskimos dozed, their arms across their chests, sleeves hanging empty,

NIAKOGNALUK

folded forward over the *iglerk* like a pair of puppets. Storm meant to them shelter; time meant nothing to them; their minds were at rest, and they slept the sleep of the unworried. I tried to do as they did, but for a long time my mind stayed awake, and the best I could achieve was to squat by a sack and hope we should not be too long.

An afternoon in an igloo during a blizzard is another element in Eskimo life the quality of which is hard to convey. It is timeless. It is colorless. The mind is void of all thought and image. A man cannot say if he is hot or cold. Is it three hours or is it twenty minutes that we have sat like this? There is no telling.

I waited, and as I waited I found myself not only thinking and feeling nothing, but actually without a mood, a state of mind. To this point, at least, I had become an Eskimo. Like them, like their dogs, I could no longer fret about time or weather. Did it matter, after all, whether I slept here or somewhere else? What was one day among all the days of a lifetime?

As I crouched with these two on the *iglerk* one of them came up out of the simulacrum of death, the seeming annihilation, that is their slumber. The other awoke at the same moment. They mumbled something, and then Peruanna took off his caribou mitts, picked up his snow-knife, and, cautiously, like a burglar piercing a safe, he cut out a small hole in the wall of the igloo. A blast of snow blew in. The man started back slightly and sat staring without a word. What he saw was not favorable, for after a moment he murmured a verdict, picked up a lump of snow, and stopped up the hole. The igloo fell back into torpor for a time impossible to measure.

It was five in the evening when they decided again to remove the block from the entry, for the dogs had to be fed.

Hardly had the block been lifted away when the snow whirled in, filling the air. They pulled the block across behind them, leaving me alone inside. I sat listening, and I could hear them wake the dogs with swift kicks, fling them their food, and swear as they cut fresh snow blocks and built a screen in front of the porch to ward off what might come in the night. Hardly was their rampart raised when the wind piled a great drift of snow against it, and over that drift I heard the smack and whistle of the angry air. They had re-set the sled-cover, but once again it was loose and flapping. I jerked myself out of my lethargy and began to brew tea against their return. They came in covered with snow—this was only the second heavy fall of the season, and there might not be another, so rare is a heavy snowfall in the Arctic. Beating their outer coats, panting with the effort and the cold, they stood in the center of a cloud of snow that came out of each *kuliktak* like dust out of an old carpet. Then we ate.

Next day the storm was over, we were again on the trail, and except in my notebooks the episode was forgotten.

We were on our way to a seal camp, and on the trail we picked up a young Hudson's Bay apprentice named L. The sight of him gave me, better than anything else could have done, a true notion of the distance I had come.

You would expect that two white men meeting in the Arctic, in mid-trail, would fall on each other's necks. But I was no longer a white man. When that young man hurried forward to greet me, I stood, to my own amazement, stock still, almost with an Eskimo's prudence and timorousness; and what was worse, as soon as we had exchanged greetings, I turned back to Utak and Peruanna. They had grown closer to me than my own kind. When we moved on—there were now three sleds, all bound in the same direction—I left L. to himself and ran beside my companions, joking and chatting with them, one of themselves. I had a great many things to say to my Eskimos, and they to me: neither of us had anything to say to L., the Kabloona. What L. said to me did not somehow reach me; it hardly struck my ear, and what I could understand of it seemed to me inconsequent, absurd. But Utak and Peruanna—even when there were no words, we understood one another, our thoughts were simultaneously of the same things, of the dogs, the load, the trail; and in the presence of that stranger, the white man, we continued to live our life from which he was excluded.

The difference between him and me was particularly striking when night fell. Utak built an igloo for the five of us which seemed to L. so tiny that he gasped. One's first igloo always looks like that—too small to hold the travellers.

"It's ridiculous!" said L. to me. "Tell him we can't all sleep in that."

But you cannot tell an Eskimo anything, especially not when you are travelling with his sled and his dogs. Besides, I knew Utak. One word, and he would flare up. I tried to explain to L. but it was Greek to him. He knew nothing of igloo life. He was like a man newly flung up on a desert island. And thanks to him, it came to me suddenly that merely to spend a night in an igloo involves a hundred details which I, unknown to myself, had learnt one by one. There is the snow to be tamped into powder with the Eskimo shovel and flung in a certain way—exactly as our masters the Eskimos insist—over the igloo. There is the building of the *iglerk* and the precise and most efficient fashion of settling oneself on it. There is the trick of beating the snow off one's clothes without covering the *iglerk* with snow,—for if you do this badly, you have to take all the hides off the *iglerk* and beat the snow off them, one by one, before you put them back. There is the fine art of arranging all your things in such a way that every one is within reach as you lie on the *iglerk*. Finally and above all, there is the rhythm of igloo life as commanded by the *Inuit* and ordained by them once and for always with rigorous precision. This is the order of installation:

Build the igloo.

Patch and shovel it outside.

Bring in everything you are going to need.

Bury the rest in the snow.

Build the *iglerk* and cover it with hides.

Place everything within reach on the *iglerk*.

Start the Primus or seal-oil lamp.

First mug of tea. (You are still wearing your *kuliktak*, for there is still work to be done out of doors.)

Bring in blocks of snow for drinking purposes, and a block for the entry.

Go out and feed the dogs.

Come in and beat your clothes with the snow-beater.

Tea, this time without your *kuliktak*.

Prepare the meal.

Smoke a cigarette.

Eat your meat (either frozen or boiled).

Tea.

Smoke.

Spread your sleeping-bag and begin to take off your clothes.

Hang up your clothes on the drying-rack.

Last mug of tea before going to sleep.

Make sure that Primus stove, needles for stove, and matches are within reach against your awakening.

Last cigarette.

Last conversation, once you are in the sleeping-bag.
Sleep.

If you know this order of things, igloo life is simple and
goes on without a hitch. But if you do not know it, everything goes wrong; you are late; you scramble; you cannot
find what you are looking for; the others are already in their
sleeping-bags and you have not even been able to find time
to eat.

Poor L. was lost. He was a landlubber on a ship, a dead
weight, in everybody's way. Not only was he no help, he was
a hindrance because he had no notion what to do and would
have done better to do nothing. In a space so small, every
false move creates trouble for some one else. But, like the
Ma-i-ke of last autumn, there was another thing wrong, and
that was that he thought only of himself. Watching him I
discovered once again that Eskimo life strips a man of ego-
ism. L. was a white man, therefore an egoist. "My tea . . .
my tin . . . my sleep." But no, Mr. L.! *Our* tea, *our* tin, *our*
sleep. Human life in the Arctic would vanish without this
solidarity among men. It is the community that remains
alive here, not the men; it is the community that has had a
poor hunting season or a good one, that is hungry or well-
fed, that has reason to rejoice or to despair.

And so I watched L. pass through those first phases of disgust and distress through which I had some months before
passed myself. But there was nothing I could do to help him.
There are no words, there are no ideas, that can convey to
the white man how one goes about living with the Eskimos.
You who sit reading these pages will say to yourselves that
this cannot be. Have I not, in this very book, "taught" you
what is necessary? But no, I have not taught you anything:
I have merely told you what I went through. One cannot be
taught in words to live with a people 20,000 years behind

one's own point of evolution. Here is an art that cannot be learnt by correspondence, like bridge or needle-point. And even on the ground, the "lessons" would be received with incredulity.

When an L.—myself some months back—sees his first igloo go up, he says to himself: "This is dreadful. It will never hold us all. Why can't they make it bigger?" Perhaps, if there is no blizzard, they can make it bigger. But they won't. And you are living with them, not they with you, so you must learn to submit. When L. is on the trail, hunger seizes him and he says to himself: "What a whopping meal I shall eat to-night!" That night he hasn't drunk three mugs of tea—preliminary to the meal—before his hunger has gone. Fatigue has conquered appetite. He is too weary to feel the desire for anything, and he sits morosely on the *iglerk* while the others attack their seal or caribou. And if he could eat anything at all, would it be seal or caribou in these early weeks? Decidedly not. Not good enough for him! Meanwhile, the Eskimos sit in a circle and eat, and they murmur to one another as they eat. What they are saying, L. does not understand; but they seem to be talking about him; he seems to be the object of their mockery. Midnight comes. He is sick at heart. They turn to him and say, *"Tee-mik!"*—"I want tea;" for it is the rule to drink a final mug before turning in. And our green Kabloona will have learnt just enough to put up a brave front (since a single scowl will assure him a wretched life for the rest of his stay among the Eskimos). He will re-light his Primus stove, serve the gentlemen their tea, pass them sugar and tobacco, and will say to himself meanwhile in despair: "So this is what I have come here for: to wait upon the *Inuit*." He will slip fully clothed into his sleeping-bag—halfway into it—and will be unable to go to sleep, while all night long the *korvik* (chamber-pot) circulates under his nose to raise his fallen spirits.

On this as on other trails we stopped fairly often. A leisurely cigarette made the going easier. Now and then the runners had to be re-iced,—which meant that the sled was unloaded and loaded again; and that took time. One of the sleds in our caravan might have been held up while its driver went after a bird, and it was only just that we wait for him. And tea! There was always a fitting moment to stop, turn an empty packing case on its side, and brew a pot of tea within its shelter. Now and then it even happened that we did not know quite where we were, and the route had to be discussed by the several drivers.

Poor L.! It was too soon for him to be habituated to the rhythm of Eskimo life, and he was desperate.

"We'll never get anywhere at this rate! To hell with this tea business. I don't want tea, do you?"

He would fume and stamp, of course to no avail.

I would say to him: "It's true you don't want tea. But they do. And whenever an Eskimo turns to you and says, 'Perhaps you would like to stop and make tea?' you had better smile and say that you were about to suggest the same thing. For what his question meant was: 'I am going to stop and make tea.'"

I am sure that L. was not convinced; but I am equally sure that he learnt in time that I was not making fun of him. I tried to tell him that the more one entered into the mood of the Eskimos, and shared their view of a situation, the better humor that put them in, and then there was nothing they would not do for one; and they can be confoundedly helpful when they want to be. The contrary was equally true, I said; and if you resisted them, or were not shrewd enough to play their game according to their rules, they had a thousand ways of making you pay for your stubbornness.

We were still on the lookout for our seal camp. From time to time the man on the leading sled would stand up on his load and try to see it; but a few igloos in this flat immensity were almost impossible to see, and already we had missed a first camp by a mere half-mile. (I thought of Father Delalande, with whom I had stayed at Coppermine. "You want to see this country?" he said to me one day. "Get up on a chair and look round. It's as flat as that and you'll see all of it at a glance.")

Evening was coming down and still we went on through the grey air, wandering to left and right but moving instinctively in a given direction nevertheless. A moment came when the sleds stopped. Men went on ahead and spoke to the dogs. The dogs were tilting their heads, pointing their ears in this direction and that, and the men watched them as if of a sudden a husky might trot straight into the camp we were seeking. Nothing came of all this and we made igloo . . . only to discover next morning that the seal camp was near by.

I do not mean that next morning we saw it immediately. We had to look for sled tracks; and we found first one and then a second, which meant we were on the right road. The dogs were whipped up, and the bitch leading the first team trotted with her nose to the snow, for she knew now where she was bound. In another hour the men sang out that the camp was in sight. I strained and strained, and saw nothing until one of the Eskimos pointed with his whip; and rather against my will I agreed that I saw what he saw. Soon what he saw became for me something as big as a pin-head; in a quarter hour the pin-heads were fly-specks; and in the end I could see that the fly-specks were in truth a camp.

Within sight of the camp we stopped. Nothing stirred.

"What now?" L. asked with a worried look.

"I don't know. We are waiting. If the Eskimos say nothing, then it's no good asking. We shall have to wait with them."

"But what do you think? Is anything the matter?"

"I don't believe so. Probably a different clan, and our people are cautious."

Eventually a child ran out of an igloo, and a man emerged and came up to us. He shook hands all round, and then, as if this had been a signal, the whole camp came alive.

These greetings are sometimes very strange. Men will come up and shake your hand courteously, then turn away and go back without a word to you. You don't know what you should do, where to chain up your dogs, where you are expected to sleep. At other times, you have hardly stopped before you are taken in hand by your hosts and almost literally carried in the arms of these men of good will. They do everything for you—push your sled up a rise; unharness your dogs; help you with your load. It all depends; and I never knew upon what.

Here we were apparently to do everything ourselves, for although we had waited to be guided and helped, no one raised a hand. We freed the dogs from their harness, dug holes in the snow where we might anchor them at a respectful distance from our hosts' huskies, and unpacked our sleds. Up to that point the sealers had merely stood by looking on. Then a cautious beginning was made in the way of conversation (two Eskimos strange to each other are warier than a pair of cats), and after ten minutes everything seemed to be settled. L. and I were to sleep in the igloo of one Paniyuyak.

Next day L. was off to his post, leaving me as indifferent to his absence as I had been to his presence.

Now something happened which would once have upset me and no longer had the power to do so. Utak decided that he would like to go back to King. I let him go without a word. Peruanna, next, became restless: he was in a hurry to reach Perry River. I knew better than to try to persuade him to stay; and as I was bound I would attend a seal-hunt, I simply arranged with another Eskimo, Ohohunuak, to re-place both my guides, and stayed on. The day they left, I went out with the natives to hunt the seal.

This camp had been a glum place on our arrival. For two days no seal had been caught; and to return empty-handed at night, when the women and children were waiting for you to bring them something to eat, was disheartening. I had told the Eskimos with a smile the night before that their luck was about to change. "You will see," I said. "To-morrow there will be fresh seal-meat for all. I have made a prayer to Nuliayuk." Their heads had come up with a jerk, and they had stared long at the Kabloona. How did the white man know about the Spirit of the Waters, she who shep-herds the seal in the recesses of the sea? Nobody spoke, and as we left next day I trembled for myself. If no seal rose, the fault would be mine, for the Eskimos are superstitious. My little joke seemed now to me serious, and on the way out over the sea, I prayed with real fervor that a seal would rise.

We reached the hunting ground. The dogs were unhar-nessed and chained up to the anchor fixed in the ice, and tea was made. Then the Eskimos spread fanwise over the sea, each with two specially trained dogs on a thirty-foot lead, and, slung across his chest, a sack containing his tackle. I ac-companied one of the hunters and saw the rest dwindle into black dots in the limitless distance. We walked the dogs up into the wind, and soon they began to pull and trot, for they knew that the chase had started. First they ran like pointers, then after a bit they stopped and started off again more slowly and cautiously, nose to the snow. Suddenly they stood quivering in their tracks and sniffing the ground. They had located the *aglu,* the seal's breathing-hole. We could not see it, for it did not pierce through the snow; but the dogs could smell it. When it was a bull-seal's hole, even the men could smell it, once the dogs had led them there.

Every seal keeps a number of holes open in the ice through which to breathe. While the ice is forming over the sea, the seal bobs up and plunges down and bobs up for air again so frequently that the sea freezes very thinly between his visits to the hole, and his body can easily break through the thin sheet of ice. All round the hole, the ice is six or eight feet deep. Above it, over the sheet of ice, snow collects and hides the hole from the passing Eskimo. What is curious also is that the seal comes up to sit on the ice, beneath the surface of the snow, at either side the hole; and here in spring the cow-seal bears her young. A sort of arch of snow is thus formed, and at either end of the arch the seal takes his ease, like a tramp under a bridge.

Our dogs went round and round, sniffing, and that they had truly found the seal-hole was confirmed by my Eskimo after a bit of gentle prodding with the handle of his harpoon. As I stood by watching, I saw him go suddenly down on his knees. He brought out of his sack a feeler, curved in such a fashion that by making only one hole in the snow, and moving the feeler round in a circle, he could tell just how large the hole was and where its center was. What he found seemed to satisfy him, for he stood up with a grunt and led his dogs about a hundred yards down-wind, where if they chanced to bark they would not be heard by the seal

—an animal practically blind but very acute of hearing. He was down-wind and the seal-hole had not yet been opened when he called out across the sea:

"*Nik-pa-rar-tun-ga!*"—"I have found the hole."

His face, as he came back to the hole, was wonderful in the concentrated purpose it expressed, the sober concern with his craft that it revealed.

Now he produced from his sack a marker of the length and shape of a long knitting needle, and sent it straight through the snow into the water that filled the seal-hole. The seal would displace the water as he rose, and with the water the marker would rise. When the marker sank, the hunter would know that the water was back in place and the seal had risen.

From his sack, again, he took a square of bearskin and stood on it about a foot away from the hole. He brought out a steel spear-head which he fastened to the point of his harpoon, and he rested the harpoon horizontally in front of him on a pair of forked sticks that stood upright in the snow. Round his hand he looped the cord tied to the detachable spear-head, and he stood now ready for the kill. When the marker rose he would take the harpoon in his hand. When it sank again, he would drive the spear straight down with one powerful stroke. The spear-head would be deeply imbedded in the seal. He would detach the handle and pull at the cord with all his strength, hauling up the hundred-pound beast.

But the kill might be long delayed. The seal, having several breathing-holes, might be hours coming or might not come at all. I myself had met a hunter who had spent three days motionless in that extraordinary attitude in which they stand, feet planted together, head down, bottom high, forced by the seal's acute hearing to maintain absolute silence,—and all to no avail. Angus Gavin, at Perry River, came back once from sealing, very disappointed to return empty-handed.

"How long did you wait at the hole?" an Eskimo asked him.

"Four freezing hours!" Gavin answered indignantly.

The Eskimo looked at him soberly. "Four days is not too many," he said.

I had been ordered by my Eskimo to move off, and it was from a distance of a hundred feet that I waited and watched, and photographed the scene. I was in great luck. An hour had not gone by before we heard a shout. A seal! As soon as a seal has been speared, the hunter cries out, "I have killed the seal!" and instantly the others abandon their *aglu* and race to be in at the kill.

We ran as fast as we could, for the winner of the race receives a choice quarter of the beast, the hunter himself taking the hindquarters, while the rest is distributed throughout the camp. It was Tutannuak who had killed the seal, and already he was hauling it out of the hole. Blood ran in streams as the beast was brought up, and the dogs bounded

over the snow, licking up the blood. The seal was dragged
a few yards from the hole, and then all the hunters knelt
round to perform their rite of thanks to Nuliayuk.

I can describe the scene, but how can I convey its solem-
nity? There was a hush as Tutannuak picked up his snow-
knife, made a small incision in the abdomen of the seal,
put in his hand, and drew out the liver, all red and smoking. The five hunters knelt in silence as he proceeded. He
put the liver down on the seal and cut it into six slices, one
for each, and he set a slice on the snow at his place and
before each of the men who knelt, still as in prayer, in that
circle. Next he cut and laid beside the liver six chunks of
blubber. Six men, members of the hungriest and most vora-
cious race on earth, were motionless in the presence of the
greatest delicacies known to the palate of their race. Blubber
and liver lay uneaten on the ice while the hunters mutely
rendered thanks to Nuliayuk for the gift of the seal. Behind
the men sat the dogs, quivering with greed, their eyes on the
seal, but no less still and motionless than their masters. Here,
before me, six men and their dogs sat worshipping the sea
from which they drew their sustenance, like sun-worshippers
adoring the source of light and life. The wide immensity,
the hush that overspread this world, lent to this scene a
measureless grandeur.

Suddenly the charm was broken. Each man picked up a
pointed stick, stuck it into his bit of liver, and swallowed
the liver at a gulp while the blood ran down his chin. Then
he popped into his mouth the blubber held in his left hand,
and joy spread over all their faces while I, outside the circle,
photographed them and prayed to Nuliayuk . . . that my
pictures turn out clear, for here was a rare scene I should
never again come upon.

Tutannuak was now free to return to camp; indeed, he

must return to camp with this good news. The others would
continue the hunt while I went back with him. We put a
hook through the nose of the seal, and two dogs dragged
it as far as the sled.

An early return to camp always meant meat, and everybody was out as we drove up. As usual, it was the children
who had seen us first and raised the alarm; and from every
side women, scuttling in their crab-like shuffle, were hurrying towards Tutannuak's igloo. We shoved the seal through
the porch, and inside the butchering began. The honor of
cutting up and distributing the meat fell to Tutannuak's
wife. She skinned the seal, and as she worked she went
mentally through the list of households and decided who
was to get which cut. The blubber was removed and set
aside, the blood was scooped out with a great ladle and
poured into a bowl, and the moment for distribution arrived. All the women in the camp were crowding into the
porch, children crawling between their legs and over their
backs, the sight and smell of meat creating a prodigious
agitation. On her knees in the porch, her head framed in
the opening, the wife of the man who had won the race to
Tutannuak held out a basin. As soon as it was filled she
made her way out, and was replaced by the next wife in
the same animal posture.

That night the men returned in high humor. My presence
had brought them luck, and now they looked upon me as
one of themselves. How simple their pleasures are! As we
were smoking and joking in the igloo, one of them stood up
and began to laugh all by himself, but to laugh as I have
rarely seen a man laugh. He stood shaking and radiant with
glee, while the others stared in bewilderment and wondered
what could have happened to make him laugh like this. No
one asked, of course; and finally he said, still shaking: . . . no,

I cannot tell you what he said; Rabelais could, but not I, though I thought his immense laughter, his gargantuan pleasure over his eupepsia, wonderfully and humanly funny. He was laughing uncontrollably as he crawled out of the igloo through the porch.

Getting away from this seal camp with Ohohunuak was different from my other departures in only one respect. The sled was lashed, everything was ship-shape, and still we were not away. But now I was as bad as the Eskimos. Now it was I who proposed a final cigarette before pulling out, I who thought suddenly of something I had forgotten, I who crawled back into the igloo to get it, and, once there, made no bones about drinking another mug of tea. And over tea, a story began, as always. The story led to another. When the second story ended I went out of doors to have a look at the weather, came back to tell Ohohunuak that the harness of one of his dogs was frayed almost through. Somebody else had a look at his snow-knife, shook his head dubiously over it, and went off to his own igloo to fetch a better knife for us. We went out of doors, and there I heard a woman call out something I could not understand, but its effect was to bring two other women out of their igloos and start a child running. The child came back with his father's shovel.

At that moment, exactly like an Eskimo, I came to myself with a jerk, swore that we were already late, and sprang on the sled. Ohohunuak, with a wide grin, flung himself on behind, and we were away with authentic Eskimo abruptness.

Leaving an igloo is not precisely like driving off in a motor car from your front stoop. The man who takes the trail carries his kitchen, his oil-burner, his lighting plant, his building tools with him. Each night when he makes a halt, he starts housekeeping over again; and each morning

it is life itself that he begins anew. Imagine an existence in
which, day after day, men leave the known for the unknown,
leave the firm for the vague, the solid for the crumbling, the
formed for the formless. Taking the trail is an adventure,
it is flinging yourself into the sea. And for me there was
never anything more astonishing in the code of the Eskimo
than the total absence of effusions, embraces, and vain words
of farewell when a man or a family left the rest on a
journey into the uncertainties of this waste of wind and ice.

At Pelly Bay, where their manners were softer than the
manners of these Netsilik, one hunting partner might—
though it was rare even there—say to another, *"Taa-va-vu-
tin?"*—"You, you leave?"—and the other would answer,
"Tag-va-vu-tin,"—"You, you stay." But not here. The nearest thing to a farewell that I ever saw was when a woman
came forward and handed her husband his igloo-building
gloves,—gloves that close at the wrist and are specially de-
signed for this purpose.

The trail is the great Book of Silence. Ohohunuak and I
sat side by side and exchanged no word. There was nothing
for us to say. I knew—on the trail—as well as he did, what
was in his mind. "The snow is soft," he was saying to himself. "It sticks, and we shall have to ice the runners pretty
soon." Or what he said to himself was: "Yonder lies such-
and-such an island. We may reach it in time to make tea
on the lee side." I knew that he was thinking these things.
When the snow was soft and the sled dragged, there was
nothing else in the world a man could think. When an
island rose into view, and it was a couple of hours since we
had drunk tea, that island had to be associated in our minds
with the next halt for tea and rest. And if, looking at the
dogs as they ran, you saw that number four—the tempera-

mental one—was cutting up again, refusing to pull her share
of the load, you could not think of anything else. You are
bound for Perry River. You have a leader who is a magnificently powerful brute. But he has one tiresome trait, he cannot stay in the track of sleds that have gone before unless the
track is very fresh. You have to keep your eye on the road
constantly or he will have tacked five points before you
know it. Well, you don't talk football or politics with a
leader like that.

In the morning, before we started out, Ohohunuak had
come to see me.

"Anore taima-ittok," he said. "The wind is from over
there."

"Over there" was the direction we were to take, and I had
let him know that we would start nevertheless. He had
made ready the harness and had come back to kneel in the
opening of the porch where he waited for me to pass him
the water and bearskin with which he was about to ice the
runners. "You still insist upon going," his reproachful glance
had said. He must have dropped a word to his neighbor
about this, for the eldest of the clan, Inoayuk, came in a moment later, ostensibly for a mug of tea but actually to feel
me out. After a moment of silence he had said to me with
an attempt to speak casually:

"You like this weather?"

I had said that it suited me well enough, and he had
drunk his tea and left.

Actually, the day had not been hard, and when, at six
o'clock, Ohohunuak and I stopped for tea the wind was not
unbearably strong. We unloaded an empty case, set it down
back to the wind, and set my Primus inside. To right and
left, Ohohunuak placed blocks of snow as further screens
against the blow. When the water was hot we squatted

inside our shelter and drank our tea, after which he looked
to the dogs while I stowed the things away.

To myself I said, What would a man from Outside say if
he could see us together like this? By what miracle was I,
so lately come from afar, able to get along with this man
of the stone age? For we do understand each other perfectly,
and the understanding seems a natural one, altogether effort-
less. Part of it goes on as between men Outside. I put my
hand into this sack, on the sled, and draw out a tin of tobacco. I pass it to this Eskimo, who takes it without a word
and rolls himself a cigarette. He passes the tin back to me.
I put it away, and I hand him a match. All that is under-
standable enough.

But this sort of thing happens, which belongs only to
Eskimo life. He and I see at the same moment that the dogs'
traces have become entangled. With one impulse, both move
to stop the sled. He on his side jumps down and, clinging
to the sled, brakes it by dragging his heels in the snow.
Simultaneously, I have flung the sled anchor overboard into
the snow and am clinging to the chain with all my might.
The sled stops, the Eskimo goes forward and puts a dog
back in its place; and at the moment when he straightens
up, I haul in the anchor, the sled glides smoothly forward,
the Eskimo drops down on it as it comes abreast of him, and
once again we sit side by side without a word. Time passes,
and Ohohunuak turns his head towards me. I see a serious
look in his face. Squall forward on the left. We stare, he
nods, and from that bobbing of his head I know that the
squall will not hit us. Still without a word we go on.

Together we spend hours like this, reading in the great
Book of Silence. He learnt its lessons in childhood; I have
come from afar to spell them out with extreme difficulty.
They have taught me, above all, to discard things—haste,

worry, rebelliousness, selfishness. It has taken me a year to learn these lessons, and I see suddenly that my year in the north has not been, as I thought it, a year of conquest of the elements, but of conquest of myself. And because of the peculiarity of my conquest, the Arctic is for me no longer a source of suffering but of joy. It is the crucible in which, slowly and patiently, the dross in my nature has to some extent been melted away. In this Arctic have I found my peace, the peace I was never able to find Outside. Except one were a monk, or such extraordinary circumstances as war and danger intervened, there was no way in which one could find this peace Outside, this sense of the brotherhood of man. Yet this sense, the Arctic had given me simply and directly. That which, elsewhere, would demand a sublime degree of abnegation, had been effected here by simple necessity. How was I going to say this sort of thing to the men of my soft world, who sat in offices during the day and played bridge at night?

Next day we had been but a few hours on the way when it became clear that we were lost. The coast was close at hand, but we were running through such a chain of islands, that what with moving through every point of the compass at one time or another, we no longer knew where the coast lay. Finally, we seemed to be running over a river-bed. What did this mean?

Ohohunuak turned towards me, and I took it that he was about to speak of what was in my mind. Not at all. "I should like your pipe," was all he said; and when I passed it to him he drew two puffs merely and handed it back with a *"Na-ma-kto,"*—"Very good," accompanied by a smile.

I should have known better. Of course he would not worry. He was an Eskimo. If he became lost, he would build

an igloo—one more igloo among so many. And sitting beside me, lost as I was sure we were, he fell peacefully asleep
behind his snow-glasses, woke now and again to urge on the
dogs, and fell once more asleep. We drove on, moved out of
the river-bed, discovered finally that we had come too far
east, and determined to follow the now recovered coastline
where we were sure we should come upon the track of sleds.

A squall blew over us, and Ohohunuak shook himself
awake. As the snow drifted through the air and turned the
islands into phantom shapes, he looked at me through his
eyelashes and I felt that he was weighing me in his balance.
Had I been found wanting? Not this time. And when, at
the height of the storm he stopped the sled and proposed
tea—a Chinese would not have played with the Kabloona
more subtly—I smiled and said, "Of course." He sent me a
broad grin and whipped up the dogs.

Ka-mo-tik! (A sled.) It was not actually a sled; but the
track of sleds was there and the sleds were clear in the
mind's eye. Tracks in this immensity speak an eloquent language that fills the thoughts of the man on the trail. How
old is this track? Who made it? We'll have a look. Seven
dogs. Sled not weighed down. Track not deep, he must have
been running fast,—like us, running out of the storm. Look
here! A second sled has moved in. The two tracks are now
one, and the haste of their drivers is evident. A gust of
warmth goes through you as you stare at the ground, for
these are the traces of men of your kind, men hurrying as
you hurry, running to shelter as you run. The unknown is
your brother.

Now a third track, and a fourth. The image comes into
my mind of railway points on the outskirts of Paris. It is the
station, the capital that we are making for. We whip up the

dogs, call them by name, and they seem to understand and to collect their second wind, for they charge ahead.

An island. Ours? Then it will be the next one. Time and the trail are both behind us, we pay them no heed for now we are sure of making port. We are not even in a hurry, now, and we sit on the sled humming softly to ourselves, almost regretting this journey's end.

There is nothing like the trail and the sled to fill a man with this sense of homecoming. The air is still, the day is dying. All fever is abated. The hush of peace has descended upon us. The dogs are weary, but they trot at a steady pace. We on the sled doze, enveloped in a strange languor in which lassitude and happiness both have their part.

A beacon rises suddenly, and we know we have reached the Post. Instantly the dream world drops away, and reality returns. Ohohunuak is thinking of what he is going to trade; I, of a slice of toast. The island revolves gently. I feel that it is not we who are approaching it, but it that is coming nearer and growing bigger, as in a film. The rest happens in the wink of an eye. One mast, then two more flow towards us. We urge our dogs on. Men come up out of the earth, and as we pull in there are shouts from every side. Someone claps me on the shoulder. Sergeant Larssen, of all people! "Well, well. Hello, Count. . . ." "What are you doing here? I thought you were at Adelaide?"

This time I ended a trail as fresh as when I had started it. What had been a nightmare for me nearly a year before was now a mere matter of miles covered. Once the trail had meant suffering, and the Post had meant a harbor of grace. All this was now changed.

I do not mean to say that I did not enjoy being idle at Perry River, where the Post Manager was Angus Gavin, he who knows more about the Eskimo than any white man in the North. I smoked innumerable cigarettes, grilled myself mountains of toast, listened to stories and told my own with an ineffable sense of having earned this ease and comfort. Yet, after a few days I grew restless again. My peace was to be found on the trail, not at the Post, and I was anxious to be off. The season was flying. But I had neither sled nor dogs, and I had to sit still. I was the prisoner of circumstance, and until some one came by to release me I should have to stay where I was. It was forty-three days before I was able to resume my journey out.

Chapter II

Spring was returning to the Arctic. The temperature rose till it stood well above zero, and suddenly one day—it was the 25th April—it mounted to 30° Fahrenheit. A nasty warm wind was blowing, the kind of wind which, at home, makes us fearful of catching an unseasonable cold. The "heat" was intolerable.

I stared through the window of the Post at the dripping icicles out of doors and thought gloomily how dreary a world this looked. Angus came up, looked out, and spoke.

"It's all over now," he said. "I shall have to shovel the snow off the roof before it melts up there and floods us all round."

The snow porch was going to pieces, slipping and slopping away and showing its framework in a score of places where the thaw had worked straight down to the wood. For the first time in many months I had to pull on a pair of rubbers over my moose-skin boots to keep out the wet.

Light had come to the northern night—or if this was not light, at any rate it was no longer darkness. The air was filled with an eerie glow; the horizon was swollen with the promise of light, and the night was a ruddy purple.

Each day that followed was different from the last, and

with each day the rush of light over the earth grew stronger. We had been plunged during our long season in darkness: like miners brought up to the surface, we were being swung back again into the day. The earth emerged, and from day to day the landscape changed so radically that we might have been in a moving train. Perspective was here again. The scene had a foreground, a middleground, a background; and the background was hazily pink. Where there had been snow, dirty grey patches were now to be seen, and rocks stood forth. To-morrow a stream would run noisily past, and in this slow-moving world would give an unwonted impression of haste. Islands were baring themselves to our sight. Valleys appeared. All that before had been smooth and flat was now hollow and humped. For the man living there, the Arctic has two topographies, one of winter, the other of summer, and to the traveller who knows only one, the other is unrecognizable.

In winter this land is white and clean; the snow purifies it. In this season it is repellent, sordid, haggard. All the skull-like stones strewn over the barren tundra grin in the dead landscape of summer. As far as the eye can see, all is brown, black, lugubrious. The Post itself seems deep in a welter of ashes and garbage now uncovered by the thawing of the successive drifts of winter. What filth we ourselves, without knowing it, were responsible for! The ignoble tins flung heedlessly out-of-doors; the empty jam pots; the rotten potatoes—all this is present suddenly to disgrace us.

Waiting here for a team to haul me back Outside, I chopped wood for want of something better to do. During several nights—for I did my chopping at two in the morning—I swung the axe by lamplight. But as the days went by the lamp became unnecessary and we had the light of the sky all through the night.

One of the most curious things was our resistance to sleep.
"Bedtime? Really?" Angus and I would say to each other;
and still we would not go to bed. Why, I do not know, but
it would have been a lesser annoyance to go to bed during
the day. I would lie down in my clothes. From the other side
of the partition I would hear Angus stir. He was as sleepless
as I was. We had solemnly said good-night, yet neither of us
would sleep. His door was open, and so was mine. Every
door now was open. Like animals, we had hibernated: now
we were ready to emerge.

Sleep would not come. I would get quietly out of bed and
go out-of-doors to sketch. Something was going on out there,
something that was not normal: I had to be part of it.

Across the northern sky stretched a band of white gold,
white and liquid, like gold in a crucible. Against this back-
cloth, the point of the island stood out with its beacon and its
thousands and thousands of dark-brown skulls. The southern sky was a hard bright blue, and so luminous that the
chaplets of islands and the faraway mountains emerged in
the distance with brilliant clarity. Over this world hung a
peace, a silence, that seized the beholder. The air was brisk
and light. But the peace of the scene, the lightness of the air,
were mere deception. Something stirring, something vibrant
was present that filled the being with a nameless agitation.
It was impossible to be still. You wanted to walk, to run, to
go on endlessly from hillock to hillock, shouting verses
aloud, singing songs you had never before heard. You were
seized by what could easily become delirium and might
move you as plausibly to religious ecstasy as to sexual explo-
sion—of itself and without the intervention of your will.
The earth was being born again. You were witnessing its
creation. You wanted harps to chant its glory; and you knew

that it was moving the missionaries to prayer and urging on
the Eskimos to their indefatigable mating.

For they were no more asleep than I was. Not the least
little thing could happen as far away as the eye could pierce
without an Eskimo seeing it, and on the instant giving the
signal. It was as if they went out every other minute to scrutinize the horizon, and peered between times out of their
porches. Let but a seal rise within a radius of ten miles and
an Eskimo has seen it, three Eskimos are running towards
it. Let a single ptarmigan come trotting over the land, and
an Eskimo woman, her child in her hood, is already after
that silly bird which, with unbroken regularity, flies fifteen
yards, rests, trots; and then flies, rests, and trots again with a
quick comical and anguished gait that seems to say, "Please,
Sir, do not annoy me. I am a respectable woman."

I had scarcely sat down to my sketch when three Eskimos
were already on their way—by different paths and methods
—to find out what I was up to. One pretended that he must
go have a look at his dogs; and on the way back it was natural that he should pass the place where I had stopped to
work. The second, who has no dogs, approached in a circle,
operated by envelopment, as it were. (He was young, and
the young are sly.) The third was an old man called
Ailennak. I watched his figure rising above the ridge, and he
came down towards me with the air of a dog afraid he
might be beaten. He came forward in a straight line and
each time that I raised my eyes he essayed a feeble grin. His
eyes were anxious. He was trying to guess what my mood
might be. Did I mind his coming up to me? He quickened
his pace, and then, when I lowered my eyes to my paper, he
stopped short, doubtful. The nearer he came and the more
the game seemed to him dangerous, the wider grew his

grin. When, finally, he had come quite close, his whole being was one vast grimace.

It was three o'clock in the morning and children were at play out on the frozen sea. Women, their mothers, sat on the point of a knoll and watched them, called out to them. Eskimos were wandering in every direction, hunting no one knew what. I saw them come in, go out again, move busily over the landscape. They will wander like this all summer long, sleeping only when they are too weary to stand, and sleeping wherever they happen to find themselves.

This is the season of Eskimo madness, particularly for the young. I remember a boy of eleven or twelve years, named Ivitaligak, who went out of his mind every spring. I do not know if this malady exists elsewhere in the same way, but with Eskimo youths it takes the form of a violent somnambulism. Ivitaligak would rove like a somnambulist, coming, going, shrieking, beating his head with his fists and screaming, "Give me a rifle! Give me a rifle! I want to kill myself!" It would not have been hard for him to kill himself before coming to. That night he picked up in both hands a burning stove and shook it violently without feeling the burns. His friends threw him down and pummeled him to try to wake him, but no one could do it. They smacked him again and again, holding him down on the ground as he twisted and contorted himself: all in vain. After a half hour of this, they gave it up. *"I-ti-bli-lerk-to,"* the old men said. (He is out of his mind.) Once awake again, he could remember nothing that had happened, and when they told him, he burst out laughing and refused to believe them. His father, Anarvik, said to me that this always happened in the spring, when the boy did not get enough sleep, wandered all night long, night after night, and stretched out occasionally on the bare ground to slumber. Angulalik's little son, Wakwak, displayed the same symptoms, though not so violently. Once they came to, the boys complained of headaches; but these things pass when they grow to be men.

At Gjoa Haven, in October, I had attended the annual winter burial carried out by Paddy Gibson to preserve his stores against the coming cold. Here, at Perry River, it was the spring disinterment that I witnessed.

"Last autumn, I was finishing the building of my house," said Angus Gavin. "We had unloaded the ship, and I had a lot of stuff for the Store piled up on shore. I went to bed one night thinking I could go on with the house and move the stuff up the hill later. It snowed that night; the drift piled up; and by nightfall everything on shore was buried. I managed to dig out some of the stuff, but the rest is over there" —he pointed; "I *think*," he added with emphasis.

I went with him down to the shore where, like a sorcerer with his wand, he walked about plunging a long harpoon into the snow and muttering to himself.

"I'm sure this is where I buried the coal," I heard him say.

At the same time, a like exhumation was being undertaken by the Eskimos. Canoes, tents, hides, boxes, even rusted sewing machines were dug up and carried home in triumph. Tents rose on every side, and before the tent of Atkaitok an admiring crowd babbled and handled the enviable riches he had uncovered.

By now the Eskimos had abandoned their humped and crumbling igloos and pegged down their tents. The igloo had grown too hot for them; but as the ever uncertain Arctic wind turned cold and whistled through their new habitations, they built ramparts of snow round the tents to keep it out. Harpoons, bearskins, kayaks, sewing machines, and dilapidated gramophones were among the articles that lay pell-mell in their tents. Empty tins, carcasses of foxes, ragged strips of hide made a dump of the shore, testifying that man was the most sordid animal in all creation. The bay itself was pockmarked with tiny pools of black water, for wherever an object had been flung and left to lie the sun had struck it square, and the ice on which it lay had melted. It was curious to see that, heavy or light, iron file or cotton rag, when the sun touched a dark object on the frozen surface of the bay, that object seemed to stand up on end, for it always sank vertically. A rag would go straight through several feet of ice, and Angus told me that often the Eskimos, out jigging, would set down a dog-dropping on the ice and let it do the work which otherwise they would have to do with the ice-chisel.

May being the great month of visiting, nearly every day there were arrivals or departures round the Post. Eskimos came here from O'Reilly Island, Lind Island; from Putulik in the north, Ellice River in the west, Sherman Inlet in the east. Many were on the move simply because the isolation of winter was at end and the blessed season of great gatherings had arrived. Others came to do their annual trading, and there were some who brought as many as a hundred and fifty or two hundred foxes. They arrived feverish and exalted by the prospect of the feasting, the visiting, the wife-trading of which Perry River was to be the scene, and the arrival of each sled was a triumph for the entire camp. Twice or three times a day, old Ailennak, whose tent was raised nearest the Post, would totter in with the news: "*A-oo-dlar!*"—"Coming!" and Angus and I would go out to greet the newcomers. Ailennak had seen thousands arrive in his long life, but each time his emotion was as fresh, his

enthusiasm as great as before: the Eskimo instinct of sociability never dies.

For me who had lost the habit of living in this hubbub,
the scene was disheartening. There were dozens of tents,
each with its dead seal, its dog-feed, its rusted rifles planted
in the snow (if you want to see what a rifle can resist, come
to the Arctic!). There were fish-nets, clusters of rusted fox-
traps flung down carelessly and to be left behind out of
simple forgetfulness. The tent-cloths flapped in the wind despite the heavy stones by which some were held down. It
was a gipsy cantonment, in bustle and agitation as in sordid-
ness.

There was a blind boy here in this season of decomposi-
tion, and in his way he was an even more sinister character
than the paederast who had dropped in on us at Gjoa Haven.
I say "boy" because I believe he was no older than eighteen,
though some said he was all of thirty. He was squat and
brutal, with powerful arms and a barrel chest, almost a
dwarf, so that even before you saw his blind man's movements as he wandered alone round the Post, you felt something disconcerting in his person. He would go forward
feeling his way, stop for a second as if studying the direction
of the wind, and be off again on his mysterious errand, gay
as a bird and clever as a monkey. I have seen him shuffle
alongside a sled to harness and unharness dogs; and when
the harness was twisted he could set it straight again as
quickly as anybody.

He used to come to talk to me; and as he had spent a good
part of his life round a Post, here or elsewhere, he had accu-
mulated a certain stock of odd bits of white man's lore about
which he used to ask me endless tiring questions. One day
he came in, peered with his sightless eyes into the room, and
told me that his eyes ached, that this day he could scarcely

see anything! Then he sat back and laughed quietly to himself. I should have been better able to bear him if he had not
the habit of coming up close to people and running his
hands over them. Also, it was a trial to be present when he
ate. Food would be set within his reach. He would fumble
for it, and when he had got his hand on something, it was
like the clutch of an octopus—a gruesome grip as of a
strangler's hand. Having eaten, he would be asked, *"Tai-
tai?"*—"Do you want more?"—and he would respond with
a rumbling grunt and stretch forth that beastly claw.

He had a gramophone, one of those cheap objects with a
cardboard horn made specially for the natives, and he spent a
great part of the day playing it. The spring in the motor was
at the end of its life, so that the sounds that came from his
horn after the first few seconds were a croaking and yowling
horrible to hear. But he would wind and wind, and play and
play. One of the two disks that constituted his stock was a
trombone solo of *Old Folks at Home*. I never hear that song
without seeing instantly the snow, the thaw, the gipsy cantonment, the gorilla-like blind boy of Perry River. I found
him one day busy with a borrowed screw-driver: he was
taking his weary gramophone apart.

Strangest and most disturbing of all was the attraction he
held for the girls. They were round him day and night, chattering, teasing him, giggling as he would catch one or other
of them in his arms, screaming with delight when he drew a
girl into his tent.

"They're mad about him," Angus would say; and then,
with a grin, "He must be awfully good."

Unlike ourselves, the Eskimos are still children of nature.
Spring, the season of rut in the animal kingdom, induces
physiological mutations in them. They change color: from

earth brown they turn purple, a red glow lies over their
cheekbones, and their eyes shine with a strange gleam. Here
at Perry River a frenzy of sexuality had spread through the
camp, embracing every member of it. Day and night they
copulated in a sort of delirium, inexhaustible and insatiable.
They talked of nothing else, and the men would arrive at
the Post, gleeful, hilarious, to recount their exploits in a
thousand details. And then, their own words working on
them, they would hurry back to their tents. Young and old,
every girl and woman participated in the excitation. Mokahainek, being without a wife, suddenly married his hunting
partner's mother, who, as she looked seventy, must have been
fifty; and he too appeared at the Post to tell his tale. Even
the little children were seized by this fever of which they
witnessed the external manifestations (for there was no
modesty in the tents); and though they knew not what they
were doing, they giggled and screamed with glee as they
pantomimed their elders. Angulalik, the Eskimo most nearly
like a white man in manner and ambition of all those I saw
in the North, turned up one day at the Post with his wife,
and it was plain that even for him the ambiance was irresistible. His little boy came in and stood motionless in the doorway, a handsome child of about five years.

"Where have you been?" the father asked. "In the tent?"

"Yes," said the boy.

"Was your wife there?" Angulalik went on with a wink
at the other Eskimos.

"Did you take her, at least?" the boy's mother put in, in a
matter of fact voice.

Even the games became sexual. Angulalik began to make
string figures, and from the normal cat's cradle he passed
quickly to the grossest obscenities, his fingers moving the
string with astonishing speed. He would stop for a second,

think of what he wanted to create and how it was done, and in a moment his fingers were flying, helped out now and then by his teeth. Often his audience called out to him to make this, or show them that; and it was not the women who were the slowest to insist upon a representation of the genitalia.

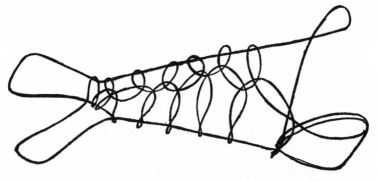

ESKIMO STRING FIGURES REPRESENTING A GROUP OF PEOPLE DANCING

Their dance in this season was consonant with the general atmosphere of inspissated amorousness. It took place in the only igloo left standing, an igloo large enough to hold fifteen people, and we stood in a circle at the center of which a single Eskimo pantomimed an amorous bear as he beat the wooden frame of a drum slung from his wrist by a cord, the women chanting an accompaniment.

The dance began with the man swaying slowly and beating the drum from time to time as he swayed on motionless feet. Then he turned slowly round and round, gazing at the onlookers and apparently trying to win their participation. After a moment one of the women (his wife) began a high-pitched lingering chant, and the man's pace quickened.

Each time that he hit the drum with his heavy stick, it piv-
oted round his left wrist, and as both drum and stick were
very heavy, and the drum was often raised above the dancer's
head, the dance was in part an exhibition of endurance and
the dancer was required to go on until complete exhaustion.
Then, in a ceremonial gesture, he would pass the drum to
some one else.

As usual—and especially here, where many of the natives
had adopted some of the white man's ways—it was the old
men who knew the tribal rites best. Ailennak must have been
sixty years old, yet when he took up the drum an extraordinary agility began to flow through all his body. To this
he added immense spirit and a remarkable sense of pantomime, so that he, in dancing, became the amorous bear he
was seeking to simulate in a mixture of the burlesque, the
lascivious, and the solemn. He handled the drum as if it
were a fan behind which his impudicity was hidden, and
the constant and unceasing repetition of the drum-beat sent
his audience into a sort of trance. After an hour of dancing
and drumming, the men and women round him had been
worked up to a pitch of hysteria. The more lubricious and
exhilarated the old man grew, the more the entranced
women fell into an ecstatic rigidity. Standing with closed
eyes, rigid to a point that seemed to simulate rigor mortis,
they chanted an endless refrain on two notes while Ailennak
bounded, crouched, sprang up again, and then squatted with
glazed eyes as if never would he be able to come out of his
delirium. The drum seemed to grow larger and larger until it
filled the igloo, and as it rose in the air and fell again each
time to earth, an intolerable impression of its weight was
suggested by the rise and plunge of the drum. Now and then
the old man seemed about to stop for lack of strength. Then

the whole audience would come suddenly out of its trance and shout to urge him on. He went on till he could do no more, and of a sudden he stopped dead, the drum hanging from his inert wrist. The air seemed to clear at once; the distorted faces and rigid bodies became normal; but the effect was still to send the audience back to their tents to continue their erotic exercises.

None of this was for me; not the sport nor those who engaged in it. These were not the Eskimos I could be happy among. They were already half way on the road to civilization, possessed treasures, hunted with rifles, could add and subtract, and some traded at the Post on open account. Whereas I myself wore the untrimmed furs of King William Land, scarcely one of them but he paraded round in a *kuliktak* covered with ornamental tails and sewn together of furs of different colors. When they came visiting to the Post their gloves hung at their sides from long cords of braided and vari-colored wool that passed under their collars and round their necks at the back. Like circus monkeys, they sat in chairs, ate only "first quality" biscuits, smoked what we called tailor-mades, and all their gestures were carefully copied from the white man. Jam was the highest delicacy they knew, and they consumed quantities of it. There was hardly a native implement to be found in their tents, and when by chance I found one and offered to trade for it, it seemed to waken a sense of shame in them, to prompt them to keep it as a reminder that they were after all *Inuit,* "Men, preeminently," and they would put a prohibitive price on it to make the trade impossible.

Besides, I was no longer the free man I had been on the trail. Here at Perry River I had found waiting for me a bundle of letters, brought out by the Police sled. I had to answer some of them, and that meant the resumption of relations with the world outside. I was five hundred miles from Coppermine—not too far, it goes without saying, to escape being hooked by the grappling iron of the radio and forced to send off telegrams. Henceforth there was nothing for me to do but to plan to return to that world outside to which I was now bound. I struggled against the thought, told myself that in the igloo I had been a king and Outside I should be again a slave; but there was no returning to the igloo. I had no means of subsistence left; and besides, it was not, I had to admit to myself, my world. Yet, graceless and ungrateful as it may seem, every impulse in me rejected my own world; and until I was out of Canada itself and had heard that the war had started, I did not want to hear of France, of my nation, of my family anxious for my return.

On King William Land, I did not miss that world in the least. It was from the worries, the complications, the agitation of that world that the Arctic had released me, and it was because of this that I had loved the Arctic. The blizzards had been my allies. Remoteness had been my safeguard,— and to such a point that the Canadian Government, which possessed a formal right to control my movements, had not known where I was and had telegraphed to the Police for information concerning the whereabouts of "Scientist de Poncins." The Police themselves could only answer that I was "somewhere west," and "somewhere west" was the address I found on the envelopes sent up to Perry River from Coppermine. I had a rare laugh out of that address.

All this was moving swiftly into the past, and between the wide grins of the half-civilized natives and the importunate messages from Outside, I sat glumly down in the Post and waited for the sled that was to take me out on the last trail.

Into the holiday fever of the camp a group of Eskimos from inland brought suddenly the news that the caribou were moving north.

For these Mainland Eskimos, much more than for those who wander among the islands in the Glacial Ocean, the caribou is the center and fundament of their existence. It represents for them not merely what wheat represents for a peasant of the Beauce or a Kansas farmer, not merely what fish means for the Netsilik kindred. Caribou means meat and stronger dogs; but it means also bone for weapons, hide for clothing, sinew for sewing thread. They live on the edge of the northward migration of the herd, and the coming of the caribou is their annual rescue from destitution.

The imagination of these natives is visual: they actually see the caribou, see meat, when they hear the name; and the news spread a fresh fever round the Post, woke the Eskimos abruptly as the French are waked by the cry, "The enemy is at the gates!"

Mokahainek and I lashed a sled and were the first down the bay and round the point into the Perry River, Kailek and one of Matomiak's sons following close behind. We travelled inland through a landscape of low hills, running some eight or ten miles over the bed of the river, calling out to our dogs in those words that seem to be the same the world over, "Gee!" and "Haw!" to guide them to left or right, while my half-civilized companions gravely pulled out watches to mark the hour, or stopped, climbed a hill, brought forth telescopes and solemnly inspected the horizon.

No caribou were in sight, and at eleven that night we made camp, four of us sleeping in a single small tent.

At a bend in the river we had come upon an Eskimo cache and had seen at a glance that the cache had been emptied by the wolverene. This amazing animal had been able, with its fantastic dexterity, to push away a mound of stones and uncover the buried meat; and after eating only a little, it had dragged the rest round and round in the maculate snow, inspired more by a spirit of destruction than by hunger. Everybody in the North believes firmly that the Devil inhabits this beast, for it is trickier than man and rarely caught. Set a trap for it: the wolverene will not, like the fox, sniff innocently and let itself be bagged: it will lie on its belly on the trap and paddle with its feet in the snow until the trap springs of itself, and the bait can be nibbled off without danger. No stones are too heavy to be removed by the wolverene from the cache they cover; no remains are too foul to be eaten by the wolverene when it is hungry.

On the second afternoon out, we sighted our first caribou. Where I had looked for thousands, millions, one of those endless herds that I had read about and seen in the films, I saw but a single, yellow-white, luminous animal, so like the snow in color that if it had not raised its head from time to time I might not have known it was there. We were standing on a ridge and it was cropping below, some eighty yards off. The caribou saw us, stiffened as if about to run, and then lowered its head to the ground again. A single shot killed it.

They skinned the beast, and then one of them took the flesh in his fingers and pinched it sharply. Two enormous lice—worms, more truly—jumped out of the carcass and looked up out of Kailek's hand with myopic eyes. Kailek felt of them as if to see if they were proper to his purpose, and he went so far as to consult me, who had no notion that

worms could be either "good" or "bad." These worms had
made their way through the thick hide from outside and
had hollowed out sockets in the flesh, where they lay imbedded, only the two yellow pin-points of eyes protruding
from the flesh. There were scores of these yellow points, and
one after the other Kailek squeezed the worms out with his
thumb and popped them into his mouth. I, who was determined to try everything once, took one up, shut my eyes,
and put it in my mouth. It was sweetish, inside its surpris-
ingly fuzzy, raspberry-like skin, and I spat out the skin and
had another, while Kailek sat with a heap of them before
him on the snow.

That night we left the monotonous mediocrity of the low-
lying land by the sea and came out into a vast plain.
It was nearly midnight when we pitched our tent and built
a fire. The dogs were fed, and then the Eskimos and I
walked up a ridge to have a look round. The eerie beauty
of this serene and tranquil land was breath-taking.

Imagine a world covered by the waters of an endlessly
wide lake, and the waters receding until only peaks emerge
like islands over the lake-bottom. There were hundreds of
these peaks as far as the eye could see, with here and there
a ridge that ran like a prehistoric river bank, its smoothly
worn slope covered with pebbles that appeared from far
away as fine as sand. Infinite in distance, hushed, seemingly
deserted by man and beast, it was the landscape of a fairy-
tale. Far away, farther away than I have ever been able to
see anywhere in the world, the sun burned on the rim of a
ridge, and every peak and slope and hillock stood bathed
in a ruddy pink light, a rose that was unreal in its liquid
softness. There were days enough when the land of the
Eskimo, with its blizzards and its grey and horizonless air,
had seemed to me in truth a ghastly world; but on this day,

seeing this immensity spread out before me, being conscious
of the solitude in which I stood gazing at it, I recognized the
right of the Eskimo to the pride he took in his land, and I
fancied that in his mind this was an offering made to him
by who knows what god, and that he too felt himself a
member of a chosen people. Here, I told myself, is their
Eden, this wide world stocked by the Great Giver with the
magnificent game that came up year after year to feed them
and arm them and clothe them and surrender itself, the
constituent fundament of their households. Seeing this, I
understood better the anguish of Tutiak when, Gibson having ordered him to remain at the Post until his lip was
cured and his fever down, he had gone defiantly off to his
hunting ground and his people.

As my eye went back to the half-civilized Eskimos who
stood with their telescopes beside me, I realized that it was
not of them I had been thinking, but of those strangers, the
Tomiaks, who had appeared from inland at Perry River a
few days before, accomplished their annual trading, and disappeared again into this inland country that was their own.
Like the Arviligjuarmiut, the Tomiaks were uncontaminated, though of the Mainland and not of the islands. My
companions of this night were of a different stamp. Their
concern was not with the land, but exclusively with the
chase, and a sudden grunt from one and then another was
the signal that the caribou had been spotted.

The animals were visible now everywhere over the plain;
not in a thick and countless herd, but in a hundred clusters
of four or five on every side. These peaceful invaders were
all female, come here to drop their young and then resume
the northward march in a day or two, when their males
would have come up to join them. As we looked on, more of
them filled the shallow valleys, and my Eskimos, content,

folded their telescopes, went back to the sleds for their guns, and vanished into the landscape.

One by one I watched them disappear while this eerie light that was not light swallowed them up. The glow over the earth penetrated the soul and filled it with a sort of exaltation. It was less properly light than atmosphere. It was not light because it struck no object with its strength but merely lay over the world, laved it, suggested itself subtly and indirectly. The sun's rim was on the horizon, but it seemed not to be rays from the sun that brought this light; it was self-created, mysterious, universally present without a source of radiation. The whole land lay bathed in it: it was no less present in the valleys than elsewhere, and the earth was shadowless. When I watched the Eskimos go off, brown against the brown earth, my eyes could not follow them; and if I took my eyes from them they vanished. The caribou, too, appeared and reappeared like this, despite their winter coat, the white bellies and yellow-white flanks colored like the snow where it still lay on the ground. Since this light had no source, there was no sharp outline to be seen; caribou and Eskimo alike detached themselves from the ground when they moved, and were reabsorbed by it when they stopped. The Eskimos had not disappeared, they had melted in my sight.

Mokahainek had remained with me during the few minutes in which I continued to inspect this crowded yet noiseless kingdom, and now I followed him as he went down to the game. He had suddenly become unrecognizable. The Eskimo who during three days at the Post had seemed to me so fraudulent, so wilfully simian in his mimicry of the Kabloona, had donned again his savage vestment. The presence of game had resuscitated the primitive in him and transformed him. Now the white man had ceased to exist

for him, and I am sure that during the few days of this
hunt Mokahainek—and the others equally—was oblivious of
my presence. He began to run, and so fast that it was hard
for me to keep up with him. As I ran, I admired the agility
with which he sprang from the darkness of one rock to the

next. We were still half a mile from the caribou when he
began to creep on his belly like a deer-stalker in Scotland.
There was as yet no need for this, but the Eskimo loves to
do it. I have seen an Eskimo take three hours to creep over
ice as level as my hand to approach a seal; and despite the
prodigious suspicion of the seal, who turn their heads every
eight or ten seconds in all directions, an Eskimo, after creep-

ing and even simulating the movements of the seal with head and arms, is able to come close enough to seize the flipper with one hand and stab the seal with a knife held in the other.

So now Mokahainek, peering with ears cocked from behind a rock, his face sober and intense, all his being concentrated upon his purpose. We were moving towards a cluster of four caribou who were peacefully cropping the tiny sprouts of lichen, some of it black and other a fine pale green, that grows beneath the snow. The caribou seem to smell out its presence, and their eyes tell them that a spot of snow no larger than my hand, but imperceptibly darker than the snow that surrounds it, conceals a tuft of lichen. They scrape with a hoof to uncover it where the snow is thicker, or they brush the snow aside with their nose where the covering is thin. As we advanced I saw again and again the jerk of their legs as their hoofs scraped the ground; and later I found dead caribou whose hoofs were worn down with this scraping.

In the two hours since we had made a start, more and more caribou had arrived from the south. Nobody can say in advance what route they will take. In one year or another it will be Perry River, or Cambridge Bay, or Burnside that will see them; but only one will see them in a given year. I was now seeing perhaps a thousand, but they have been known to pass Burnside for days on end in many thousands; and their lack of timidity is such that an Indian was able to say at the Post, without raising protest, that at Fond-du-Lac he had seen them wandering among the tents of his tribe, had shot them down without stirring from his seat in front of his tent. They follow the wind, it seems, and know no other guide. No one has ever seen them graze except nose in the wind. And what is curious, their greatest enemy is

the mosquito, who devours thousands of them in the brief
northern summer, clinging to them until the beast drops
dead, its thin summer coat invisible under the clouds of
insects.

For three days and nights we followed the caribou, shooting, wounding, killing, skinning, carving, and eating. I
remember an afternoon when the Eskimos—I myself carried no rifle—shot for ten minutes at three caribou while
they lumbered slowly and heavily on. Shot in the haunch,
they wavered, went on, stopped, and stared back at us while
the shooting continued. The slaughter was disgusting, and
the ineptitude of the Eskimos was inconceivable. Once, a
buck having been wounded at a distance, I shouted to the Eskimos to run forward and finish him off, and began to run
myself. But they behind me continued to shoot from where
they stood, like children too excited to stop what they had
started, and I had to fling myself down on the ground to
escape the 30-30 bullets that were kicking up the snow all
round me. I ran back and gave them a jawing, but it was no
good: as soon as a beast stirred, they fired another salvo. Finally, one caribou lying still, I went towards him with a
young Eskimo; and he, being two feet from the beast, could
still not contain himself but dropped on one knee and shot
the dead beast again.

Another caribou lay wounded, the blood running down
his horns. He tried to rise, stumbled, fell, tried again to rise;
and my stomach heaved at the sight of the beast as at the
sight of a horse in a bull ring. Two shots finally killed him.

When I, carrying this poor beast on my back—his weight
was about seventy pounds—had rejoined my Eskimos, I
found them butchering two animals. They skinned the caribou by inserting a hand between hide and flesh, and the
hide came away with a sound as of tearing silk. Then they

cut it up with a skill and dispatch that my troubled stomach barely permitted me to take note of, and after tearing at choice cuts of the raw meat with their teeth and gulping it down, they put the bulk of it into a sack improvised out of the hide; and this meat, with the useful bones and valuable sinew, we carried back to our base.

For fifty feet round the tent the snow was filthy with blood, entrails, heads, and legs of caribou. Back at camp they ate again, hands, faces, and coats covered and spattered in blood, squatting like cave-men in the snow and ripping the tendons out of the legs with their powerful teeth while the caribou tongues—great delicacies—were set down to dry on the ground. All round lay the dogs, breathing heavily after their enormous feast, but like the men, prepared shortly to eat again. For dogs as for men, famine was always in the offing, and while both crammed themselves I could see both grow from hour to hour fatter and greasier, the faces of the men shining and their stomachs bloated, like cannibals. Because their dreams had been of the feast they woke in the night, shook themselves out of that Eskimo sleep than which nothing is more profound; and they began again in the night to gnaw and tear and gulp.

It was on April 7, 1939 that I arrived with Ohohunuak at Perry River. On the 25th of May I went off in a caravan of six sleds, with Mokahainek as my driver, bound for Cambridge Bay. There on May 31st I boarded a Royal Canadian Police boat, the *St. Roch,* which took me to Coppermine. It was July 28th before I was able to get away from Coppermine with Art Watson as his guest, or his unpaid hand, as it may please him to remember me, in the 106-foot *Audrey*

B. which brought us into the harbour of Vancouver after
fifty-seven days round Alaska, through the Bering Sea, and
eastward across the Pacific. My journey was ended.

But the real end of the trail had been my arrival at Perry
River in April. The tents of spring, the broad light over the
North, the shacks of the ragged and impure natives round
the Post are not the Arctic that I wish to remember.

There was a night at Ellice River, two days before I
boarded the *St. Roch* and found myself again among my
own kind, when I walked to the top of a hill and looked
round. The night was marvellously serene. No bird broke
with its cry the particular hush that lay over land and
sea, that hush that makes night in the Arctic a thing un-
imaginable by men who do not know it. The air was cold
without chill; the sea lay unwrinkled and icily blue, for it
was still in the main frozen over. A seal rose; and alone in
this vast sweep it stretched itself heavily on the ice and slept.

I thought of the months on the trail, of the hardships and
even miseries I had endured, and of a sudden I began to
miss them with an intensity which amazed me and which,
since then, has never left me. For one does miss these trials,
indeed, more than anything else. One remembers them
without remembering what they made of one. Man thinks
of the thing rather than of the idea. The hospital patient,
once cured, remembers less his recovery than the bed of pain
in which he lay; and for my part I have never yearned with
as much tenderness for anything as for the polar winter and
those transient shelters in the snows.

God knows we were poor enough. Our poverty was total.
We possessed nothing: not even the snow was our own. As
a bird carries off a twig with which to make its nest, then
leaves that borrowed twig once the season has passed, so we
cut and trimmed our borrowed snow and left it to return

to the common lot, passed it on as the Eskimos bequeath
from generation to generation the stone traps in which they
catch their river fish. But there was a cheer and a contentment in our existence which I continue to muse upon and
cannot altogether explain to myself. Was it because infinite
poverty lent infinite price to the least object? There was
more to it than this. I had lost all I owned, but had found
great riches. Like a religious, I possessed the veritable treasures, those which could not be taken from me. I had lost the
world, but I had found myself, had exchanged the glitter
for the gold. Within me had lain potentialities for moral
serenity, and I had not known it. Storm and danger had
been my salvation, and without them my spirit should have
dropped heedlessly off to sleep in my flesh. There on that
Arctic tundra I had reconstructed myself from within. Up
through the lined and frozen layers of skin on my face, my
true visage had begun to emerge, the visage that God had
meant all men to show to one another; and that visage all
the blizzards, all the adversity in the world could not de-
compose.

Out in the world I had been ridiculously capable of swelling myself up to the point of filling a city: here I was dust.
Nothing informs man with humility like the Arctic wastes.
At sea one is still a man, one rides the waves and is not lost
in them. Here we creep, we are insects. As insects minutely
small we crawl over the ground by day, build our diminutive snowhouses by night; and when we seat ourselves
within, it is this sense of proportion that reveals to us the
quality of our conquest.

I say "we" but I cannot pretend of course to lend to the
Eskimos these thoughts I now express. The poverty that was
my salvation had from the beginning of time been theirs,
and so long as they were uncontaminated they lived in

obedience to the high code that it commanded. But I was rediscovering that code. I was rounding out the cycle of life in my return to a point on that cycle which the Eskimos had never left. Those men about whom I knew properly nothing at all, those beings of another race separated from me by thousands of years of the evolution of my kind, had stood shoulder to shoulder with me in the blizzard. With my friends Outside there had always been differences, we had always remained personalities, individuals. Here, after the first few weeks of my probation, none of this existed: the contact was direct, devoid of the détours of personality. Day after day a wind would rise, a sign of danger would appear in the air, and we would respond together, each forgetting himself and striving in the common cause. Outside, it wanted war and flood to give man this sense of brotherhood: here it was a commonplace of life. And if I write this now, and am moved by the memory of it, the reason is that these were the only moments of my life when I was describable not as a Frenchman, not as an individual product of heritage, place, environment, but as nothing other than, simply, a man.

I stood on the shore of Ellice Island and said to myself that I did not want to leave this land. What I wanted was to go back into the remoter regions, to live perhaps as Father Henry lived at Pelly Bay. But that was for many reasons not to be thought of. And as I turned and walked down the hill, I knew that my fate lay elsewhere; and I know now that it lies in France.

In the Connecticut village where the closing pages of this book have been written, snow lies on the ground; but here too spring has come as, a year ago, I saw it come to the Arctic. The sight of the sun on the snow after so many grey days makes even keener the nostalgia that never left me throughout the months when this book was being composed. Even as I could not stay on in the North, so I must leave this simple and peaceful village. It had seemed to me last year that the trail back ran only from King to Cambridge Bay. But for a Frenchman of our time, the trail back leads home.

ABOUT THE AUTHOR

GONTRAN DE PONCINS was a restless French aristocrat who gave up careers as an artist and a businessman to become a freelance journalist and wander the world. He returned to wartime France in 1940, and died in 1962.

THE GRAYWOLF
REDISCOVERY SERIES

BEYOND THE MOUNTAIN
by Elizabeth Arthur

STILL LIFE WITH INSECTS
by Brian Kiteley

THE ESTATE OF POETRY
by Edwin Muir

ALL THE WORLD'S MORNINGS
by Pascal Quignard

LEAH, NEW HAMPSHIRE
by Thomas Williams

THE MEN IN MY LIFE
by James D. Houston

THE PAINTED ALPHABET
by Diana Darling

DREAM HOUSE
by Charlotte Nekola

PLACES IN THE WORLD A WOMAN COULD WALK
by Janet Kauffman

A SONG OF LOVE AND DEATH: THE MEANING OF OPERA
by Peter Conrad